Countering Displacements

DANIEL COLEMAN, ERIN GOHEEN GLANVILLE, WAFAA HASAN & AGNES KRAMER-HAMSTRA, EDITORS

Countering Displacements

The Creativity and Resilience of Indigenous and Refugee-ed Peoples

THE UNIVERSITY OF ALBERTA PRESS

Published by

The University of Alberta Press
Ring House 2
Edmonton, Alberta, Canada T6G 2E1
www.uap.ualberta.ca

Copyright © 2012 Daniel Coleman, Erin Goheen Glanville, Wafaa Hasan, Agnes Kramer-Hamstra

LIBRARY AND ARCHIVES CANADA CATALOGUING IN PUBLICATION

   Countering displacements : the creativity and resilience of Indigenous and refugee-ed peoples / edited by Daniel Coleman ... [et al.]. — 1st ed.

Includes bibliographical references and index.
Issued also in electronic formats.
ISBN 978-0-88864-592-0

   1. Refugees—Cross-cultural studies. 2. Indigenous peoples—Cross-cultural studies. 3. Internally displaced persons—Cross-cultural studies. 4. Creation (Literary, artistic, etc.)—Cross-cultural studies. 5. Resilience (Personality trait)—Cross-cultural studies. I. Coleman, Daniel, 1961–

JV6346.C69 2011   305.9'06914   C2011-907438-9

First edition, first printing, 2012.
Printed and bound in Canada by Friesens, Altona, Manitoba.
Copyediting and proofreading by Joanne Muzak.
Maps by Wendy Johnson.
Indexing by Judy Dunlop.

All rights reserved. No part of this publication may be produced, stored in a retrieval system, or transmitted in any form or by any means (electronic, mechanical, photocopying, recording, or otherwise) without prior written consent. Contact the University of Alberta Press for further details.

The University of Alberta Press is committed to protecting our natural environment. As part of our efforts, this book is printed on Enviro Paper: it contains 100% post-consumer recycled fibres and is acid- and chlorine-free.

The University of Alberta Press gratefully acknowledges the support received for its publishing program from The Canada Council for the Arts. The University of Alberta Press also gratefully acknowledges the financial support of the Government of Canada through the Canada Book Fund (CBF) and the Government of Alberta through the Alberta Multimedia Development Fund (AMDF) for its publishing activities.

A Canada Research Chair Symposium for Diversity in Canadian Literary Cultures Project.

CONTENTS

Acknowledgements VII
Introduction IX

1   **Displacing Oil** 1
    Towards "Lyric" Re-presentations of the Alberta Oil Sands
    JON GORDON

2   **Citizenship Studies and Migrant Illegality** 31
    JEAN MCDONALD

3   **Israel's Wall, Displacement, and Palestinian Resistance in the West Bank** 59
    MAZEN MASRI

4   **Theatricality and The Exposure of Exclusion** 87
    Théâtre du Public and Theater for Everybody's Les Murs Tombent, Les Mots Restent *(Walls Fall, Words Live On)*
    CATHERINE GRAHAM

5   **Mapping Manipur** 115
    PAVITHRA NARAYANAN

6   **The Refugee and the Government**   151
    A Saga of Self-Rehabilitation in West Bengal
    SUBHASRI GHOSH

7   **Stirring the Cultural Fire**   177
    Mohawk Filmmaker Shelley Niro's It Starts With a Whisper *and* Suite: INDIAN
    AGNES KRAMER-HAMSTRA

8   **Creativity as a Form of Resilience in Forced Migration**   205
    MAROUSSIA HAJDUKOWSKI-AHMED

Works Cited   237
Contributors   261
Index   265

ACKNOWLEDGEMENTS

THIS PROJECT would not have been possible without the generous help of many people. Our thanks go, first and foremost, to conference presenters at the "Displacements: Borders, Mobility, and Statelessness" conference (March 2008) whose work inspired the themes of this book. Sincere thanks are also due to conference volunteers: Carolina Moulin Aguiar, Phanuel Antwi, Petronila Cleto, Karen Espiritu, Marnie Goheen, Mauroussia Hajdukowski-Ahmed, Nick Holmes, Emily Johansen, John Kirstein, Andy Kramer, Anna Kramer, Christine Lyons, Graeme MacQueen, Robert Miltner, Dilia Narduzzi, Sharlee Reimer, Anne Savage, Laura Wiebe Taylor, Lisa Vargas, and Riisa Walden.

Thanks also to the Department of English and Cultural Studies at McMaster University, particularly Antoinette Somo and Aurelia Gatto whose help was invaluable. Thanks to Department Chair, Mary O'Connor, and James Erskine Taylor, of the Taylor family, for their warm words of welcome. The John Douglas Taylor fund and the Canada Research Chair for Diversity in Canadian Literary Culture provided essential financial support to make this project possible. We are grateful to the Filipina caregivers and the Salameh theatre troupe for generously volunteering their time to perform at the conference and for allowing us to post their performances in our online archives. A special thanks to The Pearl Company whose willingness to accommodate the conference when it had to move venues in the midst of a massive winter storm was key to its success.

We have benefitted from the help of many people in organizing and revising materials for the book and the website, especially Elizabeth Shultis, who edited and posted conference videos on the website; Lauren Murphy, who compiled an early version of the manuscript; and Elizabeth Jackson, who saw us through the editing stages of completing the manuscript. We are also grateful to the writers of the chapters in this volume. Without them, none of this would have been possible.

Wafaa would like to especially thank Omar for his unwavering and loving support and extend a gratitude to Nader, Suhair, Khaled, Wafa, Bessma, Riisa, Esmat, Mervat, and the Pearsons for their encouragement. Erin would like to thank the Goheen, Glanville, Goldsmith, and Groen families, and Mark, who together have provided a sense of place from which to work in the two continents she straddles. A motley assortment of people from Agnes's kin, including Fran, Shirl, Sara Ann, as well as Marvin, MaryLou, Debbie, Linda, Shirley, June, Sheila, Nan, and Andy: I am so grateful for the ways each of you consciously and without knowing, spurred me on. Daniel offers his thanks to Wendy, whose love makes solid ground.

INTRODUCTION

Prefatory Remarks

THE CHAPTERS gathered in *Countering Displacements: The Creativity and Resilience of Indigenous and Refugee-ed Peoples* highlight the creativity and agency of people who have been displaced. Each author, addressing a distinct case study of displacement, points to the ways in which the experience of displacement and the possibilities and realities of resilience are creatively expressed in the cultural domain. The relationship between indigenous and refugee-ed experiences of displacement and of agency is directly addressed in a number of the following eight chapters and is further opened up by the conversation offered amongst the chapters.[1] Contexts of study range from the Americas to the Middle East and the Indian subcontinent.

The volume begins with two foundational articles. The first introduces creative acts of narration as a form of agency, and the second offers a theorization of creative acts of citizenship. Jon Gordon's "Displacing Oil: Towards 'Lyric' Re-presentations of the Alberta Oil Sands" explores the literal displacement of the earth under our feet (as in the stripping away of land in the Alberta oil sands project) and that process's eventual displacement of indigenous people. Displacement, here, is uniquely extrapolated from its anthropocentric assumption and is instead situated within a complex relationship amongst land, ecosystem, economy, and human experience. His essay reminds us that human displacements are fundamentally about removal of and from the land. And, by showing how creative "lyric" and literary expression have been used to protest the oil sands project, Gordon draws our attention to the way displacement is often countered in cultural forms. The essay that follows, Jean McDonald's "Citizenship Studies and Migrant Illegality," parallels Gordon's topographical groundwork by providing a theoretical grounding for the volume in her literature review of citizenship studies. Her essay familiarizes our readers with the conversations in international relations regarding nation-state sovereignty. McDonald's focus on the work of No One Is Illegal illustrates how those who are excluded from statehood and citizenship can creatively express their protest and, by taking up their own assertions of citizenship, erase clearly defined lines between insiders and outsiders.

The next four essays by Mazen Masri, Catherine Graham, Pavithra Narayanan, and Subhasri Ghosh outline various experiences of displacement and the complex relationships between indigenous and refugee-ed populations, ranging from studies in Israel and Palestine to Manipur and West Bengal. Masri and Graham both address Palestinian displacement. Graham examines a play about a Western male journalist at an Israeli checkpoint who is certain that he can be "objective" and thereby detached from the huge imbalance of power in this situation. His mindset in fact deepens the displacement that the Palestinians at the checkpoint are experiencing. Displacement through detachment is also the subject of Masri's chapter, but his focus is on how the Israeli-built segregation wall detaches Palestinians from the necessities of life: public justice, livelihoods, access to health care, and freedom of movement. While Graham depicts theatre as a witness to this displacement and as a confrontation with a supposedly objective audience, Masri demonstrates the many ways that the illegitimacy of the wall is highlighted through organized political resistance outside of conventional citizenship paths.

In her contribution, Narayanan describes the way indigenous peoples of the Manipur region have experienced internal displacement, first by the British Raj and then by the state of India, while Ghosh's chapter focuses on refugees who fled East Pakistan and squatted on marshy lands outside Calcutta. Both chapters trace the initiatives displaced and disempowered peoples have taken up under very adverse conditions. In response to the government in New Delhi making life in Manipur increasingly precarious through the abuses of the Indian army and through intentionally keeping the area underdeveloped, Narayanan describes how women's groups, called Meira Paibis, have organized themselves to patrol neighbourhoods and guard them against military abuse. For her part, Ghosh shows how refugees around Calcutta have organized in creative ways over the years to win clear title to their once marginal, now valuable lands. Even as these four essays describe detailed conditions of displacement, they focus on the ways in which the peoples' agency and resilience gives birth to theatrical performances and other creative forms of protest that declare "we are here" and insist upon their own citizenship.

The final two essays bring the volume back to the place where it is being edited and published (Canada), to specific internally displaced indigenous and refugee-ed communities here. Both essays highlight how they have creatively found ways to speak in their own voices, rather than being represented or spoken for by others. Agnes Kramer-Hamstra's chapter explores how Mohawk filmmaker Shelley Niro's work takes up stereotypical representations of Indigenous peoples in Canada, replacing "cardboard characters" with Aboriginal actors who translate their own tradition so that it reverberates in contemporary contexts. While Niro counters inert stereotypes of internally displaced First Nations people, Maroussia Hajdukowski-Ahmed's chapter draws our attention to the resilience of women who have been forced to migrate to Canada. Her study of women's healing from traumatic experiences of displacement through art contributes to the volume's focus on the complex relationships between indigeneity, migration, colonialism, and settlement, as well as the role of human agency and creativity in navigating these experiences.

As they emphasize the cultural domain's relation to the explicitly political one, our contributors' discussions of creativity, agency, and indigeneity in relation to refugee-ed people brings a fresh voice to broader studies of displacement. The volume as a whole offers a study of the cultures of displaced people from within the discipline of cultural studies. Eschewing associations of culture with an elite or with "high art," the version of cultural studies associated with Raymond Williams examines the everyday life that people engage in to discover the complex ways their activities and practices shape a public culture. Our emphasis on the agency of displaced peoples is informed by this focus on the "ordinary."

A helpful link can be made between Williams's comments on the advent of mass media in the 1950s and our take on displacement studies. Both share a concern with the way a complex context and diverse peoples can become simplistically fixed in the public mind. Refugee-ed and internally displaced indigenous peoples often have had to struggle against reductive definitions of their identity that have little to do with their lived reality. However, as Lawrence Grossberg puts it, "For cultural studies, the fact that people do use the limited resources they are given to find better ways of living, to find ways of increasing the control they have over aspects of their lives, is significant, not only in itself, but also in terms of understanding the structures of power and inequality in the contemporary world and the possibilities for challenging them" (75). Compared to studies that examine displacement in relation to political economy, international relations, or citizenship law, then, we focus on the cultural domain in order to track and emphasize people's everyday agency. The case studies in this volume each document how particular peoples have, in their unique responses to displacement, been active in reshaping their lives in public ways. Collectively, these case studies demonstrate the resilience of displaced people, creatively countering unequal political and cultural power through political, communal, and artistic acts, taking up and speaking back to discourses that appear to be "natural, universal and eternal" (Hebdige 363–64; see also During 6).

We want to avoid the tendency towards determinism that can occur in some cultural studies theories on power and ideology. Instead, we celebrate the "ordinary" that Williams and Grossberg and many other cultural studies scholars have insisted on: that is, the agency of humans as it is expressed in everyday neighbourliness, in daily life, and social interaction. Because of our focus on everyday agency, we are reluctant to portray culture exclusively in terms of the machinations of power elites or static power hierarchies. Rather, the studies of culture in the following chapters emphasize the limited power of oppressed people that is nonetheless used for enablement (Masri, Hajdukowsk-Ahmed, Ghosh, Narayanan), the essential interdependence between the human and non-human communities (Gordon), and theatre and film that challenge mass media representations and invite audiences to share in the narratives of displaced communities (Graham, Kramer-Hamstra). As they highlight the many voices that make up each particular context, these case studies are manifestations of neighbourliness and of insistence on neighbourliness.

More often than not, refugee and Indigenous studies have been disconnected. The definition of a refugee and the challenges of refugee populations have been addressed thoroughly in refugee studies, while the displacements of Native peoples have been addressed in the field of Indigenous studies. Rarely are refugee and Indigenous studies brought together into one volume, and so this dialogue, in tandem with our cultural studies focus on creativity and agency, uniquely contributes to the conversation on displacement.[2] What follows is our introductory essay on these themes, split into three sections: Displaced Native Populations, Claiming Agency in Displacement, and Countering Displacements with Creativity.

Displaced Native Populations

It has become a truism to say that we live in an age of massive human upheaval and migration; more people than ever before no longer live where their ancestors did. Some have moved from their ancestral regions because moving helps them participate in a global economy of circulating goods, labour, and capital. Others have been unwillingly displaced by environmental, economic, social, or political adversities. We use *displacement* to refer to the experiences of this latter group, those who have been unwillingly uprooted. The displaced, as compared to migrants, expatriates, and other kinds of travellers, are usually people who have been seen as standing "in the way of development" (Blaser, Feit, and McRae 1–21), and, as a result, they have been either forcibly removed from their ancestral lands or have had the authority of their experience on the land denied and the ground itself redefined beneath their feet.[3] Two populations mark opposite vectors on the continuum of displacements: Indigenous peoples, who may still live on their ancestral lands but whose relationship to that land has been abrogated; and refugee-ed people, who have had to leave their homes usually without passports and visas, and who therefore live outside of the provisions of a nation-state. Despite the fact that the refugee is, ultimately, a displaced native, these two populations are not often discussed in relation to one another. In public policy and social sciences research, this separation emerges from the fundamental difference between legal categories applied to internally displaced people, who have not left the nation-state within which they live, and to refugee-ed people, who are defined by having crossed an international border.[4] Our concern as academics in the humanities has been to understand not only the legal and the political but, more broadly, the *cultural* causes, effects, and possibilities of displacement, and, by this means, to encourage an interdisciplinary dialogue that might bridge the gap between Indigenous and refugee studies. With these goals in mind, the editors of this volume hosted a conference over the weekend of March 6–9, 2008 entitled "Displacements: Borders, Mobility, Statelessness" at McMaster University in Hamilton, Ontario, Canada.[5] Most of the chapters of this volume were presented in an earlier form at the conference, while we have solicited others since then. On hearing the papers at the conference and before editing them for the volume, we were struck by three central themes, which, in turn, have shaped the three main purposes for this volume: 1) to generate the dialogue between Indigenous and refugee displacements mentioned above; 2) to provide an arena where suppressed or contested narratives of displacement could be re-narrated and therefore "witnessed" in a public forum; and 3) to highlight the agency and creativity of displaced people who are often represented as objects rather than subjects of their experience.

While there are comprehensive literatures in the fields of citizenship studies, international relations, and refugee studies on the displacement of refugee-ed people and undocumented migrants, and there is an equally large literature on the displacement of Aboriginal peoples in the field of Indigenous studies, the two are seldom studied in relation to one another.[6] Despite their common experience of displacement, however, there are often tensions between these two populations, with refugees from one region displacing people who already live in the place to which they flee. This history of displacements includes many variant examples. Among them are Irish potato famine refugees who migrated to Turtle Island (North America) in the nineteenth century; Jewish refugees who migrated to Palestine during the nineteenth and twentieth centuries to flee racial discrimination and genocide in Europe; Hindu and Muslim South Asians migrating in opposite directions during the partition of India and Pakistan. This is the complicated reality whose tensions include the indigenous right of land and the refugee right of migration, tensions we do not wish to separate. Instead, we wish to examine how the displacement of refugee-ed people who have fled economic, political, or natural adversities is complicated by the ways in which their flight was facilitated by colonial and neo-colonial projects. The new homes in the places where they sought refuge were often created by imperialist or nationalist movements that were aggressively displacing people indigenous to the place. Because such examples of displacements invoke strong political and social investments, as well as disciplinary ones, there can be a desire to keep the discussion of these two displaced populations in separate, and often virulently opposed, accounts. Our examination seeks to show how the figures of the native and the refugee are inherently bound to one another in the larger narrative of multiple, and often intersecting, displacements.[7]

By attending to the displaced in this volume, we take a critical step back from the tendency in postcolonial diaspora studies to focus on the kinds of hybrid cultural fusion and processes of creolized adaptation that occur across the generations as migrants encounter other cultural influences in the large metropolitan centres of the ex-empires.[8] We admire the project of these studies to recognize the creative forms of self-redefinition and cultural cross-pollination that dislocated people invent. Yet the multi-generational long view of diaspora studies can overlook those populations who live in more immediately urgent and radically disenfranchised circumstances—in refugee camps, detention centres, border zones, reservations, residential schools, and other special, hidden zones where they have limited access to the basic protections of international human rights law. To focus on displacement, then, is to focus on a series of interconnected and often contradictory losses: from the literal loss of land to the loss of an affective connection to home, language, or culture; from the loss of legitimacy in a region to the loss of control over the symbols, stories, and laws that define that region; from loss of citizenship in a nation to forced submission to the laws of a colonizing foreign nation; and from loss of freedom of movement to loss of the right to stay in one's home.

Because of the dehumanizing effects of these kinds of loss, one might think that the laws of universal human rights would be decisively implemented to protect those who have been displaced. But as Giorgio Agamben has famously observed, neither international human rights organizations such as the United Nations nor individual nation-states have been capable of guaranteeing human rights to people outside the parameters of the nation-state: "The paradox here is that precisely the figure that should have incarnated the rights of man *par excellence*, the refugee, constitutes instead the radical crisis of the concept" (116). Agamben traces this failure to the way the rights of the *citizen* have always overwhelmed those of the human being *as human* ever since the formulation of the French Declaration of the Rights of Man and of Citizen in 1789. He thus identifies the refugee as a key challenge to the belief that the modern nation-state exists to protect the rights of the human, because "by breaking up the identity between man [*sic*] and citizen, between nativity and nationality, the refugee throws into crisis the original fiction of sovereignty" (117). To put it simply, the nation-state system may be able to protect (some of) the rights of citizens, but not of people who exceed the national bounds of citizenship. Agamben's work has stimulated a large body of scholarship scrutinizing the nation-state's borders, where, in Linda Bosniak's apt phrase, nations' provisions for their citizens are characterized as *"hard on the outside and soft on the inside"* (*Citizen and Alien* 4, emphasis original). For those on the inside of citizenship, who have passports and citizenship papers in place, border crossings are a mere inconvenience, but for those who do not have the required documents or who do not fit the acceptable criteria for welcome, the border becomes a hard edge where one can be transformed into an "alien," searched, detained, turned back, or interned.⁹

This scrutiny at the border—whether a border checkpoint, airport immigration desk, or immigration office in a refugee camp far removed from any national boundary—unavoidably raises the spectre of fear. In his study of the 1951 UN Refugee Convention's definition of a refugee as a person who, "owing to a well-founded fear of being persecuted…is outside the country of his nationality" (UN qtd. in Nyers, *Rethinking Refugees* 47), Peter Nyers observes that this rendering of refugee-ed people undermines their dignity, reinventing them as "human beings 'in the raw,' so to speak, because they are motivated by a *feeling*—the subjective emotion of fear—rather than by *rational deliberation*" (*Rethinking Refugees* 61, emphasis added). Nyers goes on to trace how this dehumanized refugee derives from Thomas Hobbes's idea that state sovereignty was founded to subdue the fearful chaos of the pre-national "state of nature," a state of constant warfare where "every man is Enemy to every man" (Hobbes qtd. in Nyers, *Rethinking Refugees* 53). To return to Bosniak's formulation, the chaos and fear posited outside the nation-state demand that it harden its exterior to protect its citizens within. The same spirit that sets feeling in opposition to the ability to reason seems to be at work in the UN Convention's portrayal of the refugee as one who is defined by the irrational fear that opposes the domestic peace of the nation.

But Hobbes's own human denizens of the state of nature were not refugee-ed people; rather, his examples were "the savage people in many places of *America* [who] have no government at all; and live at this day in that brutish manner" (qtd. in Henderson, "Context" 16, emphasis original). According to Hobbes, people in a state of nature have "no Knowledge of the face of the Earth; no account of Time; no Arts; no Letters; no Society; and which is worst of all, continually feare" (qtd. in Henderson, "Context" 16). In the Hobbesian pedigree to the UN Convention, then, we see once again the deep and long connection between Indigenous people and refugees, both of whom are figured as subjects of fear in the state of nature, outside the rational rule of law, and both, by this logic, reduced in dignity and agency. Chickasaw legal scholar, James (Sákéj) Youngblood Henderson writes, "The theory that Indigenous people lacked positive law had certain self-serving implications for Europeans. If they had nothing resembling European law, then they had no government until they allied themselves with a European Crown" ("Context" 20). Here we see the interrelations between discursive displacement and material displacement; if the inhabitants of the Americas can be portrayed as people with no culture or government of their own, then they can be removed from their land with impunity and replaced by refugees from the Highland clearances, the Irish potato famines, or various European wars. They can be removed to reservations, or can be taken from their homes and placed in residential schools where they will be shorn of their culture and language and forcibly immersed in Euro-American values; they can be reduced from citizens with their own forms of jurisprudence to wards of the state without basic provisions for self-government or independent livelihood. Subsequently, descendents of the European refugees, now citizens protected by the civil and rational laws of the colonial settler state, can redefine and literally displace the land so radically that it will be unrecognizable to its original inhabitants.[10]

A recent and telling example of the relations between settler-colonial displacements of Indigenous peoples and the state's rejection of (fearful) refugees can be seen in Australia's notorious "Pacific Solution." According to Suvendrini Perera, national alarm in 2001 over the arrival of Lebanese asylum-seekers on board the MV *Tampa* on Christmas Island off of the north coast caused the Australian government to excise 4,000 islands from the country's "migration zone." This excision meant that any refugee-ed people who attempted to land on any of these islands would not be considered to have landed in Australia or to have recourse to

Australian law. They would then be sent to Australian-established internment camps in Indonesia. After another refugee ship, the *Minasa Bone*, was escorted by the Australian navy from Melville Island in 2003, one of the Aborigine islanders told the press, "We know what it means to be non-Australians. If that boat comes back, we'll welcome them and give them food and water. You know why? Because we're all one group—non-Australians" (qtd. in Perera 212).

The islander's rejection of the nation-state that had excised Melville Island from its official territory demonstrates that, while nations may attempt to make their margins hard on the outside, their borders are nonetheless "alive, mobile, resourceful, and operating to multiple rhythms under different temporal and spatial conditions" (Soguk 285). Borders are imposed (and, in this case, moved) by the power of states, but they are also constantly contested by those who inhabit what Prem Kumar Rajaram and Carl Grundy-Warr call "borderscapes" (xxxiv). Their term borderscapes incorporates the whole range of zones where insidership and outsidership are negotiated and contested, from deep within the territory of the nation (such as refugee hearings, detention centres, or migrant workers' camps) to the borderlands where immigration offices, squatters' villages, and camps string along an international boundary.[11] Ranging even further outward, this borderscape includes undocumented outposts of the nation on ill-defined foreign soil where would-be immigrants are screened or untried prisoners of war are incarcerated, such as Australia's refugee camps in Indonesia or the USA's infamous detention camp at Guantanamo Bay, Cuba.

The islander's statement also reminds us that, for all the people who seek asylum and the rights of citizenship, there are as many who reject the citizenship that has been forced upon them. This latter point is a key reminder that all displaced people do not seek the same solutions to their circumstances. While many asylum-seekers and undocumented migrants spend years and significant resources seeking UN-sanctioned refugee status or citizenship within a hosting nation, many Indigenous peoples resist citizenship in an effort to retain a previous national identity that was denied by the Hobbesian theory of the state of nature. As Canadian Indigenous people's canny decision to name their political association "the Assembly of *First* Nations" indicates, many Aboriginal people contest, rather than seek democratic inclusion in, the nation-states that have displaced them. Indeed, they seek a full realization of the nation-to-nation relations outlined in the treaties they originally signed with incoming colonial powers. For example, Henderson observes that to invite Aboriginal people to take up Canadian citizenship

> *ignores the fact that the rights of aliens to Canadian citizenship are derived mostly from the Aboriginal sovereign's conditional permission to the British sovereign to provide for settlements, rather than as is frequently argued, from British sovereignty alone and delegated legislative authority. Aboriginal peoples do not have to join Canada and become citizens; Canada and its citizens have to acknowledge their Aboriginal foundation.* ("Sui Generis" 419)[12]

Henderson's reminder that the settler colony's legal legitimacy depends upon a prior recognition of Aboriginal sovereignty (otherwise, why the need to sign treaties, if Indigenous North Americans were merely savages living in a state of nature?) stands as a witness to a political history usually repressed and forgotten in the official histories of colonial states. Accordingly, if a first purpose of this volume is to generate dialogue between refugee and Indigenous vectors of displacement, a second purpose is to provide such re-narrations of official history as forms of witness. Paul Ricoeur summarizes Hannah Arendt saying that "the meaning of human existence is not just the power to change or master the world, but also the ability to be remembered and recollected in narrative discourse, to be *memorable*" (100), and he adds that "to give people back a *memory* is also to give them back a *future*" (109, emphasis original). Part of our purpose in collecting the essays in this volume, then, is to remember narratives of displacement and to therefore resist both their disavowal and the ways in which their suppression from memory can make their effects seem natural and fixed.

One danger of drawing attention to narratives of traumatic displacement, however, is that such narratives can reduce the displaced person to the status of an object, a victim of larger powers who lacks her or his own agency or creative capacity.[13] One sees this phenomenon in the many media representations that portray refugee-ed people as being absolutely dependent upon humanitarian intervention if they are to survive. So the third, and most important, aim of this volume is to highlight the agency and creativity of those who have been displaced. If the chapters in this book call attention to the imposition of military force on the northeastern Indian state of Manipur, to Israel's building of the so-called security fence in the West Bank, or to the mass production of stereotypes about Indigenous people in North American popular culture,[14] they also witness the ways people subjected to these impositions of power counter them. Insisting upon telling their own stories, they resist officially sanctioned narratives of their marginalization or disappearance, and not only oppose but transform the violence and trauma they have encountered. By drawing attention to their insistence on narrating their own experiences, we hope to show how these forms of creativity, as Maroussia Hajdukowski-Ahmed points out in her essay, generate agency and resilience. Thus, the chapters in this volume are not just about displacement but about *countering* displacement, insofar as they emphasize the ways in which those who have been displaced remain active, potently political, and remarkably resilient, even when they have very little access to official power.

Claiming Agency in Displacement

Refugees, "illegal" immigrants, and internally displaced people are increasingly taking up and asserting political subjectivities that are not legitimated by the liberal nation-state system. While national borders purport to draw clean delineations between who belongs and who does not, Nevzat Soguk argues that borders are "forever insufficient to...challenges and pressures" of human need (285). This volume is emerging at a time when "no border" movements are growing all over the world, calling for "an end to displacement worldwide, the free movement of people and committed support for indigenous struggles for traditional land and self-determination" (Nyers, "Abject" 1080). The volume also emerges in the context of Indigenous calls for a "transnational indigenous identity" (Alfred, *Wasáse* 143) that is now fragmented by processes of colonialism but originally stems from traditional teachings (144). As this volume exemplifies, such transnational or global social movements test the borders of the nation-state system.[15] Interestingly, these movements are initiated by both concerned rights-bearing citizens and also the subjects who are excluded or constrained by borders. As illustrated in Pavithra Narayanan's chapter about the women's Meira Paibis movement in Manipur and Subhasri Ghosh's chapter about West Bengali refugees' political organizing in Calcutta, activism takes the forms of protests, rallies, street patrols, and legal action. It also takes the forms of storytelling, re-narrations and re-presentations of history and identity.

Indigenous peoples have often sought to contest, rather than to seek democratic inclusion in, the nation-states that have displaced them. In his book *Wasáse: Indigenous Pathways of Action and Freedom*, Mohawk scholar Taiaiake Alfred argues that the imperative of the state has historically tended towards "homogenization and singular control" through "force and legitimacy" (136). So for him, the tendency for some social movements to utilize the "conventional 'indigenous rights within the law' approach" only "redistributes existing legally constituted authority" and "is not transformative in the least" (133). He equates this internalist or reformist strategy to "an acceptance of assimilation" and the eventual loss of the Onkwehonwe [Mohawk term for "original people"] culture (133). For him, the liberal state, whose core function is "to integrate pre-existing social and political diversities into the singularity of the state, assimilating all cultures into a single patriotic identity," cannot be reformed to include pluralistic forms of governance and legal plurality (155). Instead, Alfred moves away from the strategy of reform to promote the autonomy of the Onkwehonwe peoples the world over.

Alfred notes that "a more rooted indigenous peoples' movement has been emerging globally over the last thirty years as a movement *against* the state and *for* the re-emergence of Onkwehonwe existences as cultural and political entities unto themselves" to promote a pluralistic worldview (133). For Onkwehonwe, finding agency in (internal) displacement means retaining memories of difference and cultures of indigeneity. Indeed in his text he refers to "being indigenous" as a practice of resistance (139–40). He is struck at the way Isabel Altamirano, a political scientist at the University of Alberta who is Zapoteca from Oaxaca in southern Mexico, is comfortable as she is "dressed amid the suited academics in the traditional clothing of her people" (140). For Alfred, her resistance is "in her blood" and she "knew what it was to live it" (140). Ultimately, Alfred encourages a form of everyday agency or subjectivity that does not seek to define itself against the state but as different from and independent of the state, seeking to disrupt the dialectical relationship between the state and those outside it. Instead of reconciliation, he argues for restitution or "purification"; instead of recovery, regeneration; and instead of resolution, resurgence, which includes "courageous acts against injustice."[16] Alfred promotes an Indigenous agency that is not focused on recuperating or resolving the colonial problem, but in transcending what has been done to Aboriginal peoples (151). These strategies, he argues, move away from a kind of futile dialectical engagement with the modern liberal state. For Alfred, the logic of a modern, settler nation-state is fundamentally steeped in the plundering of Indigenous resources and in unsustainable economic and environmental practices. His energies toward and his encouragement of a global Indigenous movement are based, then, in the re-taking of the Indigenous movement itself.

A similar impetus towards regenerating communal identity rather than simply resisting state-imposed labels exists in many *sans-papiers* and refugee communities. During an interview with Soenke Zehle, Amy R. West, author of a number of articles on refugee policy and human rights, answers the question raised by refugee researchers "are refugees political agents?" by saying, "of course refugees are political....Refugees are capable of supporting one rebel group over another, swaying policy decisions in the host or home country, and maintaining instability in a region if they so choose" (410). Within camps, refugees elect leadership, organize security forces, hold court, and start postal systems (412). This image of refugees as agents in public debates and events and as civic participants upends the dehumanizing refugee definition of the UN Convention and provides a basis for understanding the complicated agencies that refugee-ed people take up in the midst of displacement.

In "Abject Cosmopolitanism," Peter Nyers shows how the contemporary creation of "no border" social movements and public acts of citizenship challenge the sovereign order (1090). "In France for example, much of the energy in immigrant rights campaigns has come from the undocumented themselves, as demonstrated by the...*sans papier* movement" and its impact on public life (Nyers 1081). According to Nyers, all over Europe and North America "self-organised migrants" participate in rallies and hunger strikes, raise public awareness, and organize political and legal responses directed at governmental policies at such meetings as the European social forum, and the EU and G7 Summits. One example of such activism is the Action Committee for Non-Status Algerians in Montreal, which is "composed of people who are most directly affected by the exclusionary practices of the Canadian state" (Nyers 1082). The non-status refugees have "themselves taken the lead in the campaign to stop their deportations and regularize their status in Canada and Quebec" (Nyers 1082).

These groups' actions sometimes take on the state and other times transcend it to target international or transnational conferences and organizations. They use slogans like "we are here because you destroy our countries," "'no one is illegal,' 'no borders, no nations, no deportations,' and 'neither here, nor elsewhere'" (Nyers 1080). In this way, these social movements are evoking global relationships that challenge the seemingly impermeable borders of the nation-state. They evoke international economic policies that "create the conditions of poverty and war that force migration" (No One Is Illegal) and to counter displacement.

However, "no border" social movements do not always bypass the nation-state. They often simultaneously critique state policies such as the deportation of refugee-ed people back to home-countries that are declared unsafe for travel for their own citizens (Nyers 1081, 1083). Such movements engage in "taking-politics," which can include "delegation visits" to immigration offices that "allow the non-status, those who have 'no part,' to assert their political voice" (Nyers, 1084). Nyers reports that immigration staff often have been moved to tears on hearing individual stories that have humanized the "number" that is the refugee. Nyers suggests that "the audacity of such tactics threatens to subvert the entire framework of 'authoritative citizen' versus 'passive refugee'" (1085). "That abject agents sometimes make an appearance—to take space, to take voice" is a form of "radical democratic politics" (Nyers 1087), and, in combination with the creation of sanctuary zones, "an abject cosmopolitan political agency" can be created (Nyers 1084).[17]

Like Alfred, however, Nyers is not completely convinced that the politics of claiming space and a voice in the public sphere with the aim of *reforming* the state system will not be appropriated by sovereign power because the sovereign order "itself relies on such subversions for its own condition" (1087). It is true, Nyers admits, that "Abject cosmopolitanism...burrow[s] into the apparatuses and technologies of exclusion in order to disrupt the administrative routines, the day-to-day perceptions and constructions of normality" (1089). When abject or excessive humans take up space and voice, they are provoking foundational questions about politics: "Who speaks? Who counts? Who belongs? Who can express themselves politically? In short, who can be political?" (1089). This intervention is effective in challenging nation-state borders and disrupting the citizen-government relationship as the only legitimately political one.[18] However, according to Nyers, this movement does "not aim for a higher ground" (1089). Like Alfred, Nyers points out the inherent violence in the modern system of states: "our received traditions of the political *require* that some human beings be illegal" (1089, emphasis original). However, the transcendental notion that "no human is illegal" might be a more comprehensive politics because it calls into question "the entire architecture of sovereignty, all its borders, locks and doors, internal hierarchies, etc." (Nyers 1089). Nyers argues that "radical takings" made by "foreigners are always at risk of being deflected and absorbed by the non-democratic re-takings of sovereign power for the purposes of national and international (re)foundings" (Nyers 1090).

Difficulties in enacting *effective* agency are exemplified by the experiences of many diasporic Palestinians who face the dilemma of choosing between indigeneity or access.[19] Noora, a Palestinian-Canadian York University student with a Palestinian ID number, was faced with such a dilemma in 2008. Israeli nationals and foreigners with European or North American passports are often

Introduction XXVII

allowed to cross into Israel via Elat, through Taba, Egypt. Although Noora has a Canadian passport and is a Canadian citizen, she was told by the border guards that because she had a Palestinian ID number she could not enter the West Bank or Gaza. The Palestinian ID number is an "in-process" number that gives Noora the theoretical right to a Palestinian passport. Her mother, who was travelling with her at the time, was told she could enter because her ID number had expired. Noora, however, was told to try entering through the King Hussein/Allenby Bridge border in Jordan. At that border, after ten hours of waiting, she was told again that because she held a Palestinian ID number, she could not cross. According to Noora, the Israeli officer gave her two options: 1) she could enter if she forfeited her ID number (and therefore her right to a historical claim to the land and a right to return under international law), or 2) she could keep her Palestinian ID number and give up the possibility of entry. If she gave up her ID, however, she would only be able to enter for a maximum of three months on a tourist visa and this access could be denied at any time. Alternatively, she could meet with Palestinian officials in Gaza to obtain a Palestinian passport through her ID number. But this option was simply lip service to legal alternatives as she was not allowed to enter Gaza. In any scenario, Noora is forbidden from entering the West Bank or Jerusalem if she retains her Palestinian ID, which is her claim to indigeneity in the region, her form of retaining her *historical evidence*.

Although Noora's options were bleak, she could have given up her ID number in order to see her family, friends, familial home, religious sites, and ancestral land. But Noora refused to give up the ID number. After taking time off of work and school, travelling overseas, paying for flights and taxi rides, and waiting for hours at borders, Noora decided to forego access in order to hang on to the documentation of a past that has the potential to challenge contemporary and future borders. Keeping one's identity number at the cost of sacrificing home *today* is a kind of agency in a situation where there seems to be no real choice.

Noora's position makes state demarcations of outside and inside highly tenuous in a particularly unique contemporary case of exclusionary ethnic-state politics. Her choices are not determined by the conventional coordinates of state and citizen. Noora's act of agency and resistance is informed by a history that validates her ID number as a political right to the land (and as evidence of another story like that of *Nakbe*[20] and the ensuing Right of Return). Her subscription to a logic outside of the state/citizen logic parallels Alfred's and those of the *sans-papiers* refugees mentioned above. And while Alfred and Nyers show that outsiders stand as part and parcel of state logic that *needs* outsiders to define itself and that activism needs to aim for "higher ground," it becomes endlessly more complicated to think through where Noora's and *sans-papiers* movements' resistance fall within this outsider/insider dichotomy. Such delineations rely heavily on human narratives and resulting imaginings of human-land networks and connections.

The oft-repeated representations of the "desperate" or "fearful" refugee or displaced person who is acted upon is countered in powerful ways by the many Aboriginal people who seek healing and sovereignty outside of or extraneous to the state and who do not work towards integration into the democratic modern nation-states. Amid the complex realities of displacement, the innovative and creative ways people voice or re-take their voice speak to the intimate relationship between human agency and social context.

Countering Displacements Through Creativity

The creative countering work of those who have been affected by forced displacement often remains hidden behind the sheer mass of current scholarship that focuses on the injustices done to the millions of people displaced every year throughout the world.[21] Our choice of the term countering over other options such as "resisting" or "undermining" deliberately draws on the word's flexibility and on its constructive connotations. To counter a force is both to meet it in strength and also to strategically undermine it, to prepare for a future onslaught and to question injustice in the very moment of displacement. The *Oxford English Dictionary* suggests that "counter" often carries with it the notions "of rivalling or outdoing, checking or frustrating that action" and of "balancing, checking, sustaining thrust." The flexibility of the term and its ability to join numerous other verbs and nouns into a compound word reflects the myriad ways displaced people choose to act in the face of their own displacement (consider the differences between counteracting, counterbalancing, and counterattacking, for instance). More than simply *en*countering displacement, countering encompasses the varying activities of creative and strategic agents.

Countering displacements also connotes more than a dialectic relationship with displacing forces; it suggests an alternative to displacement. Just as a counterargument does not stop at pulling apart the opponent's logic but goes on to provide a new and convincing set of proofs, communal memory-keeping, creative performance, and acts of citizenship[22] cultivate alternative interpretations of national identity and more complex understandings of refugee-ed identity. Nurturing those counter-actions can contribute to the regeneration of subject identities, both communal and individual, of people in displacement. In the countering of displacement, indigenous cultures continue to change and grow and refugee-ed people are more than fearful victims.[23]

Human creativity that gives voice to the layered experience of a particular displacement is "*dangerous* in the best sense of the word" as displaced playwrights, artists, theatre troupes, journalists, poets, or groups of refugee-ed women intervene on any report that normalizes displacement (Ricoeur 106, emphasis original). Their interventions are dangerous in a vital sense as they speak over against and trouble, for example, reductive language and other representations that generalize what it means to be refugee-ed or internally displaced. They are dangerous in that they challenge unquestioning adherence to official stories; they complicate news media sound bites that pass for authoritative reports. Ricoeur claims that "human creativity is always a response to a regulating order" and that the task of the imagination is to take "established laws" and to "make them function creatively, either by applying them in an original way or by subverting them; or indeed both" (107). As they articulate and give voice to the nuances of displacement, refugee-ed and internally displaced people subvert, for example, notions on which established laws for immigration are based, which render them invisible, passive, and speechless people. Their voices wedge open the carefully contained and managed space of the official story, the "objective" news report.

As refugee-ed people engage with reductive stereotypes and as internally and culturally displaced peoples regain their vision, their imaginative articulations and reorientations produce a "play that is formidable precisely because it is loose in the world, planting its mediations everywhere, shattering the illusion of the immediacy of the real" (Ricoeur 107). Countering the illusion that the present conditions define refugee-ed people, their imagination mediates between the past, present and future, between internal displacement and all that a people, culture, or community has been and is in a place over time. The play of the (collective's as well as individual's) imagination can take and recreate a community's memory in a way that gives them strength to speak to the present context.

This creative play takes up the conventional ways of thinking about many things, not just identities that fix a people as "postcolonial"; as this play redefines the legacy of an Indigenous people, it can also shake up colonial assumptions of what civilization means. Take for example Métis architect Douglas Cardinal's Museum of Civilization. As it faces the buildings of the Canadian Parliament from across the river that marks the border between the provinces of Ontario and Quebec, it imaginatively counteracts the boundaries that explicitly assume Canada is a nation-state founded on the legacy of English and French colonialism.

Besides offering a Métis counterbalance to the primary divide between French and English in the national mythology, the museum's design brings other voices to the question of where civilizing power comes from. The museum's undulating lines refuse a "rage for measurement and calculation," suggesting instead that human building needs to be founded on a careful listening and response to the organic life of the environment (Lefebvre 122). With its "repertoire of curving forms" that echo Cardinal's "hopes for an architecture in dialogue with landscape and river," his design implicitly critiques the way humans abstract themselves from the living organism that is the environment and suggests that civilizing power lies in humankind's rerooting itself by heeding the sophisticated wisdom gained by Indigenous peoples who have lived in step with a particular place for millennia. The museum's design (conceived in the early 1980s) asserts that civilization is closely related to the life of the earth; it explicitly critiques "nature's new managers in Geneva," who, in declaring a specific area a UNESCO World Heritage site, empty it of the peoples indigenous to an area, peoples who have never made the separations suggested by the term "wilderness," but who have conceptualized this place as a "moral world where humans and nature are mutually constituted" (Cruikshank 251). Cardinal's design utters a dangerous call for an alternative view of civilization, in the best sense of the word.

Acknowledging his own uneasy relationship with a culture that internally displaced indigenous views and civilizations, Cardinal speaks of "the problem [of]...how to be a Native in the true sense and be able to live and work and contribute to a society that has its roots in a foundation that is totally different, totally adversarial" (Armstrong and Cardinal 44). He responds to this problem by making a connection between creativity and the particular spirituality that fuels his hope and vision and which he identifies as a vital part of his Métis heritage: "The design of each building," he says, "is a spiritual act that demands from all those participating in it the very best of their endeavours" (Armstrong and Cardinal 112). The resulting design also reflects what he has learned from Native people, which is that

> *the most powerful force is soft power, caring and commitment, together....You can have visions and dreaming but* how you realize them depends on caring and commitment. *Soft power is more powerful than adversarial or hard power because it is resilient. By its nature, soft power is giving and flexible but strong.* (96, emphasis added)

Cardinal's conception of soft power as a kind of resilience allows him to re-present civilization so as to suggest alternatives to the hard borders mentioned above.

The undulating lines of the museum also speak of Cardinal's own resilience as he creates an alternative to an adversarial system that is often founded on polarization, not only separating nature from culture, and peoples indigenous to an area from what has suddenly been reconfigured as "wilderness," but also creating opposition between tradition and the development and use of technology. Technology, identified often with modern and white culture, is separated from tradition, identified with Indigenous cultures, as if a particular culture must choose either one or the other. Cardinal counters this persistent stereotype as he relays how he was given a vision at the ceremonial lodge "of taking technology and creating something positive with it and maintaining my way of being in doing it" (Cardinal and Armstrong 112). While technology is commonly caricatured as the always "new" and, implicitly, better, and tradition as frozen, out of time, and fixed, Cardinal counters these oppositions by developing an approach to technology that serves the dynamic unfolding of a tradition he has come to identify as his own.

Cardinal's architecture is not the only form of imaginative play that counters the many ways a people are displaced. As it provided a public space for stories of displacement to be told and discussed, the Displacements conference, for which most of the following chapters were originally written, was itself an attempt at countering displacement. Recognizing the potential for the conference discussion to remain within networks of people who have never been displaced or to stay at the level of critiquing displacing institutions and policies, we intermingled presentations by cultural workers from a variety of fields: theoretical papers, activist talks, poetry readings, stories of writers in exile, and theatrical performances (see www.literaryculture.ca for video of many of these performances). The many forms of displacement narration that were presented over the course of three days together stood both as a witness to the complex losses inherent in dislocation and to the ingenious imaginings, long-haul sacrifices, and new life growing in displacement. Two performances were particularly powerful in witnessing to the vitality of displaced communities and their struggle to "be at home," in the sense of being recognized as social, political, human actors in their new surroundings: excerpts from *Operetang Maynila*, written by Petronila Cleto[24] and performed by Filipina Live-In Caregivers from Toronto, Canada; and *Finding Our Song*, written by Hazem Jamjoum[25] and performed by Salameh Theatre Troupe from Mississauga, Canada.

Both performances' scripts and actors came out of diasporic community organizations in the greater Toronto area. They highlighted the voices of local stakeholders and in so doing, they avoided conversations exclusive to a managerial or scholarly elite, such as those that Amy West sees at work in the refugee policy of the UNHCR and other international agencies: "Key international actors are well-connected to global communication networks, but disconnected from local stakeholders" (415). Each performance was the result of collaborative work that expressed concerns immediate to a displaced community. *Operetang Maynila*[26] is a theatrical distillation of the stories that Cleto gathered from Filipinas who came to Canada as part of the federal government's Live-In Caregiver Program.[27] Cleto, a member of PEN Canada's Writer in

Exile Network, solicited caregivers to act in the play, and the caregivers helped Cleto to decide which pieces of the script needed to be emphasized and which most resonated with them. On the day of the performance, the women arrived having just participated in the International Women's Day March in the midst of a snowstorm. Marching on the streets of Toronto and then acting on the stage at an academic conference were complementary pieces of their struggle to have a voice within a legal structure that does not recognize their voice. Their very presence and performance at the conference was the political and creative act of "taking space and voice" in the kind of "radical democratic politics" that Nyers describes ("Abject" 1087).

In the play, unscrupulous employers are reframed as small-time mafia sharks, holding complete power over a few people, making decisions motivated only by personal profit, and dishonestly manipulating contracts to benefit themselves. Vignettes of the employees' lives show women working hard in silence and solitude for hours, reaching out to each other through brick walls but never connecting; a woman reading a letter from her own child while she cares for her employer's baby; a woman praying about her faraway husband, unsure if he will remain faithful to her; and women being ordered by their employers to do things that are not in their contracts. One woman explains, half to herself, half to the audience

> *I can't say anything. Otherwise she will fire me. I don't want that to happen. I may not be able to complete my two years of living-in by the deadline. I can't complain now. It doesn't look like I can get out of this, this prison. (Goes back to baby's room.) Alright, when those two years are over, I will complain. Then I'll have rights. (Pause) I think. (Operetang Maynila)*

In these few excerpts the silencing force is portrayed effectively as the "LCP Machine" (i.e., Live-In Caregiver Program); it is emotionless and will not take responsibility for what it has set in motion by bringing the women to Canada. The machine says

> *Well, I cannot feel pity—I have nerves of steel and a heart of aluminum! So I cannot give you any money.*
> *I don't have a conscience, so I do not feel anything.*
> *And I can do anything I want with you—I was built that way!*
> (Operetang Maynila)

Here is the moment where the displacement of live-in caregivers, who may appear to be free agents in migrating to Canada, is made clear. So long as they accept the actual loss of rights that accompanies their status as temporary workers in Canada, they are merely well-oiled parts in the economic machine. But in choosing to voice the need for change in that machine, they find themselves standing in the way of "progress" and easily delegitimized as not belonging to this place.

For caregivers, the borders of Canada are soft because their labour is needed. Once inside, the hardness of the border reasserts itself in the form of citizen-employers who appear to have free reign in policing the border within their own homes. In a Hobbesian ideal state, the border is meant to keep chaos at bay and to protect its citizens within. But through provisions such as the Live-In Caregiver program, the Canadian nation-state can introduce an exception to its own labour laws by creating a special, temporary, immigration category, whose relations to domestic labour laws are ambiguous at best.[28] Employers of Filipino caregivers can use their privilege as citizens in Canada both to manipulate international inequities for their own financial gain and also to hold the caregivers' temporary status as a threat over their work security. Caregivers find they are the exception to the rule, though they have come to Canada depending on its legal order. *Operetang Maynila* both humanizes live-in caregivers by embodying their individual stories onstage and also levels a critique at unfeeling structures that treat caregivers as commodities rather than stakeholders. Remarkably, faced with their own powerlessness, these stakeholders still choose, in the words of the play, to "open up their hearts" and "offer a poor woman's love" to the children they care for, revealing an alternative ethic at work. (In comments following their performance, some actors expressed surprise at the way that their employers did not value the work of raising children.) Caregivers "speak to their hearts" and "pray" as a way of grounding themselves. These poignant scenes of self-reflection remind the audience that countering displacement requires a deep-seeded knowledge of one's identity.

The struggle to understand one's own identity in displacement is precisely what was expressed in another theatrical performance on the opening night of the conference. In *Finding Our Song*, the young actors in the Salameh Theatre Troupe established a very different tone from the Filipina Live-In Caregivers, taking their voice as Arab teenagers in a university conference hall with humour and strength.[29] The skit begins as the theatre troupe gathers for a rehearsal and tries to determine what their theme song should be. As they try out different musical styles their central question is, how will we sing in this new Canadian setting? And, what song represents us and our culture here? The performance opens with one character swaggering onto the stage, carefully adjusting the collar on his white shirt before playing a flamenco riff on his guitar.[30] His playing is interrupted by the "yo YO!" greeting of a rapper dressed in a hoodie, who interjects rhymes throughout the group's discussion, drawing the proud flamenco player into the rhythm he creates. The rapper's rhymes cannot represent them because his assimilation into black Atlantic culture has resulted in his own rejection of the label "displaced" and his unrecognizable performance of Arab identity. The flamenco guitar player is equally unable to represent them, but for an opposite reason: his performance as a new immigrant does not yet engage with the new land. Wanting to acknowledge that they are "settlers here on Native peoples' stolen land," one of the group members suggests and teaches the rest a Native "honour" song he has learned from AIM—the American Indian Movement. At this point another group member interrupts by raising the issue of cultural appropriation, arguing that "their land is stolen...and we are going to start stealing their songs too?" There is a deep affinity with Indigenous displacement because of stolen land that the theatre troupe recalls through its name: *Salameh* is the name of "the largest Palestinian city before the *Nakba* (the Catastrophe) of 1948," when it and "over 500 villages were destroyed and over 700,000 Palestinians were expelled" (Salameh). But the group members do not want their acknowledgement of Indigenous people to further disenfranchise First Nations people—an experience they can understand because of the Canadian appropriation of Arabic foods for the nation's multicultural identity. So they return to their search for a song that will do justice to their identity. An Arabic popular love song by Amr Diab is dismissed as "too cheesy" and someone raises the question of value ("just because it's popular doesn't mean it has meaning"). Another person suggests that they write their own words to a 100-year-old Arabic folk song, "*Ala Dalona wa Ala Dalona.*" They focus approvingly on the meaning of the original lyrics, which are "about rich and poor, about the dignity of the working class despite poverty." Finally they use the tune to write their own song, which recognizes "who we are, where we are, whose land we're on...and also alsO, yo [the rapper joins in] that our culture is alive, that it's changing and that the changes are good, GOOD!" Their song is in Arabic and the translation allows the non-Arabic speakers in the audience to hear that

> *even if they displace us....expel us....humiliate us....We remain Arabs, with all our heritage/ Music, theatre, and all our arts....We're building a future for our grandchildren/ To dignify the memory of our grandparent's resistance and memories....Our Glorious, beloved people; May they stay safe/ With the history of our land.*

In the translation of the final verse one can hear traces of the rapper's influence:

If you liked this skit, your place is hona (here)
Division is no good, we need this unity
Your hands in my hands for the community
Every one of us has the ability
Together we are strong and not alona (alone).

This verse signals many things, including the importance of the dialogue between the troupe and its audience, which suggests that the audience is invited to step away from the role of being a detached observer. This invitation turns on its head the idea that there is power in being such an observer, as the rest of the verse suggests this detachment and non-participation means one is "alona," and that this actually weakens one's identity. Besides this challenge to Salameh's immediate audience, they promote dialogue between black culture, diasporic fused cultures as represented by flamenco, Indigenous culture, and the working poor.

In creating this song, the troupe suggests one of many ways to answer the implicit question of how communities can recall the disaster that has displaced and threatens to erase them but in a way that will not repeat this devastation. Salameh acknowledges the devastations of the past as well as the influences of other voices and generates out of them a new form of self-expression, one that brings together the past and the future in a meaningful present. Their creativity helps them find their way through many languages—Arabic, English, the musical languages or traditions of Arabic music, rap, flamenco, the discourses of their own and Native American displacement—and they form a song that they can meaningfully sing, bringing together these many voices in a new way.

This creative process enacts what Ricoeur describes as he wrestles with the relationship between giving meaning to the past, hope for a future and creativity: "To 'repeat' our story, to retell our history, is to re-collect our horizon of possibilities in a resolute and responsible manner" (104). In asking how and what to sing in this new place, the characters create this horizon of possibilities. As they imaginatively explore their particular relationship to displacement and a new place, they respond with a new song that gives their new circumstance a particular shape. The song they sing cannot be an old song that their parents used to shape their response to another time and place. One character protests to the old lyrics: "but, I never lived in a village!" And yet, the new song recalls who they continue to be ("we remain Arabs"). Their song is creatively retrospective as well as prospective, looking back and looking forward in an imaginative way.

▶ Throughout the Displacements conference, participants raised questions about the values and losses inherent in solidarities and alliances between differently displaced communities, amongst those who are seen to stand in the way of progress. Alfred's distinction between non-transformative reconciliation and substantial regeneration reminds us that the way forward for displaced people is not found only in alliances with people who are well-placed but also in building communities and identities that have the strength to be a counter to displacements.

The refrain repeated at the end of each scene in *Operetang Maynila* offers an important warning against the additional silencing force of what has been called "violent humanitarianism":[31]

> *They don't beg for your pity.*
> *Can you hear their hearts?*
> *They don't beg for your tears.*

This refrain is then followed by the sudden vulnerability of a single voice asking her audience, "Do you feel anything?" Basilia, the single voice here, reminds her audience that the caregivers' struggle to counter displacement often takes place in the solitude of domestic work and that words spoken in hope often go unheard. Yet the caregivers do not fall silent. The strength of the voices in chorus, speaking in the third person and so mediating the perspective of the viewer, breaks into the thoughts of the audience members and reframes for them what they have just seen. The scenes of loneliness and of broken trust are not reason to pity the caregiver's situation or to weep cathartically with their pain, and the actors do not beg despite the deep vulnerability they demonstrate. Certainly, the viewer is called to *feel* in contrast to the character of the LCP Machine. Yet the greater call from the mediating chorus is for the audience to actually "hear" the "hearts" of the displaced; to listen; and to support their radical democratic vision of acting politically even without the legal stamp of citizenship.

In a place where *(y)our* memories hold no meaning, where *its* people, geographies, and past events do not trigger memories and therefore cannot provide you with the strength of communal identity, the countering work of creativity in displaced communities begins the rebuilding of relevant memories and connections. In a place where you *do not count*—in other people's memories, in historically significant places, in important communal events, and in civic and legal conversations—even in this place, the activities of creating and staging (whether in art, theatre, protests, or literature) can make public places into significant memoried spaces for displaced people and produce events in which the voices of the displaced *count*. The processes of production and performance create a place where the personal memories and the private experiences of the displaced become publicly relevant, where agency can be enacted, where all that has been kept internalized can finally be insisted upon in public, where new, shared stories can begin.

DANIEL COLEMAN
ERIN GOHEEN GLANVILLE
WAFAA HASAN
AGNES KRAMER-HAMSTRA

NOTES

1. In using the term "refugee" we are aware of at least three contextual uses. The first is as a noun and legal term used by the international human rights community both as a way of providing access to protection and, less admirably, with the effect of imposing a standardized description of refugeeness on a variety of experiences. The second is as an adjective indicating forced displacement as an imposition on a person's identity. In this and the previous context, turning the noun "refugee" into a third term, the adjective "refugee-ed," is a form of discursive activism. "Refugee" suggests that this temporary state is a permanent identity, while the adjective "refugee-ed" suggests a person's ongoing formation of identity always exceeds its present state. The third usage is as a claimed identity by people who have been refugee-ed and want to draw on the strength of the term ("I am a refugee"). Throughout this introduction we use whichever version of this term is most appropriate to the immediate context.

2. In many ways, our volume serves as a companion to *Narratives of Citizenship: Indigenous and Diasporic Peoples Unsettle the Nation-State*, edited by Aloys Fleischmann, Nancy Van Styvendale, and Cody McCarroll and also published by the University of Alberta Press (2011). Their volume was in press when the essays were written for *Countering Displacements* and therefore not available to our contributors. The two books parallel one another in focusing on the domain of culture and in bringing together studies of Indigenous and diasporic people's challenges of the nation-state and its power to determine citizenship. Our volume differs from *Narratives of Citizenship* in its focus upon Indigenous and refugee-ed people's creative agency in responding to displacement. Broadly, diasporas can include some powerfully privileged peoples, so our focus on refugee-ed people rather than on diasporas more generally emphasizes the phenomenon of creativity despite extreme adversity.

3. Among the definitions for displacement in the *Oxford English Dictionary* we find these: "**1.** Removal from an office or dignity; deposition. (The earliest sense, but somewhat *rare*.). **2. a.** Removal of a thing from its place; putting out of place; shifting, dislocation. **b.** *Physics*. The amount by which anything is displaced; the difference or geometrical relation between the initial position of a body and its position at some subsequent instant.... **f.** *Psychol*. The substitution of one idea or impulse for another, as in dreams, obsessions, etc.; the unconscious transfer of intense feelings or emotions to something of greater or less consequence... **3. a.** Removal of a thing by substitution of something else in its place; 'replacement.'" In addition to these physical, social, and psychological meanings of displacement, Angelika Bammer reminds us, in her

introduction to *Displacements: Cultural Identities in Question*, that Derridean theory depends on an understanding of discursive displacement, whereby the meaning of any given sign depends on *différance*, the endless deferral of meaning along a chain of differentiated signs (xiii).

4. For an argument for keeping the legal definitions clear between refugees and internally displaced peoples, see Barutciski. The discussion continues in articles published in the *Journal of Refugee Studies* and with the emergence of forced migration studies; see Zetter and Chimni.

5. For more information on the conference, including a program as well as videos of talks and performances, go to www.literaryculture.ca, click on "Ongoing Projects," and proceed to the Displacements conference archives by clicking on "Read More."

6. For a survey of citizenship studies' discussions of refugees see Jean McDonald's essay in this collection; for a sampling of studies of Aboriginal displacements in the field of Indigenous studies see Cardinal; Adams; Todorov; Wright; Blaser, Feit, and McRae; and Milloy. While most Indigenous studies scholarship focuses on the settler states of the Americas and Australasia, this volume attends to indigeneity as it plays out in regions such as India and Palestine, as well as North America.

7. A similar conversation is launched in Ann Curthoys's book chapter, "An Uneasy Conversation: The Multicultural and the Indigenous." Her chapter has led to a debate in cultural studies and race studies, though mostly limited to the Australian and New Zealand contexts.

8. Of the many writers at work in this field, we are thinking here primarily of influential work by Homi Bhabha, Chambers, Gilroy, Hall, Radhakrishnan, and Rushdie.

9. For a brilliant rendering of the hardness of national boundaries, see Greek-Cherokee writer Thomas King's short story, "Borders," where a Blackfoot woman and her son are detained for two days at the Canada/US border because she identifies herself as "Blackfoot" and refuses to declare her citizenship as "Canadian" or "American." See also Catherine Graham's chapter in this volume, which examines a Palestinian-Belgian theatre troupe's rendering of the contrasting experiences of border-crossing between a European journalist and Palestinian workers at an Israeli checkpoint.

10. See Jon Gordon's essay in this volume on the literal displacement of land—topsoil and substrata—in the massive oil sands project near Fort McMurray, Alberta, Canada, and the project's effects on the environment, as well as the Indigenous people who live in the region.

11. In his chapter in this collection, Mazen Masri traces how the wall constructed deep within Palestinian territory in the West Bank by Israelis has created radical displacement for Palestinians, walling them in and cutting them off from their work, from hospitals, from the rest of their communities. He also records how the systemic and daily interference of the wall and the checkpoints has been resisted, by such people as the villagers of Bil'in who have been joined by Israeli and other activists in weekly protests since 2005 (see http://www.bilin-village.org/english/).

12. Henderson refers to Canadian treaty history in support of his claim for preexisting Aboriginal sovereignty. See James Tully for references to similar treaty constitutionalism in United States history and see also the famous Mabo trial in which Australia's official policy of *terra nullius* was overturned in the 1980s in recognition of pre-colonial Aboriginal land rights. David Mercer's two articles give a sense of the debate over Australian aboriginal land right claims continuing since the Mabo trial. In other contexts, Aboriginal status is germane to current debates over land rights. See, for example, Israeli references to Biblical Jewish aboriginality in Palestine as a way to contest Palestinian claims for indigeneity and the right of return (Parkes qtd. in Rejwan 118–19).

13. Flannery O'Connor, the American short story writer, calls attention to this problem in her story, "The Displaced Person," by having a Polish refugee's every action scrutinized and interpreted by the other characters in the story and never allowing the Polish man to speak for himself. Eventually and symbolically, when his hard work begins to threaten the jobs of other farm workers, one of them releases the brake on a tractor and the man is run over and killed.

14. See Narayanan on Manipur, Masri and Graham on Palestine, and Kramer-Hamstra on First Nations resistance of stereotype, respectively.

15. The nation-state is a legal and political structure of governance, represented by a prime minister or president (O'Brien and Szeman 208). In this system humans are *subjects* to the political state and are expected to "observe the obligations of citizenship such as voting, paying taxes, obeying the law, and so on" (208). The nation-state often works to create a feeling of unified purpose and belonging. It has historically excluded or colonized others (Grewal and Kaplan 151) while preserving a sense of "horizontal comradeship" and creating a dominant culture (Anderson 7 qtd. in Grewal and Kaplan 218).

16. For further discussion on these forms of agency see Alfred, *Wasáse* (151–54).

17. Sanctuary zones have a long history and are rooted in the idea of "sacred space" that is free from governmental intervention. One example of such a

sanctuary can be seen in the International Cities of Refuge Network (ICORN), formerly known as the International Parliament of Writers in the early 1990s. ICORN is a loose network of cities and regions that offers a two-year residency to writers who "have consistently been targets of politically motivated threats and persecution" in their home countries (http://www.icorn.org/index.php).

18. Consider the battle against government-sanctioned displacement and citizen-ed landlords that was undertaken by refugees on the outskirts of Calcutta and supported by the United Central Refugee Council, as it is chronicled in Subhasri Ghosh's chapter in this volume.

19. For a more detailed look at Palestinian displacement see Mazen Masri's chapter in this volume.

20. *Nakbe* is an Arabic term for "catastrophe" used to reference the displacement of Palestinians from Palestine in 1948.

21. As a single example of the scale of displacement occurring in the world today, consider the Democratic Republic of the Congo. In the first six months of 2009, 800,000 people were displaced in the east of the country alone. See "Democratic Republic of Congo" at http://www.internal-displacement.org.

22. "Acts of Citizenship" was the title of the Displacements conference's first plenary panel session. In that session Peter Nyers along with Mohan Mishri and Anne McNevin explored the strategy of redefining citizenship as presence and action in a place in order to "inform a more effective advocacy for those most excluded from the social and political rights that come with citizenship" (McNevin). See www.literaryculture.ca.

23. See Agnes Kramer-Hamstra's article in this volume for an analysis of how filmmaker Shelley Niro counters the warrior image of First Nations people, a stereotype that represents their culture as frozen in history, not dynamic or contemporary.

24. Filipino journalist Petronila Cleto came to Canada in the 1990s to spread word about the persecution facing journalists in the Philippines. She was the writer in residence at McMaster University's English and Cultural Studies Department from January to April in 2008.

25. Palestinian Canadian Hazem Jamjoum is the editor of *al-Majdal*, the English language quarterly magazine of the Badil Resource Center for Palestinian Residency and Refugee Rights in Bethlehem, Palestine and hosts Kan Ya Makan (on CKLN 88.1 FM), Toronto's only Arab community radio show.

26. Literally translated as "Operetta Manila." For a video recording of the performance, please see www.literaryculture.ca, click on "Ongoing Projects," and proceed to the Displacements conference archives.

27. The Live-In Caregiver program was introduced by the Canadian government in 1992, in place of the Foreign Domestic Movement program of 1981–1992. Since the 1950s, Canada has invented various programs such as these to allow foreign workers into the country without guaranteeing them citizenship or the rights of Canadian workers. In the Live-In Caregiver program, for example, caregivers must live in the home in which they serve as nannies or as caregivers for seniors for at least two years, and they may only apply for landed immigrant status after that time. There are many ways in which caregivers have been abused under such confines (see Stiell and England; Hodge). See also Jason DeParle's *New York Times* article "A Good Provider is One Who Leaves," a study of the way the Philippine government encourages its citizens to find work elsewhere. This political manoeuvring crosses party lines, beginning with Ferdinand Marcos and continued by his staunch opponent Corazon Aquino; so many Filipino workers are encouraged to leave that "migration is to the Philippines what cars once were to Detroit: its civil religion" (DeParle).

28. The nation-state of the Philippines, which relies on the remittances sent "home" (more than one billion dollars a month in 2006) to cover its own lack of will to address poverty, does not advocate for its workers abroad. Rather, in 2006, a million or one in seven Filipino workers who migrated abroad were called "modern heroes" by then president Gloria Arroyo (DeParle).

29. The riveting performance was enacted by Leen Ramli, Hisham Shokr, Saleh Fadel, Yamen Fadel, and Radi Hilaneh. The Salameh Theatre Troupe meets under the auspices of the Palestine House Educational and Cultural Program. *Finding our Song* can be viewed at www.literaryculture.ca, click on "Ongoing Projects," and proceed to the Displacements conference archives by clicking on "Read More."

30. Flamenco originated in Andalusia in southern Spain and owes its unique sounds and rhythms to the dynamic fusion of cultural influences of the region's migrating inhabitants: Roma people, Persians from Rajasthan, Spaniards, Indians, Sephardic Jews, Moroccans, and Egyptians. The playwright's choice of flamenco at this point in the play may also be a specific reference to Arab control over the region from 711–1492 and to the influence of Persian music on the genre, specifically the modal theories of flamenco, which appear to be influenced by Medieval Islamic calls to prayer (see "Flamenco").

31. See Nyers's chapter "On Humanitarian Violence" in *Rethinking Refugees* for an explanation of the term "violent humanitarism." For an excellent analysis of how violence can occur in humanitarian work, see Sherene Razack's book,

Dark Threats and White Knights, on Canadian peacekeeping in Somali during the early 1990s.

1

DISPLACING OIL
Towards "Lyric" Re-presentations of the Alberta Oil Sands

JON GORDON

FEBRUARY 2008: Environmental Defence warns that, in tailings ponds created from oil sands mining, "The toxicants are so concentrated that birds can die by landing" on them (Hatch and Price 7).

MARCH 1, 2008: A rally at the Alberta Legislature calls attention to the health and environmental consequences of development in the oil sands, especially for the area's Native populations.

MARCH 29, 2008: The play Swallow, at Edmonton's Azimuth Theatre, places two migrant workers on the shores of a tailings pond; their job is to keep birds off the toxic water, even at the expense of their own health.

APRIL 29, 2008: Public outrage is focused on Syncrude's Aurora tailings pond when an estimated 500 ducks die after landing there.[1]

THESE FOUR MOMENTS in the ongoing narrative of the bituminous sands of the Athabasca region each counter the official story that dominates the struggle to represent what is happening in and around Fort McMurray, Alberta. Dominant representations of the oil sands establish a particular view: capital speaks as freedom and nature is spoken for as resource. Despite the dominance of this narrative, funded by government and industry, alternatives persist. The challenge is to create space to listen to these voices. The above examples suggest some emerging counter narratives, which may displace the droning monologic justification of the status quo through the idealization of "sustainable development" that has dominated in Alberta for many years. This chapter considers industry and government rhetoric, which seeks to speak for both humans and non-humans so as to determine what the future of the oil sands will be, and juxtaposes that rhetoric with an exploration of Jan Zwicky's concept of "lyric" through a reading of two texts by Rudy Wiebe.

Wiebe's short story "The Angel of the Tar Sands" (1982) and *Far as the Eye Can See: A Play* (1977) counter industry and government rhetoric by re-presenting those dominant narratives so that what they exclude becomes apparent. Following Gayatri Spivak, I want to note the difference between "representation as 'speaking for,' as in politics, and representation as 're-presentation,' as in art or philosophy" (256). "Speaking for" tends towards appropriative ventriloquism, while "re-presentation" offers the possibility of new understanding and insight. While it is ultimately impossible to maintain this distinction, moments of re-presentation are necessary if there is to be any change in the relations between those who are speaking and those being spoken for. Literature can and does re-present the necessity of ecological coherence and the threats posed to it by industrial capitalism; we have a responsibility to listen to these alternatives and live our lives differently after we've heard these stories (King, *Truth About Stories* 29).

Literature can offer a practice in vulnerable listening, attending to otherness, the marginalized, the unsayable—as in Wiebe's texts. In "The Angel of the Tar Sands" we meet the superintendent of a bitumen project, whose certainty about the need for particular actions to keep the plant operating at capacity are momentarily called into question when an angel is unearthed in the bitumen deposit. In Wiebe's play, *Far as the Eye Can See*, the defeat of a proposed coal mine due to local opposition and the last-minute intervention of Peter Lougheed—Progressive Conservative Premier of Alberta at the time of the play's creation—is suffused with irony over the political pragmatism of Lougheed's decision. In the story, the superintendent's silence when confronted with the angel requires the reader to attend to the angel's alterity. In the play, the conclusion's irony requires the audience to attend to the persistent threat posed by technocrats and the world they seek to create.

Literature, then, is one place to look for alternative narratives that reveal what is left out of progressive and teleological myths, alternatives like that suggested by Wiebe's angel. Even if literature does not tell us what we should do, it can suggest that something is missing in what we are currently doing. Speaking at the University of Alberta in October 2007, poet and philosopher Jan Zwicky, argued that "technocracy prevents us from living authentically if we follow its agenda." She suggests "lyric" thinking as a way of accessing what is left out of purely rational-analytical thought, what is left out of thought focused on extracting oil from sand by any means necessary. She explains elsewhere that her

> use of "lyric" quite deliberately sets aside surface historical associations with Romantic poetry in order to pursue what might be called its deep epistemological structure. The word has been used to characterize things as disparate as Vermeer's paintings and Schubert's use of diatonic tonality, and what is common to them all...is thought whose eros *is coherence.* (Wisdom n.p.)

One of the things lyric thinking can help us recognize is that ecological value, the value of functioning wholes, cannot be reduced to either use or exchange value, is always beyond the humanly convenient. Its eros, its desire, is to recognize the interconnectedness of human and non-human nature, the coherence of the whole. Human concerns—culture, economy, society—exist within a larger order, one in which human needs are not primary. "The Angel of the Tar Sands" and *Far as the Eye Can See* suggest what remains outside anthropocentric narratives and point to the coherence of which humans are only a part. Before considering what the story points beyond, though, we need to establish the field in which it is intervening.

The massive and various displacements required by the oil sands developments surrounding Fort McMurray—of land, labour, and prior communities—continue to be justified by a political representation of a "common good" of prosperity, equality, and independence that is on the way and can be achieved through work. For example, Leslie Shiell and Colin Busby, writing for the C.D. Howe Institute, argue that "all Albertans, including those yet to be born, are entitled to an equal share of resource-based spending" (3). This guarantee of continued "unprecedented prosperity" (1), though, depends upon sacrificing the finite ecological diversity on which all life, including human, depends. The process of extracting oil from sand involves removing "overburden" to access bitumen;[2] burning natural gas to create the necessary heat to separate oil from sand; drawing water from the Athabasca River for use in various extraction processes, some of which actually sterilize the land (Shukin 136, Pratt 16); and constructing tailings ponds for the now toxic water polluted with the byproducts of upgrading the oil. David Finch elaborates:

> *To get one barrel of oil, 2 tonnes of tarry sand have to be dug out of the ground...some bitumen goes to the plant through a pipeline, after being broken up and mixed with hot water. When the oily sand*

> gets to the plant, hot water helps release *the oil from the sand as the whole mixture gets shaken and stirred. Bitumen rises to the top and goes off for further processing, and more oil gets squeezed out of the slurry.* Even then, it still has to go through an upgrader, which makes it lighter using diluents or lighter oil, before it can go into a refinery. (111, emphasis added)

The verbs in this passage highlight that this method is a form of analysis, defined as "separation of a whole into its component parts" (Zwicky, *Lyric* 5). Humans are very good at analysis, as the "success" of the oil sands shows, but once the rich complex of something whole is taken apart, dis-integrated, it cannot be put back together. Bureaucratic doublespeak about reclamation implicitly recognizes this inability when it states that "companies are required to replace what was there before industrial activity with a landscape of 'equivalent capability.' This means the land should be able to support similar, but not necessarily identical, uses after reclamation is complete" (Brooymans, "Oilsands"). Such a focus on "uses" ignores the ecological point of integration: value lies in functioning wholes as well as in the production of useful or exchangeable parts. Regardless of this narrow and troubling definition of reclamation, it is worth noting that as of March 2008, only 104 hectares have received certification as reclaimed, and these 104 were never mined (whereas, 40,000 hectares in total in the tar sands area *had been mined*). Rather, the 104 hectares were used to store the overburden taken from land being mined.

The crucial point, for my purposes, is that once the disintegration of analysis has occurred, there is no system available for reintegration. Although, the Alberta government requires bitumen companies to pay a security deposit against the cost of reclamation, the "companies calculate the cost of their own security deposits," and there is no opportunity for public input in this process (Grant, Dyer, and Woynillowicz 46). It is important to note, then, as Pembina Institute researchers Jennifer Grant, Simon

Dyer, and Dan Woynillowicz do, that "the fact that virtually no reclaimed sites...have been certified suggests not only that the true costs have *not* been identified, but that they *cannot* be identified" (46, emphasis original).³ Therefore, the subsequent recommendation that "liability bonds [should be] conservative to ensure that Canadians are protected" (46) rings hollow. If the true costs of reclamation cannot be identified, then the only way Canadians and others, not to mention non-human others, can be protected is by not dis-integrating the sites to begin with. If humans continue to pursue fiscal independence through resource extraction we incur an incalculable debt as a result. The consequences are unaccountable.

The dominant progressive narrative puts nature at humans' disposal. This narrative is apparent in histories of the Fort McMurray region. These histories tend to start with accounts of a man named Wa Pa Su (or Wa Pa Sun) bringing "a sample of oil laden sand" to Hudson's Bay Company explorer Henry Kelsey at York Factory in 1719 (Humberman 4). This moment of first recorded contact with the Indigenous inhabitants of the area does two things. First, it provides an origin and teleology for the narrative of the region, one that will reach its climax in our own time when the oil can be displaced from the sand. Second, it also implies a continuity with Indigenous practices; since Natives burned the sands and used them to seal their canoes, contemporary uses are simply logical and natural extensions of Indigenous ones, operating on a larger and more efficient scale. Robert Bott, in "Canada's Oil Sands," expresses it this way: "Aboriginal people were already using oil-sands bitumen when the first European explorers arrived in the 18th century" (11). In Wiebe's play, *Far as the Eye Can See*, William Aberhart and Crowfoot—who, along with Princess Louise, make up the "Regal Dead"—discuss Calgary Power's plan to expropriate farmland and build a coal mine. Wiebe has stated that the current debate surrounding the oil sands is "exactly the same issue" as the fight over the Dodds-Round Hill power plant represented in *Far as the Eye Can See* (Babiak).

> CROWFOOT. *A hundred years ago this year we gave this earth away and now the white man has at last decided he will chew it up and spit it out like a beast eating itself.*
> ABERHART. *No no no, chief. You never knew about all the food this land could grow, the grain, the cattle, the beautiful gardens, the potatoes and flowers.*
> CROWFOOT. *We had flowers.*
> ABERHART. *All right, flowers, but the power to grow all these other things was already there in the soil, waiting to be released. And we whites found it there, released it! Fed millions, all over the world. Now this other enormous power of coal, waiting to be released, placed there by God, is waiting to be released to lift man to his next stage of progress. These Albertans, in 1977, will develop the treasures* under *the earth, as my generation reaped them from the earth, as your people gathered them upon the earth. It is all there, the marvelous gifts of God, for us to use, for us—(Wiebe 68, emphasis original)*

This progressive logic continues to operate in narratives like Bott's, which connect current and previous actions through a focus on *use*. However, while Bott's and Aberhart's version of history may suggest some recognition of "the dependence of oil sands capital (like fur trade capital before it) upon native informants/knowledges, this debt is relegated to the distant past and ultimately reversed as corporations such as Syncrude depict themselves as benefactors bringing economic development to Aboriginal communities" (Shukin 144). Thus, while maintaining continuity and establishing Indigenous validity for using the oil sands, "First Peoples' knowledge of the oil sands is relegated to the past, insinuating that true knowledge of the oil sands begins at the moment when it ceases as use-value and is measured in terms of exchange-value" (Shukin 145). This abstraction is fundamental for the system of modernity, which "*consists in turning the productive origin inside and representing it as simply another factor within the system*" (Angus, *Border* 188, emphasis original). This turn radically reconfigures humans' relation to the non-human world: instead of owing our existence to it, it is an object to be bought and sold by us. Hence the irony of the conclusion of Wiebe's play: the crisis is resolved, or, at least, deferred, by Peter Lougheed descending in a coal bucket as *deus ex machina* to protect agricultural land, choosing it over electricity generation. Rather than Lougheed saving the day, though, the stage directions suggest, "nothing human has been resolved by this [Lougheed's] mechanical statement" (124). His statement is a rhetorical performance aimed at the "voters" (124) of Alberta, and while Lougheed declares his "government is committed to provide every citizen with adequate electricity…this project would disturb too much prime agricultural land" (124). The decision is a human-centred one, defending one type of human land use over another. The play ends thus:

> CROWFOOT. *A hundred years ago the white man took this country, and now they know the black burning stone is under the earth; and they will not be able to leave it alone. White men can never leave, anything, the way it was.*
> LOUGHEED. *We have listened to you, and we have understood you. Thank you.* (125)

The irony is multiple here, pointing to the dominant group's belief in its understanding of the Native worldview, a paternalistic dismissal of that worldview, and a suggestion that such a dismissal will create precisely the situation Crowfoot foresees: us eating ourselves. While Lougheed fails to really listen or understand, the play offers the opportunity for the audience members to listen and to recognize, in their own views of the world-as-resource, the hubris of Lougheed's response. Stopping a coal-fired generator development to protect agriculture leaves one form of commodification of the land in place, but it does not amount to leaving something the way it was. Lougheed does not see an alternative to a version of private property and commodity markets.

The cover letter from the Alberta Royalty Review Panel's report *Our Fair Share* shows the logic of this commodification at work. It structures the problem of royalty rates in terms of owing, but, instead of considering what humans owe the non-human world due to our objectification of it, it considers what is properly *owed* to Albertans, the *owners* of resources. Chairman William M. Hunter writes, "Alberta's natural resources belong to Albertans...a royalty and tax system for energy resources therefore must justify every dollar that does not go to the owners" (5). This language always already introduces a provisional understanding of the concept of *owing*, one inextricable from *owning*. The possibility of "responsible" or "sustainable" development of Alberta's oil and gas requires a more radical understanding of owing, one that is not contractual or provisional. Re-presenting such an understanding so that people will listen is increasingly difficult, as suggested by the very few people in the audience the night I attended *Swallow* and the low turnout at the legislature for the rally. But it is not impossible.

In the November 2007 issue of *Alberta Views*, a number of pieces focus on the effects of development in northern Alberta and point to what is sacrificed by the provisional views justifying that development. In an article entitled "The Standard is Zero," for example, Dr. Rosalie Bertell critiques the Cantox Health Sciences International assessment of the North West Upgrading Project.

> *Regulatory guidelines are risk-versus-benefit trade-offs, with little or no protection for the public against mistakes, miscalculations or even "acceptable" cancers and deaths. Courts and most people see regulations as if they were protective of human and environmental health...[but] regulations are frequently based, as is the case here, on*

> "acceptable" deaths to humans and unknown effects on the environment. (19)

While such trade-offs are standard practice in our modern, pragmatic political system, where the only protection against negative consequences is to make sure we are adequately compensated by receiving "our fair share" in taxes and royalties, we can hear in Bertell's words an echo of an alternate conception of responsibility. An understanding of this echo can be found in the work of Canadian philosopher and theologian George Grant. He has, arguably, thought through the consequences of a fully realized technological society in the Canadian context more completely than anyone else. In his last collection of essays, *Technology and Justice*, he writes that

> the limitations put upon creating by the claims of others, whether nationally or internationally, are understood as contractual: that is, provisional. This exclusion of non-provisory owing from our interpretation of desire means that what is summoned up by the word "should" is no longer what was summoned up among our ancestors. What moderns hear always includes an "if": it is never "beyond all bargains and without an alternative." (30)

This "should" beyond any "if" is hinted at in Bertell's words, but such a conception of responsibility is continually silenced in public discourse dominated by the rhetoric of resources, a rhetoric that understands our relationship to the world as one between human freedom and natural raw material.

The consequences of this view are that human and non-human nature can be, and is, sacrificed within the logic of the market. Rather than maintaining that some actions should not be taken under any circumstances, anything may be done if the price is right. Grant writes:

> *Politics is the technology of making the human race greater than it has yet been. In that artistic accomplishment, those of our fellows who stand in the way...can be exterminated or simply enslaved. There is nothing intrinsic in all others that puts any limit on what we may do to them....Human beings are so unequal that to some of them no due is owed. (Technology 94)*

While extermination and enslavement might be stronger language than contemporary bureaucrats, technocrats, and capitalists are willing to use, the exclusions and exploitations that even so-called "sustainable" resource extraction requires amount to the same thing for some. Jeremy Klaszus writes of the health problems of the population of Fort Chipewyan arising from pollution of the Athabasca River: "Premier Ed Stelmach famously said there's no such thing as touching the brake on oil sands development, and the environmental concerns of people in Fort Chip aren't significant enough to slow anything down" (32). Since Klaszus published that article, not only was a rally held at the legislature to try and get the government's (and the public's) attention, but lawsuits have been launched by the Chipewyan Prairie First Nation, the Woodland Cree First Nation, and the Sierra Club against the province (Lillebuen).[4]

Increased health problems for residents are not the only social consequence of industrial growth in the oil sands. Cheryl Mahaffy describes the lives of prostitutes in Alberta's boomtowns: "Often driven by poverty, addictions, or both, and unable to find affordable housing...most are homeless or barely housed. They lack access to showers, let alone health care" (38). The standard of suffering is not, as Bertell points out, zero: poverty, addiction, homelessness seem to be accepted consequences of growth. What royalty rate would be fair compensation for these consequences? Such a question can only be asked when certain assumptions are taken as self-evident. If we start from the premise that "there is some connection between what we think other species to be (let alone our own) and how we treat them" (Grant, *Technology* 65), this connection becomes evident when we examine the language of sustainable resource development: other species, and members of our own, are objects to be used, and, if anything is due to them, their extermination or enslavement can be compensated for with a share of the profits.

Ezra Levant, responding in the *National Post* to the public outcry over the duck deaths on Syncrude's tailings pond, trivializes citizens' concerns and re-inscribes a utilitarian view of nature as "common sense": "Even the Prime Minister called the deaths a 'terrible tragedy.' I agree. I can't believe that 500 ducks were wasted that way. Imagine all the lost foie gras." Never mind that foie gras is made from goose liver, Levant's sarcastic point seems to be that there is no consequence of development that cannot be compensated for, and the only tragedy is that the ducks' lives were lost without being commodified. While public discourse allows for debate over what the human relationship to oil in northeastern Alberta should be, the primacy of that relationship is rarely questioned: the debate is organized by terms such as "sustainability," "responsible development," and "stewardship." Humans will manage the resource in our best interests; what these interests are and what the best management looks like are the debatable topics. However, these debates remain caught within a liberal, rational, technological, humanist narrative of progress founded on a premise of autonomy over a future in which the productivity of nature will be guaranteed through increasingly efficient systems of management. Attempts to tell stories other than that of human autonomy are rare and marginal.

Internalization of productive natural origins is expressed in the economic term "fungibility," which Levant describes without naming: "If oil-thirsty America—and China and India—stop using oilsands oil because it's duck-insensitive, they're just going to buy their oil from somewhere else." That is, any barrel of oil is economically equivalent to any other. However, while this may be true on the global market, other factors exceed the market's accounting. Again, Levant notes some of these as justification for oil sands development.

> *Pretty much everywhere oil comes from is worse than Canada—even with our new reputation as duck murderers...most oil producing nations are dictatorships in the Middle East, or quasi-dictatorships like Nigeria, Russia and Venezuela. Political accountability doesn't exist there, and property rights are weak. The idea of political parties or even a free press championing the environment is a fantasy.*

In distinguishing Canadian oil from "global" oil, he wants to have it both ways. Oil sands production is *indistinguishable* from global oil once it enters the marketplace, but it is also *better* than other oil because it does not depend on dictatorship, misogyny, genocide, etc. The fact that it does depend on these things, at least to some extent, is not considered: Mahaffey's analysis of prostitution in the area indicates misogyny and the widespread indifference to the concerns of First Nations suggests a continuation of a colonial genocidal policy.[5] Levant's conclusion is simple: "It's true, the odd duck gets hurt—as with any other massive industrial project. But to portray the oilsands as unethical is positively false." And he encapsulates progressive modernist logic: the odd duck, or person, or ecosystem may get hurt, or killed, or become extinct, but that is not unethical *if* property rights are protected, and that means honouring contracts made with oil companies and, at best, getting "our fair share" as owners of the "resource." We *should* be concerned about the ducks, as Levant facetiously suggests he is, but only *if* it is in "our" best interest. That interest will be viewed through the political lens of "progress," and this view maintains that "environmental issues are largely local or regional in geographic scope while the economic benefits are provincial if not national" (Babiuk 13). "The Angel of the Tar Sands" points to a context beyond the national or even the global that needs to be considered. The "unscientific shape" of the angel disrupts the idea that environmental issues are simply local (189).

Within the progressive view, the productivity of nature and its fecundity, on which systems of exchange are founded when land, for instance, becomes a commodity, is partially captured within systems as a profitable yield (Angus, *Border* 197). However, the process of capturing these yields does not, and cannot, account for all of the productivity; an uncommodifiable excess, something unaccountable like the angel, remains. Ian Angus says, "human domestication of the excess that defines the wild shapes the wild order into a humanly convenient one, reduces diversity, and takes the excess for itself" (*Border* 197). But, while "excess keeps the system going," it "finds no recognition within it, only the belated and diluted recognition of a yield" (Angus, *Border* 197). The natural productivity is not recognized as an origin, simply as one commodity among many; the failure of the characters to account for the angel, to fit it into the system of commodity exchange, points to a need to consider the world in terms that are not merely humanly convenient. The idea of reclamation in the Alberta oil sands explicitly perpetuates this bias towards human concerns, as we will see below. While many environmental lobbyists, think tanks, and policy analysts are publishing important critiques of industry and governments' ecological conduct, their alternatives tend to be politically pragmatic calls for improvements to the system rather than recognition of what inevitably escapes systematization. The sacrifice of this excess needs to be recognized if we are to determine what we *should* do, beyond all the bargains that have been struck and the profits to be made. Lyric thought offers one mode of attending to this sacrifice.

Zwicky contrasts the disintegration of analysis with lyric: "The aims of analysis are explicitly disintegrative" (*Lyric* 6), whereas "lyric is an attempt to comprehend the whole in a single gesture" (*Lyric* 134). The primacy of analysis over lyric results in "the ability to see some thing as an object, external to oneself," which "is necessary before one can cease to care about that thing sufficiently to regard it as nothing more than an object one can use" (*Lyric* 234). Thus, the ecological diversity of the Athabasca River watershed is seen as useful because of the marketable objects it is capable of producing. Since wild ducks, for example, are not competitive as commodities in a global market with oil, and, as Levant has it, they are "a species that is as far from extinction as, say, the rat," their sacrifice is acceptable. For Grant,

> *object means literally some thing that we have thrown over against ourselves. Jacio I throw, ob over against; therefore, "the thrown against."...Reason as project (that is, reason as thrown forth) is the summonsing of something before us and the putting of questions to it, so that it is forced to give its reasons for being the way it is as an object.* (Technology 36)

This, he says, results in a paradigm in which "we have knowledge when we represent anything to ourselves as object, and question it, so that it will give us its reasons. That summonsing and questioning requires well defined procedures. These procedures are what we call in English 'experimental research'" (Grant, *Technology* 36). A great deal of "experimental research" has been, and is being, thrown against the oil sands to force them to give their reasons for being the way they are and to enable their analysis and separation. As Bott puts it, "the future of this resource will be decided in the laboratory" (38).

Objectifying reason, however, ignores the degree to which we are integrated with what we objectify. Ecologist Stan Rowe argues that "people are made from clean air, clean water, and clean humified soil—all those things that exist in Earth's green surface film. To these their healthy bodies are adapted" (117). However, he continues, "*Homo sapiens* ignore...this fundamental knowledge, secure in the belief that human errors can be...cured by science and technology" (117). As a result, humanity "makes a virtue of mining and releasing into air, water and soil the many poisonous materials that used to be safely sequestered underground: heavy metals, radioactive minerals, long-chain hydrocarbons such as coal and oil" (117). Former Syncrude president Jim Carter, in contrast to Rowe's critique of techno-utopianism, asserts, "The solution [to ecological disturbance] is in technology" (qtd. in Marsden 166). That is, the cause of the problem is also the solution; further objectification and disintegration will create "sustainability," despite the fact that, as William Marsden states, "nobody at Syncrude claims that they can restore [the land] to what it used to be. They can't replace the ecosystems, the vast networks of peat bogs, fens, rivers and wetlands. Those are gone, probably forever, along with the unique flora and fauna that once inhabited this region" (Marsden 168). Those ecosystems, part of the life-sustaining "green surface film" redefined as burdensome overburden, are sacrificed for the bitumen beneath. However, the acknowledgement of this fact by Syncrude takes a particular form: they assert that reclamation makes the land "more productive than it was when we got here" (Marsden 170). Marsden quotes Peter Duggan, a production advisor for Syncrude, as saying the company is "doing nature a favour" by "cleaning out this dirty oil out of the oil sands" (170). In "Canada's Oil Sands" Bott explains that reclamation "does not mean 'tree-by-tree' restoration, but rather that the region as a whole should form an ecosystem at least as healthy and productive as what existed before development" (Bott 31). This discourse of productivity asserts that the land will be more humanly useful, more profitable, because its productivity will be oriented to marketable ends. Planting cereal crops and trees and raising bison for profit constitute "reclamation." Grant, Dyer, and Woynillowicz show how the government's use of "the Land Capability Classification for Forest Ecosystems in the Oil Sands" to evaluate reclamation projects supports these economic endeavours (21). This classification primarily has "a focus on commercial forestry" and "implies that economic or productivity factors dictate the reclaimed target landscape—a forested ecosystem" (Grant, Dyer, and Woynillowicz 21, 22). Replacing wetlands with forests, they argue, can then be construed as an "improvement" to the land, creating "a perverse situation where oil sands proponents claim there will be an improvement in land capability after reclamation" (22). The land will produce more "merchantable timber" (Grant, Dyer, and Woynillowicz 5) and is, therefore, better than what preceded mining operations.

The human capacity to create moments of resonance and integration even out of waste and detritus should not be underestimated, as Patricia Yaeger argues in the March 2008 edition of *PMLA*. However, this does not mean that we should "drop the concept of nature" (Morton qtd. in Yaeger 324). There is a necessity, in the postmodern condition, to reveal the aesthetic beauty possible within even the most "manufactured landscapes"—to borrow the title phrase of Jennifer Baichwal's 2006 film based on Edward Burtynsky's photographs—and the persistence of wilderness, as that which precedes, exceeds, and succeeds human's rational-analytic projects, among our garbage. Nevertheless, though waste and debris may well be able to do the "subject-making" work once accomplished by a now marginalized and always-already contaminated "nature" (Yaeger 325), this perspective only recognizes nature's value for doing a kind of traditionally human-oriented integrative work associated with Romantic "lyric." Zwicky wants to set those associations aside in favour of a higher order context.[6] At the same time, while wilderness will persist, regardless of humans' destructive activities, something of more than contingent value will also be lost. Dropping the concept of nature opens the door further to a view of the world in which nothing can be said "as to why we should be glad that there are polar bears or parrots or why they are worth working to preserve" (Grant, *Technology* 64). Dropping "nature" furthers a purely contingent worldview that enables a belief that the boreal ecosystem of northern Alberta is actually *improved* by oil sands strip mining.

Slowing the pace of development, though, is an answer of *degree* to a problem of *kind* as it advocates "sustainability" or "responsible development," which Okanagan writer Jeanette Armstrong has described as "another way of (ab)using such that enough remains so that we can continue to (ab)use" ("Literature"). It substitutes one form of analysis for another. Armstrong suggests an alternative of "unqualified regeneration" that requires recognition of human dependence on and interconnection with the ecological whole. Such recognition is incompatible with the belief in autonomy asserted by Syncrude in their "2006 Sustainability Report," which claims that the corporation will "create [its] own future" (11). The human power of creativity can work for or against such discourses of mastery. However, "ethical self-mastery, political mastery over unruly and aberrant Others, and epistemic mastery over the 'external' world pose as the still-attainable goals of the Enlightenment legacy" (Code 19). The narrative of this legacy remains pervasive, and both sides in the debate around the oil sands have tried to claim its rhetoric as, for example, when Christopher Hatch and Matt Price write, "Technologies are available to curb the damage" (2). That is precisely the type of language Syncrude and other companies have become very adept at using; "sustainability" is a key term for both sides and has become, in an Orwellian way, meaningless. However, if "more responsible knowings than the reductionism endemic in the positivist post-Enlightenment legacy" are to arise, then what is excluded by this reductionism needs to be recognized through what Spivak calls re-presentation (Code 9). If we can begin from a recognition of what is excluded and sacrificed by mining's analytic dis-integration, then we can have a different kind of public debate over the future of the oil sands. This debate will put regeneration (as restoration of natural productivity not oriented to human ends) rather than reclamation or "sustainability" (as manufacturing a new kind of profitable landscape to be exploited) at its centre to avoid positivist reductionism. Wiebe's "The Angel of the Tar Sands" points us toward such a recognition by calling attention to what is left unspoken by the dominant narrative of technological progress. This story also highlights what remains unspeakable for many of its critics: our own vulnerable, limited, dependency.

Given the literary challenge of coming to terms with the geographic vastness of Alberta, Wiebe has famously stated that

> to touch this land with words requires an architectural structure; to break into the space of the reader's mind with the space of this western landscape and the people in it you must build a structure of fiction like an engineer builds a bridge or skyscraper over and into space. A poem, a lyric, will not do. You must lay great black steel lines of fiction, break up that space with huge design, and like the fiction of the Russian steppes, build giant artifact. ("Passages by Land" 259)

This might be, at least in the most straightforward reading, an accurate description of what some of Wiebe's earlier fiction does, with its tendency towards monologic didacticism. However, both his short story "The Angel of the Tar Sands" and his play *Far as the Eye Can See* do something else. As Jonathan Kertzer puts it, the story shows "how the matter-of-fact must yield to the marvelous" (xxiv), while the play's "ironic moments" (Whaley 46) arise from some characters' failure to understand anything beyond the matter-of-fact. The ironies in Aberhart's statement about the right to use the land however humans see fit and in Lougheed's claim to have understood Crowfoot's warning about leaving things alone, quoted earlier, suggest their inability to accept dependence on what is beyond the matter-of-fact. Zwicky describes the process of yielding to what is beyond the matter-of-fact in writing when she says, "lyric achieves integration only to the extent that words are bent to the shape of wordlessness" (*Lyric* 256). The building with words, the huge design, will not succeed in enclosing meaning in the structure of words, but can suggest integration by yielding to silence; a writer's design can break into the reader's mind by building around and toward the landscape. Thus, human creativity works to touch the land but not enclose it, to build a structure of fiction but not in the service of domination. Such building is "lyric" in Zwicky's sense regardless of whether it occurs in prose or verse, music or architecture, paint or steel.

Still, the economic logic of development persuasively embodies the promise of prosperity and an end to human suffering and hunger. Robert Kroetsch, in *Alberta*, his history of the province, states the view succinctly: "Ultimately, I am told, petroleum products from places like the Athabasca tar sands might not only run our cars and surface our highways, but *feed us* as well" (274). In "The Angel of the Tar Sands," the lyric moment occurs after the three characters in the story—Tak, Bertha, and the unnamed superintendent—encounter an angel. It is unearthed by Tak, "the day operator on Number Two Bucket" (188); Bertha recognizes the "shape" (188) as an angel; and the superintendent, when faced with something so "unscientific" (189), loses "all words" (190). This loss suggests a failure of reason, an inability to apprehend something beyond the rational understanding of oil sands mining as oriented toward human ends: fueling the economy, feeding human needs. For Zwicky, "lyric is a direct response to the fact that the particular capacity for language-use possessed by our species cuts us off from the world in a way, or to a degree, that is painful" (*Lyric* 246). Further, "We experience *the burden of our capacity for language* as loss—though we rarely recognize that *this* is the burden, that what we have lost is silence" (*Lyric* 246, emphasis original). Recognizing this burden as loss is a precondition for lyric, and "lyric art is the fullest expression of the hunger for wordlessness" (*Lyric* 246). This hunger, I would suggest, is acknowledged by Bertha at the end of Wiebe's story in her act of quitting her job; she is not willing to go on sacrificing whatever perfection she has apprehended in her encounter with the angel. Further, her assurance to Tak, "Next time you'll recognize it…And then it'll talk Japanese" (191), opens the conclusion out to the reader by suggesting that, like Tak, we should be ready for the appearance of the divine in our world, and, if we are, then we will be able to listen to it as it will speak our language.

Bertha is the only character who can understand what the angel says, as it speaks "Hutterite German," but she is unable to translate that speech into English or even repeat it as she has "forgotten" how (190). Although it is not silence, as such, that she has lost here, she is rendered silent by the angel's speech: "She was listening with an overwhelming intensity; there was nothing in this world but to hear" (190). She is unable to speak, is connected to something beyond language. The angel's words are unrecorded in the story—we don't get the Hutterite German, don't know what the angel said—and so, even though we are told the angel spoke, its words are an absence, a silence in the text. We, too, are connected to something beyond language through the language of Wiebe's story. For Angus, silence "is the discovery of a moment beyond language, though the beyond of language cannot be discovered outside language, but is that within language that allows its outside to appear" (*(Dis)figurations* 249). The superintendent, though unable to understand the angel, at least glimpses this too as he replies to Bertha's "I quit...Right this minute" with "Of course, I understand" (191). However, he struggles against the silence imposed by the angel, attempting to speak and "pleading for a voice" (190), and his recognition is quickly covered over when he instructs Tak to literally cover the evidence of the angel's presence by "run[ning] [his] bucket through" the sand where the angel had been (191). The production of oil is of tantamount importance so that any other story is too costly to listen to: the superintendent initially fears Tak has found "*another* buffalo skeleton" and the "bifocalled professors" that it would bring (188). He will hide evidence of the land's alternative stories in order to maintain productivity. Tak acquiesces to this request, becoming complicit when he says, "You're the boss" (191); he is just following orders. Bertha points out that "It doesn't matter how fast" they erase the evidence because "It was there, we saw it" (191). A parallel might be drawn here to the public response to the duck deaths on Syncrude's tailings pond (see Figure 1.1). People were presented with images of death and suffering on a relatable scale clearly and directly tied to oil sands industrial activity. However, the initial emotional response passed through a combination of rationalizing, as with Levant (there are millions of ducks and humans need oil), and apologies, with Syncrude president and CEO Tom Katinas' "promise to do better."[7]

In Wiebe's story, the return to "business as usual" does not quite occur immediately. First, the superintendent "had a vision" (191).

> *He saw like an opened book the immense curves of the Athabasca River swinging through wilderness down from the glacial pinnacles of the Rocky Mountains and across Alberta and joined by the Berland and the McLeod and the Pembina and the Pelican and the Christina and the Clearwater and the Firebag rivers, and all the surface of the earth was gone, the Tertiary and the Lower Cretaceous layers of strata had been ripped away and the thousands of square miles of black bituminous sand were exposed, laid open, slanting down into the molten centre of the earth. (191) (See Figure 1.2)*

In this one moment, which encompasses the entire Athabasca River watershed in a single sentence, the superintendent feels the meaning of the words of Psalm 51—"*O miserere, miserere*" (191)—in which David seeks God's mercy and forgiveness for his sins. This moment relies on a particular Judaeo-Christian conception of the world as David comes face to face with the particular devastation he has caused and repents in humility. The question of complicity must be raised here. For Grant, "what has made Western culture so dynamic is its impregnation with the Judaeo-Christian idea that history is the divinely ordained process of man's salvation" (*Philosophy* 40). However, Wiebe's conception also offers an alternative understanding of humanity's place in the world, one that

FIGURE 1.1: Syncrude Tailings Pond (Greenpeace).

FIGURE 1.2: Suncor Mine (Greenpeace).

questions the liberating role of science and technology. As Slavoj Žižek argues, science's "function is to provide certainty, to be a point of reference on which one can rely, and to provide hope (new technological inventions will help us against diseases, and so on)" (446). Further, "The paradox effectively is that, today, science provides the security which was once guaranteed by religion, and, in a curious inversion, religion is one of the possible places from which one can develop critical doubts about contemporary society" (Žižek 446). Thus, the angel reveals a lack in the dynamics of Western culture, for which Christianity is an origin, and forces the reader to raise doubts about contemporary society.[8]

Rather than human dominance over nature, submission to an Other determines what our relationship to the world should be: "The sacrifice acceptable to God is a broken spirit; a broken and contrite heart" (Psalms 51.17). David recognizes how he has abused his power and brought ruin on his neighbour. His recognition and subsequent confession are quite different than the mastery embodied in "The huge plant" in which "oil ran...gurgling in each precisely numbered pipe and jointure, sweet and clear like golden brown honey" ("Angel" 191) (see Figures 1.3 and 1.4). Regardless of our opinion of the consequences of Christianity in North America, and without calling for some kind of "return to religion," Wiebe's story envisions something lost in the pursuit of human freedom, the freedom pursued through the precise analysis of numbered pipes. Such alternative visions are necessary if we are to displace the displacements justified in the name of independence and mastery through progress, if we are to recognize the lyric coherence of which we are a part but do not control.

Bott claims:

> *Human ingenuity has already accomplished a great deal by making the oilsands economically competitive with conventional oil. Environmental and social challenges are being engaged. Continuous improvement in science, technology and management are helping to*

FIGURE 1.3: *Suncor Upgrader* (Greenpeace).

FIGURE 1.4: *Syncrude Plant Oil Mining from Tar Sand, Alberta, Canada* (Greenpeace).

> overcome the remaining challenges to meet society's expectations for sustainable development. *(39)*

The problem with "sustainable development" remains its continued orientation toward human needs and its assumption that these needs are knowable in an accountable way. Bott provides the standard definition of sustainable development: "development that meets today's needs without compromising the ability of future generations to meet their needs" (31). Shiell and Busby use sustainability "to mean that a given policy can be continued at the current level indefinitely" (2). Both of these definitions indicate a view in which the Enlightenment promise of "the end of history" continues to be persuasive: we can solve the problem of scarcity on a worldwide level indefinitely. As Grant has it, "Modern human beings since their beginnings have been moved by the faith that the mastery of nature would lead to the overcoming of hunger and labour, disease and war on so widespread a scale that at last we could build the world-wide society of free and equal people" (*Technology* 15). However, while "one must never think about technological destiny without looking squarely at the justice in those hopes" (Grant, *Technology* 15), one must also consider the need for justice for the human and non-human nature commodified and sacrificed in the pursuit of those hopes. Lyric points to this alternative call for justice.

Lyric is continually marginalized as an alternative by those who suggest it is comprised of "smoke and mirrors...just metaphors" (Zwicky, *Lyric* 326). Zwicky acknowledges that lyric moments "are just metaphors" and explains, "If there is someone who truly has no idea what I mean by 'analytic style' or 'resonance,' then these remarks will have no meaning for that person" (Zwicky, *Lyric* 326). After his lyric vision, the superintendent cuts himself off from that moment of resonance and recognition of sinfulness and loss; he turns back to the oil, "sweet and clear like golden brown honey" (191) in a moment that may be read as analogous with Lougheed's claim to hear and understand Crowfoot. The oil compensates for the loss of the surface of the earth, for our inability to leave things alone.

While I fear that oil executives and members of government, like Lougheed in Wiebe's play, may well have no idea what values exist beyond their rational-analytic understanding, or choose, like the superintendent, to deliberately turn away from such moments of recognition, I am more hopeful that Albertans are looking for a new story around which concerns over ecological destruction can coalesce, around which a different story, a lyric story, can find resonance. In the findings of "The Oil Sands Survey: Albertans' Values Regarding Oil Sands Development" (2008), Cambridge Strategies found that "Albertans see the ecological issues of wildlife, Greenhouse Gases [sic], water and reclamation being of very significant concern" (4), with 73 per cent believing water usage is determined by the needs of industry and 66 per cent believing the reclamation pace is set to serve industry needs (5). However, despite the considerable dissatisfaction with the status quo that these numbers suggest, when asked which current political party leader Albertans trusted to responsibly manage Alberta's growth, 43 per cent chose "none of the above" (6), while 33 per cent chose Progressive Conservative Premier Ed Stelmach, and 11 per cent chose then Liberal Leader of the Opposition Kevin Taft. The authors of the survey conclude that Albertans "are very clear in that they want a green lens to trump any economic or growth dynamics" (6), but there also seems to be a belief that viable alternatives are not to be found in the political realm. This belief was echoed on Monday, March 3, 2008, when 58 per cent of Albertans chose not to vote in the provincial election.

For Zwicky, lyric cannot offer a positive political alternative (Lecture). But, in revealing the qualitative values that are marginalized by political narratives of progress, lyric can open us to possibilities for what we *should* do "beyond all bargains and without an alternative" through recourse to a higher order context, a recognition of our ecological relations and of our dependence on them. The political apathy, instead of being cause for despair, may be a hopeful sign that the modern contractual compromise between owing and owning is breaking. While this is not evidence that people are listening to alternatives, *not* voting might suggest that people have stopped listening to the "sustainable development" monologue.

In "The Angel of the Tar Sands" the superintendent's final actions are a rejection of the revelation the story contains, but the story itself opens an alternative for readers. When the angel in the story first moves, the characters "staggered back, fell" (189), and "the superintendent found himself on his knees staring up at the shape which wasn't really very tall, it just seemed immensely broad and overwhelming" (189). The angel interrupts the status quo, the liquidation of the tar sands, the superintendent's commitment to keep the plant running at "capacity" (188), to "shut up the environmentalists" (188). The angel's completely unexpected appearance suggests that the land is more than the characters have yet imagined. The public outcry over the duck deaths, though only momentary, indicates a similar recognition. Seeing "the layers of strata…ripped away" and feeling the meaning of Psalm 51 (191) open a gap in the superintendent's initial assumptions, re-present them, in Spivak's sense. Although the superintendent rejects this alternative in the end, if readers listen to the story and attend to the meaning that the superintendent "could not have explained" (191), but which is acted upon by the character Bertha, then we can glimpse an alternative beyond the realm of rhetorical representations. We need not be satisfied with giving up what we owe to others, and to otherness—that indefinable, absolute, uncommodifiable, useless alterity, whose best name is wilderness—*if* we make enough money in the trade. Alternatives exist. Listen for them.

AUTHOR'S NOTE

My thanks to Agnes Kramer-Hamstra for her thoughtful comments on earlier drafts of this chapter, especially for pointing out the connection between the angel and the buffalo as alternative stories present in the land and for suggesting how Bertha's reference to "God's glory" in Isaiah 6 indicates the presence of that glory in the ecology of the tar sands.

NOTES

1. That estimate was subsequently more than tripled (Brooymans, "Syncrude").
2. "Overburden" is often used to describe everything that overlies bitumen deposits. Grant, Dyer, and Woynillowicz describe the process of preparing a bitumen mining site this way:

   > Before mining can begin, the forest, wetlands, and mineral soil are cleared, drained, and removed. Rivers and streams are diverted and forests are clear cut, with merchantable timber being harvested and the remainder being piled and burned....The layers of wetland and muskeg (water-soaked vegetation that consists of mainly decaying plant material) must be drained and excavated.
   >
   > The muskeg layer lies about 1–3 metres (m) thick above the overburden (the material that overlies the ore deposit). Prior to the muskeg layer's removal, it must be drained of its water content...The overburden is then mined with large shovels and moved by dump trucks to be placed in above ground waste dumps (called overburden dumps) or mined out pits. The overburden may also be compacted into large dykes, creating dams that will eventually contain tailings.
   >
   > With the boreal forest and overburden removed, the oil sands ore is exposed and can then be mined. (5)

3. The Pembina Institute describes itself as an organization that "creates sustainable energy solutions through research, education, consulting, and advocacy. It promotes environmental, social and economic sustainability in the public interest by developing practical solutions for communities, individuals, governments, and businesses. The Pembina Institute provides policy research leadership and education on climate change, energy issues, green economies, energy efficiency and conservation, renewable energy and environmental governance" (Grant, Dyer, Woynillowicz ii).
4. These lawsuits focus on an alleged lack of government consultation when approving bitumen leases and a failure to ensure constitutionally enshrined

5. treaty rights to continued hunting, fishing, and trapping on traditional Aboriginal lands. People downstream from the mining operations have been complaining for years about high cancer rates in their communities.

5. The suggestion that Alberta is a dictatorship has some support as well; see Nikiforuk, "The First Law of Petropolitics" (152–66) in his book *Tar Sands: Dirty Oil and the Future of a Continent*.

6. Zwicky explains that she does not use "lyric" "in a sense that emphasizes the role of the individual ego: the 'outpouring of subjective emotion' connected with the rise of Romantic poetry. That sense is corrupt and is based on a subversion of the desire which fundamentally underlies lyric expression—relinquishment of the individual ego rather than celebration of it" (*Lyric* 126).

7. Since this passage was written, charges were laid under provincial environmental legislation and the federal migratory birds act, a trial was held, guilty verdicts were returned, and a fine of $3 million was levied against Syncrude. A great deal could be said about this trial, but it must suffice here to note that despite claims by Syncrude's defense that "The oilsands industry will be 'doomed' if Syncrude is found guilty of a crime as a result of birds dying on its tailings pond" (Henton), the performance of justice in the legal system enabled the return to the status quo. That is, to those who critiqued the regulatory framework, the response could be "the system works."

8. Bertha refers the superintendent to "Isaiah chapter six" (189) as proof of her understanding of the angel's anatomy, but the reference also indicates that the angel is a seraph, a creature who declares "the whole earth is full of [God's] glory" (Isaiah 6.3). This glory, then, also includes all the relationships of which the tar sands are a part.

2

CITIZENSHIP STUDIES AND MIGRANT ILLEGALITY

JEAN MCDONALD

RECENT SCHOLARSHIP on migrant illegality has led to a critical rethinking of citizenship, sovereignty, and migration. In this chapter, I discuss the ways in which studies of migrant illegalization help to broaden understandings of citizenship in today's world. Indeed, I argue that such studies of illegalization, often ignored in citizenship studies, have become necessary given the mutually constitutive relationship between citizenship and migrant illegality. This relationship has become integral to the organization of global inequalities and the production of racist and nationalist ideologies that legitimate contemporary forms of global capitalism. I examine the potential of the study of migrant illegality to broaden the scope of citizenship. I argue that the issue of migrant illegality has tended to be ignored within the field of citizenship studies. The displacement of illegality from studies of citizenship mimics the social and political invisibility often faced by migrants with precarious immigration status and the processes of illegalization that produce an erasure of their legal personhood. Rather than ignoring processes of illegalization, scholars of citizenship should begin to see migrant illegality as integral to the study of contemporary citizenship due to the constitutive relationship between the socially, politically, and legally constructed categories of nation-state citizen and illegal migrant. Specifically, it is the everyday lived experiences of migrants with precarious immigration status that are necessary to more fully understand the constitutive relationship between formal nation-state citizenship and migrant illegality.[1] First, I describe the context of migrant illegality within the context of Canada and a contemporary challenge to migrant illegality as posed by the "Don't Ask, Don't Tell" campaign in Toronto, Ontario. Second, I explain the paradox of citizenship in Western liberal democratic nation-states. Third, I examine conceptions of postnational and denationalized citizenship to examine the ways in which these particular conceptions are challenged when processes of illegalization are taken into account. In the last section, I outline the ways in which the issue of illegality in the context of citizenship has been engaged within the body of literature that I have examined in this chapter, and I summarize three key ways in which engagement with migrant illegality broadens studies of global processes of inclusion and exclusion.

Challenging Migrant Illegality in Canada

The "Don't Ask, Don't Tell" campaign, launched by No One Is Illegal-Toronto[2] in March 2004, is comprised of a coalition of women's shelters, anti-poverty organizations, unions, immigrant rights groups, drop-ins, neighbourhood centres, legal clinics, and community health centres. Working to affirm the right of all members of the metropolis to use public services, the campaign poses an important challenge to state definitions of migrant illegality by working towards creating communities that are not dependent upon formal citizenship as a marker of belonging. In many instances, the illegality of a person surfaces when their lack of state-issued documentation produces their identity as an outsider and bars them from necessary services. Consequently, everyday forms of marginalization, exploitation, surveillance, and repression have a significant impact on the daily lives of people with precarious forms of immigration status in Canada.[3] A municipal policy that prohibits questions about immigration status and denies city workers or service providers the ability to pass on immigration information to federal agencies circumvents the increased surveillance that racism and discrimination invoke in many situations—whether attending school, going to the hospital, applying for social housing, accessing emergency shelter services, or calling for police assistance. The campaign also challenges state definitions of migrant illegality that a priori criminalize, through an erasure of legal personhood, the identity of people living with precarious immigration status.

I use the term illegalization to refer to processes that *make* people illegal, processes that *illegalize* certain bodies in particular spaces within the globalizing nation-state system. In Canada, we can see the ways in which people are made illegal through the classist, gendered, and racist processes of selection and exclusion that are engendered through the Immigrant and Refugee Protection Act (IRPA). The majority of people living with precarious immigration status do not meet the strict requirements of the point system, which emphasizes particular work skills and high economic status, while privileging education from white-dominated countries, such as Australia, the US, and the UK. I use the phrase "precarious immigration status" to refer to the fluidity of impermanent forms of immigration status. A person with precarious immigration status is someone who may have a student, visitor, or work permit, or have overstayed his or her permit. They may be in the process of applying for a refugee claim or family sponsorship. Others may have failed these claims and decided to remain in Canada rather than face persecution in their country of origin.

While legality may be officially defined at the federal level, processes of illegalization can be identified through an examination of ideological borders that arise in everyday life. For many people living without legal status in Canada, simple everyday activities such as working, driving, and going to school can become endeavours that may result in detention and/or deportation. In examining access to services, it becomes clear that the nation-state border is not just a physical geographic territorial marker that simply excludes or keeps people out. Instead, we can begin to understand the ways in which nation-state borders are also ideological, used to paradoxically *include* non-citizens through exclusionary practices that maintain conditions of exploitability and marginalization. In this sense, borders exist when non-status immigrants come into contact or confrontation with institutional settings, such as schools, hospitals, social housing offices, food banks and emergency services, all of which require some form of identification. Indeed, if one examines the ideological borders that arise through service provision, a challenge to these ideological borders may also pose a challenge to processes of illegalization, and thus to the production of illegality itself.

How do people become illegalized in Canada? Migrant illegality can be better understood when examined as the product of a set of processes rather than as a given state or status. While the flow of migratory labour tends to be understood and produced through state policies and practices as the sole responsibility of the individual, conditions of poverty, unemployment, displacement, and other consequences of capitalist globalization should be recognized as central factors of global migrations. Saskia Sassen argues that large-scale global migrations are structured through various transnational and geopolitical processes (including colonial and *de facto* colonial relationships) that can only be partially regulated through national immigration controls (*Losing Control*, 76). Thus, global migratory flows impact the ways in which migrants are produced as illegal in Canada. Sassen points out that because global migratory flows occur regardless of national immigration controls, fears of a "control crisis," or the "flooding" of migrants into a national territory, are largely unwarranted (*Losing Control*, 74). This indicates that migrants will arrive in Canada regardless of legal avenues for entrance. When one avenue of legal entrance is closed off or minimized, numbers will increase via other channels (Sassen, *Losing Control*, 74). In Canada, changes in immigration policy have further minimized avenues for people to legalize their status. Take, for example, the repeal of Section 34 of the 1967 Immigration Act in 1972 that bars potential applicants from applying for permanent residency from within the nation-state. As one of the processes of illegalization, global migrations also function to fulfill the needs of the national economy—satisfying the demand for cheap, exploitable, and disposable labour. The consequences of global capitalism, such as displacement, poverty, and unemployment, are among the driving forces behind global migration. Global capitalism is, in many ways, dependent upon a system of global apartheid within a globalized nation-state system, and this global apartheid is reproduced through global migrations.

Nandita Sharma asks whether citizenship regimes are simply exclusionary and examines the tendencies of a nation-state system of global apartheid to *include* via an exclusionary framework. She writes, "Like past forms of apartheid, global apartheid is not based on keeping differential people *apart* but instead, on organizing two (or more) separate legal regimes and practices for differentiated groups of people *within* the same space" (Sharma, "Global Apartheid" 72). The existence of global apartheid is often denied, Sharma argues, because it continues to be associated with race-based legal differentiations and there are almost no legally based race distinctions found in immigration law today (72). The nation-state system of global apartheid, however, legitimizes both global inequalities and the use of coercive force, such as detention and deportation, against non-citizens and also naturalizes classed, gendered, and racialized exclusions to national membership (Sharma 72). Apartheid in this global sense does not mean to physically prevent a group of people from entering a territorial space; rather, it means that via this exclusion, people are *included* through their categorization as "illegal" or "unlawful." This categorization fosters exploitability through an erasure of legal personhood for a specified group of people/workers. Critical scholarship has demonstrated the tacit acceptance of irregular migration by the state, as a means to access and produce flexible, mobile, deportable, cheap, and compliant labour (McNevin, "Political Belonging" 140). Anne McNevin notes, "Under these conditions, irregular migrants are incorporated into the political community as economic participants but denied the status of insiders" (141). Like Sharma and McNevin, Nicholas De Genova argues that processes of illegalization also "socially include [undocumented migrants] under imposed conditions of enforced and protracted vulnerability" (De Genova, "Migrant 'Illegality'" 429). In this sense, the production of illegality is inseparable from the practice of citizenship. As such, the liberal ideal of citizenship can be understood as a tool of state power.

Inclusion, Exclusion, and the Paradox of Citizenship

Within recent citizenship studies, scholars have pointed to a paradox, tension, or ambiguity inherent in the concept of citizenship. The meaning of this paradox, however, varies in the many different conceptions of it. For several scholars, this paradox lies with the inherent nature of citizenship to be at once inclusive and exclusive. Other scholars identify a tension within the global system itself, between human rights on the one hand and national sovereignty on the other, and examine the effects of this tension on practices of citizenship. These two central ways that scholars have critically examined citizenship are not mutually exclusive and, in fact, can be understood as constitutive of one another. In this sense, we can look at the ways in which appeals to human rights are made in order to promote greater inclusivity within citizenship regimes, while claims to national sovereignty are used to legitimate the exclusivity of citizenship. This constitutive relationship also opens up possibilities for questioning the oft-assumed binary relationship between exclusion and inclusion; as we will see, exclusion from citizenship often occurs in ways that function to include certain populations under particular relations of power, often of vulnerability and marginalization.

James Holston and Arjun Appadurai succinctly summarize the tension between inclusion and exclusion that lies at the heart of the paradox of citizenship. To do so, they point to two integral aspects of citizenship. The first is the importance of nation-state citizenship in being recognized as a "member of society" (1). The second point to which Holston and Appadurai refer is the simultaneous inclusivity and exclusivity inherent in citizenship. They note that, historically, citizenship has developed upon ambiguous lines both revolutionary and conservative (1). Correspondingly, Linda Bosniak identifies an "ethical ambiguity" within the concept of citizenship: "The idea of citizenship is commonly invoked to convey a state of democratic belonging or inclusion, yet this inclusion is usually premised on a conception of a community that is bounded and exclusive" (*Citizen and Alien* 1). She notes that ideally citizenship would work against subordination; however, she argues that citizenship is also a practice around which subordination revolves (*Citizen and Alien* 1). Bosniak echoes Holston and Appadurai's point about the historical development of citizenship by arguing that modern regimes of citizenship have tolerated, and often concealed, social exclusion and injustice (*Citizen and Alien* 132). However, Bosniak develops Holston and Appadurai's argument by pointing to the ways in which regimes of citizenship legitimate the exclusion and subordination of non-citizens. In doing so, Bosniak refers to the production of illegality and the precariousness that results from policies and practices of nation-state citizenship. Similarly, Jacqueline Bhabha argues that a central feature in the production of citizenship is, in fact exclusion from it (13). Peter Nyers argues that, paradoxically, citizenship is understood as a remarkable, even revolutionary achievement, yet the successes of citizenship are realized in highly unequal and exclusionary terms ("Introduction" 203). In this sense, the production of migrant illegality, or "alienage" in Bosniak's terminology, can be understood as a key process in the construction of nation-state citizenship.

Bosniak provides a counterpoint to the concept of citizenship when she argues that alienage is constructed within law as "a hybrid legal status category" that is at the intersection of "two legal and moral worlds" (*Citizen and Alien* 38). She notes that while they are territorially present persons, "in this world, aliens appear to be at once *indistinguishable from citizens and precisely the sort of social group that requires the law's protection*" (*Citizen and Alien* 38, emphasis added). Alienage, like citizenship, is an ambiguous category that raises issues of national sovereignty and exclusionary membership and human rights. The "Don't Ask, Don't Tell" campaign in Toronto is fighting for an expansion of social and legal rights for non-citizens with precarious status so they will be able to access community services. The need for this expansion has captured the attention of local media. A *Toronto Star* article reports that federal immigration officers with a deportation order removed children who were attending two Toronto schools in April 2006 (Kalinowski). In one of these cases, the intention of the officers was to force the children's parents out of hiding. The cases reveal a tension between the rights of children to access education on one hand and the Canadian state's ability to define national membership on the other. Another article in the *Toronto Star* explains that when immigrant women with precarious immigration status in Canada attempt to press charges on abusive partners, they often face detention and deportation (Keung). Nicholas Keung points to a tension between human rights and the sovereign right of a nation-state to define political membership through access to rights and services. These scenarios exemplify the ways in which liberal conceptions of formal citizenship in a nation-state often conceal and legitimate social exclusion and the denial of political rights to those refused access to formal citizenship. These examples also allude to a process of illegalization manifested in policies, codes, regulations, and practices in which immigration status can impact access to political rights and public services.

If the institution of citizenship defines the boundaries of membership in a particular state and thus enacts a form of inclusion, as De Genova points out, it simultaneously defines who is *not* a citizen and is thus excluded from the nation-state as aliens, foreigners, or outsiders (*Working* 216). De Genova notes that the liberal ideals of universal inclusivity tend to mask the exclusions legitimated through claims of national sovereignty and that national identities are produced hegemonically through processes of citizenship (*Working* 216). While citizenship offers a beacon of hope in terms of democracy and human rights, migration policies "have largely undermined the emancipatory potential or equalizing promise of the 'evasive grail of citizenship'" (Stasiulis and Bakan 11). Sassen posits immigration as a lens through which we can understand the contradictions of formal citizenship in a nation-state, as immigration tends to be central to the intersection of tensions between human rights and national sovereignty in the definition of national membership (*Territory* 239).

In this section, I have argued that regimes of nation-state citizenship are paradoxically inclusionary and exclusionary. The inclusionary nature of citizenship within liberal democratic states is purportedly based upon the equality of citizens within a given polity. This inclusion, however, is based upon the exclusion of others from political membership. While practices of citizenship can be understood as both inclusionary and exclusionary, it is important to examine the complexity and contradictions of this paradox. For example, formal citizens of a liberal democratic state may be formally included in political membership, yet substantially excluded in varying ways that reflect racialized, gendered, classed and other forms of hierarchical relationships. Furthermore, resident non-citizens, legal and illegal, are included under the terms of their exclusion, often through the conditions of deportability and detainability that render their labour distinctly exploitable. What Sharma describes as "global apartheid" can be understood as one of the elements that produce and uphold emerging forms of capitalist globalization. Changing historical and political conditions of globalization have opened up questions of human rights, national sovereignty, and the viability of the nation-state system. Furthermore, these changing historical conditions have led many scholars to identify and conceive of a variety of new forms of citizenship, including postnational, denationalized, global, transnational, cosmopolitan, flexible, negotiated, and neoliberal. For the purposes of this essay, I will address the first two conceptions of citizenship: postnational and denationalized citizenship.

Citizenship as Postnational or Denationalized

Yasemin Soysal conceptualizes postnational citizenship to refer to a shift in the allocation of rights previously defined as national that are currently legitimized on the basis of personhood as governed by an international human rights regime, including such international bodies as the United Nations and the European Union (3). She claims that citizenship has been reconfigured in the post-World War II era from one that is particularistic and national in nature to a model that is more universal—in other words, based on personhood rather than national membership (137). Soysal primarily identifies this reconfiguration of citizenship in Europe, but extends her analysis to Canada, the United States, and Australia. She identifies the basic rights accorded to legal non-citizens as an extension of membership to guest workers, which make national citizenship "peculiarly less important" (29). While Soysal's conception of postnational citizenship is compelling, she may have been too quick to claim that formal citizenship in a nation-state is less important in securing rights and defining political membership, as her critics (including Ong, Bosniak, Bhabha, Stasiulis and Bakan, and Varsanyi) attest. Soysal's conception is predicated on the assumption that the non-citizens she is referring to are *legal*. In making this assumption, Soysal ignores *illegal* non-citizens and this absence is an example of the theoretical displacement of this group of people within many studies of citizenship.

By arguing that rights and entitlements previously accessible through formal citizenship in a nation-state are now legitimized on the basis of personhood, Soysal accepts the denial of legal personhood to those who cannot access these rights and entitlements. One could say that the argument for extending rights and entitlements to non-citizens (legal or illegal) is often based on a recognition of personhood for those denied such rights and entitlement; yet, to argue that this is already established is to deny the personhood of those without legal status. Within this logic, it would seem that illegal aliens are displaced from the realm of personhood. A more complicated analysis would demonstrate the often fluid nature of immigration status, as it fluctuates between gradations of legal and illegal. So while Soysal refers to guest workers and the rights that they may hold in their host countries, she does not point out that if a work permit expires or a conflict arises with an employer, this legal status can quickly and easily become illegal. Thus, Soysal's concept of postnational citizenship displaces the issue of migrant illegality. This displacement creates a conceptual blindspot in which the precariousness of immigration status is not considered. When it is considered, a different conclusion emerges.

Aihwa Ong, for example, critiques Soysal's argument that the limited rights accorded to migrant workers constitute a form of postnational citizenship by pointing out that the gains made in terms of migrant rights are largely exaggerated (*Neoliberalism* 15). Ong notes that an increased denial of rights is simultaneously underway despite the dominant discourse of international human rights (16). Similarly, Monica Varsanyi points out that in spite of rights gains made by migrant workers, "*the legal right to remain must not be considered insignificant*" (237, emphasis added). In other words, the condition of deportability is extremely important in outlining national belonging. Bosniak points out that empirically identifying postnational citizenship will vary differentially according to one's definition of citizenship, whether one is addressing citizenship as legal status, as rights and responsibilities, as political activity, or as an identity or solidarity ("Citizenship" 452). She argues that while Soysal's model may or may not accurately apply to migrant workers in Europe, the postnational has limited application, including within the United States, where the tension between citizenship and personhood is often experienced through very nationalist terms (Bosniak, "Citizenship" 460–61). Rather than search for an empirical basis for postnational citizenship, Bosniak argues that the concept can be used for political advocacy, one that for her is driven by an ethical desire to fight marginalization and domination ("Citizenship" 490, 502). Much like the "Don't Ask, Don't Tell" campaign, Bosniak supports a movement away from formal citizenship towards residency as a marker of belonging and a means to access rights. Rather than being cited as an established empirical fact, postnational citizenship is a concept that advocates for migrant justice can draw upon in their work towards this new notion of community and belonging.

Like Bhabha (12), Stasiulis and Bakan argue that nation-states remain the primary site of governance in securing citizenship rights and responsibilities (13). They point out, however, that the power relations that define formal citizenship reflect wider global relations of power in the nation-state system (Stasiulis and Bakan 13). Stasiulis and Bakan note that there are two major obstacles that proponents of postnational citizenship must face: the absence of democracy in international human rights regimes and the reality of state sovereignty (37).

Sassen, on the other hand, points out that the notions of postnational and denationalized citizenship often become blurred or confused, and she argues that these terms should be distinguished in order to account for reconfigurations of citizenship that may be taking place within a national frame and as they alter the meaning of this frame (*Territory* 287–88; "Repositioning" 88; "Denationalized" 576). Sassen differentiates between postnational and denationalized citizenship largely in terms of scope. Postnational citizenship, she contends, is "located partly outside the confines of the national" and may account for new forms of citizenship emerging outside of the traditional framework of the nation (*Territory* 305). Denationalized citizenship, on the other hand, focuses on the transformation of the national through global and denationalizing dynamics that tend to emerge within the national frame, disrupting the idea that the domains of the national and the global are mutually exclusive (Sassen, *Territory* 305; "National Territory" 523). These dynamics include policies linked to globalization (from privatization to the international human rights regime) and the emergence of actors, groups, and communities that are increasingly unwilling to identify with the state and that work to destabilize previously bundled historic and embedded elements that make up the categories of the citizen and the alien (Sassen, "Denationalized" 80). This destabilization has produced openings for the emergence of new political subjects and new political spaces, signaling a deterritorialization of citizenship practices and identities and nationalist discourses of loyalty and belonging (Sassen, "Denationalized" 80). Sassen argues that both conceptions of citizenship, postnational and denationalized, are viable and are not mutually exclusive of one another (*Territory* 305).

Citizenship Studies and Migrant Illegality

The subject of migrant illegality, while often sidelined or ignored, has been taken up in a number of different ways within recent studies of citizenship. These studies are most useful as they examine the ways in which illegality is produced and take into consideration the daily realities of life for people living without full legal immigration status. For example, De Genova focuses on the legal production of citizenship and illegality, aiming to denaturalize the idea that migratory movement can be equated with transgressions of the law. In doing so, De Genova demonstrates how the law has been used in calculated ways in order to generate migrant illegality (*Working* 2). He contends:

> *The legal production of migrant "illegality" has never served simply to achieve the apparent goal of deportation, so much as to regulate the flow of Mexican migration in particular and to sustain its legally vulnerable condition of* deportability—*the possibility of deportation, the possibility of being removed from the* space *of the US nation-state. It is deportability, and not deportation as such, that has historically rendered Mexican labor to be a distinctly disposable commodity.*
> (De Genova, Working 8)

De Genova argues that the production of migrant illegality performs an erasure of legal personhood, creating a social space of enforced invisibility, marginalization, exclusion, and domination that follows non-status immigrants wherever they go ("Migrant 'Illegality'" 427). Highlighting the everyday-ness of illegality, particularly the everyday forms of surveillance and repression, as experienced by the Mexican migrants with whom he worked during his ethnographic research, De Genova examines "the heightened policing directed at the bodies, movements, and spaces of the poor, and especially those racialized as not-white" (*Working* 246–47). He notes that illegality may be irrelevant during most of their daily activities, only to emerge in particular contexts where legal reality is suddenly superimposed in everyday life, reproducing the national border in innumerable places in the interiors of migrant-receiving states (De Genova, "Migrant 'Illegality'" 422).

Étienne Balibar, inspired by the *sans-papiers* movement in France, conceives of citizenship as an active process, one that is engaged and enabled through assemblages of various components including (but not limited to) formal legal status, access to social services, right to use to public spaces, social and political obligations, and the ability to make claims on society and state ("What we owe" 42–43). In conceptualizing active citizenship, Balibar makes an important intervention by recognizing the political agency of the *sans-papiers* in France. Immigrants with precarious status are systematically denied the right to make claims on the state, yet many are refusing this denial. As Balibar notes in reference to *sans-papiers* within France, *droit de cité* and citizenship are not primarily "granted or conceded from above but are, in an essential respect, constructed from below" (*We, the People* 48). A similar assertion can be made in respect to the No One Is Illegal migrant justice movement in Canada in general, and the municipal "Don't Ask, Don't Tell" campaign in particular. The "Don't Ask, Don't Tell" campaign, as explained above, mirrors American campaigns that have created "sanctuary cities," effectively moving away from formal citizenship as a central marker of belonging.

In her later work, *Territory, Authority, Rights*, Sassen conceives of undocumented immigrants as types of informal citizens who are unauthorized and yet recognized as participants in a community, "political subjects not quite fully recognized as such," who have partial rights in society (*Territory* 294, 280). In opposition to "unauthorized yet recognized" citizens, she conceives of "authorized yet not fully recognized" citizens, such as minoritized citizens and mothers. Sassen's conceptions of "unauthorized yet recognized" and "authorized yet unrecognized" are useful; however, Sassen's work would be strengthened by examining the ways in which these categories also overlap and blur. For instance, non-status immigrants could be both mothers and "minoritized." Because Sassen does not ground her theorizations in the lived experiences of undocumented migrants, she runs the risk of generalizing her subject matter, and missing important detailed information that would likely result in more complex conceptions of formal and informal citizenship.

Ethnographic and other forms of qualitative research, including participant observation, interviews and group discussions, would add a more dynamic element to Sassen's work in this area. Qualitative research is important to engage the day-to-day experiences of migrants with precarious status, and to develop a nuanced understanding of the varied impacts of migrant illegality on the lives of those directly affected. As it currently stands, Sassen's work may be misleading because she does not forefront the marginalization, vulnerability, and exclusion through proscribed inclusion that many people with precarious status face. She writes that undocumented (im)migrants participate in their communities as citizens do, but does not mention conditions of deportability and detainability—conditions that severely limit the everyday existence of people with precarious status. Nor does she discuss the issues of variable access to services and fluidity between legal and illegal statuses for non-citizens.

In my own research it has become clear that deportability and detainability have a substantial impact on the lives of people living with precarious status in Toronto, particularly on people who have overstayed their visas or failed refugee claims and have limited options for legalizing their status. Social isolation is common, as it is difficult for people to form close relationships for fear that their status will be discovered. School children, for instance, would not be able to participate in field trips without health coverage. Similarly, young adults would not be able to go out to clubs with friends without identification. Mental health issues, more specifically depression, are often produced through the ongoing trauma of fear and the virtual impossibility to plan for the future.

Like Sassen, Engin Isin argues, "Formal citizenship is neither necessary nor a sufficient condition for substantive citizenship" (265). Isin makes only brief mention of "illegal aliens," noting that illegal migrants are non-consenting and un-consented to by the nation-state (270). Likewise, Holston and Appadurai focus on "legally resident non-citizens" to the exclusion of illegal resident non-citizens (4). When studies of citizenship focus upon legal non-citizens to the exclusion of "illegal migrants," scholars are enacting a theoretical displacement that echoes the exclusion of migrants with precarious status from political and social rights and the denial of their legal personhood. Avoiding the study of migrant illegality means avoiding the ways in which immigration status is a fluid process wherein migrants often slip between statuses defined as legal or illegal by the nation-state. Sassen, Isin, Holston, Appadurai, and others miss an integral process in which liberal conceptions of formal citizenship in a nation-state legitimate the denial of human rights to specifically categorized persons, even as they normalize their social and political exclusion from national membership.

In contrast to these works, however, Stasiulis and Bakan argue that formal, legal citizenship continues to be exceedingly important from the vantage point of non-citizens in order to access a variety of rights, not least of which is the legal right to remain within their chosen country (140). Ong notes that legal migrant workers in Malaysia have limited employment rights but cannot apply for citizenship (*Neoliberalism* 83). Illegal migrant workers, on the other hand, have no legal or social rights and, if exposed, face deportation with no right of appeal (Ong 83). Ong argues that the contingent legal status of migrant workers in Malaysia "reinforces their 'biopolitical otherness' as non-citizens and lower-class subjects," (201) thus recognizing the instability of legal and illegal non-citizens. Bosniak contends that discrimination against "aliens," whether status or non-status, and the corollary privileging of citizens reflects a tension between its legitimation as an extension of the regulation of national borders and its delegitimation as a violation of legal equality (Bosniak, *Citizen and Alien* 14). She writes, "Undocumented immigrants live among the nation's formal members, often perform their menial labour, and are subject to local law, but ordinarily have no prospects for acquiring legal status or citizenship" (*Citizen and Alien* 63). Like De Genova, Bosniak notes that the state's immigration power is manifested in its territorial interior as well as at its physical national borders, a condition that creates "internal 'borders' to full membership, or citizenship" (*Citizen and Alien* 50). In other words, the power of the state to deport "substantially constrains 'undocumented aliens' sometimes acknowledged rights as territorial persons" (Bosniak, *Citizen and Alien* 70). Thus, Bosniak asks whether the violation of national borders should be relevant in determining differential treatment under the law, and differential access to constitutional rights (*Citizen and Alien* 64). Bosniak refers to undocumented migrants as "impossible subjects"; while their territorial residency brings them into national normative concern, their deportability leaves them vulnerable to subordination and marginalization (*Citizen and Alien* 139). Drawing attention to similar tensions between territorial residency, rights, and membership, Susan Bibler Coutin contends that the labour performed by migrant workers incurs an obligation of the state to recognize them as full social and legal persons and may provide grounds for their regularization or legalization (589–90).

Seyla Benhabib's portrayal and analysis of the category of "undocumented immigrants" is often contradictory and almost haphazard. In arguing for a cosmopolitan theory of justice that incorporates "just distribution" and "just membership" on a global scale, she writes:

> *Such just membership entails: recognizing the moral claim of refugees and asylees to* first admittance; *a regime of* porous *borders for immigrants; an injunction against denationalization and the loss of citizenship rights; and the vindication of the right of every human being "to have rights," that is, to be a* legal person, *entitled to certain inalienable rights, regardless of the status of their political membership.* (Benhabib, Rights of Others 3, *emphasis original*)

While these suggestions would indeed have a meaningful impact on the lives of non-status immigrants in terms of alleviating conditions of deportability and detainability, Benhabib does not significantly challenge the legitimacy of the nation-state system itself. Instead, she tends to uncritically re-inscribe traditional categories of the state such as refugees who are to be afforded privileged entrance over others. She does not explain how refugees and asylum seekers will be differentiated from other migrants or who will make these decisions. In Benhabib's conception, migrant illegality is only the result of "bureaucratic mishaps and mistakes" or human smuggling rather than a global system of unequal nation-states and national citizenships that renders certain persons disposable, deportable, and vulnerable (215). Furthermore, "just membership" is only available to the alien who fulfills "certain conditions" (Benhabib 3). Benhabib writes, "The status of illegality does not stamp the other as an alien. Clearly, a democratic adjustment of the practices of legal incorporation is needed so as to normalize undocumented migrants" (215). Here, Benhabib describes the production of migrant illegality in a way that does not acknowledge how it is produced through the logic of national sovereignty and how it upholds the inequalities legitimated and enforced through the nation-state system. Rather than examine the production of migrant illegality as legitimated through the hegemony of the liberal-democratic state, Benhabib simply notes that migrant illegality is incompatible with this political context and a violation of human rights (3). She notes that state sovereignty, as a doctrine that justifies permanent alienage, must be challenged but she does not take the next step of challenging the centrality of the nation-state system (3–4). In this way, Benhabib continues to uphold and uncritically reproduce hegemonic discourses of liberal democracy and its corollary conceptions of formal citizenship within the nation-state system.

As demonstrated above, liberal conceptions of nation-state citizenship tend to conceal and legitimate the social exclusion and denial of political and legal rights to non-citizen actors. As Nyers points out, received liberal democratic traditions of the political "*require* that some human beings be illegal" ("Abject" 1089). To challenge processes of illegalization, then, "is to call into question the entire architecture of sovereignty, all its borders, locks and doors, internal hierarchies, etc." (Nyer, "Abject" 1089). To confront the production of migrant illegality, scholars must challenge liberal conceptions of nation-state citizenship and, in turn, conceptions of the globalized nation-state system itself.

Migrant Illegality: Broadening the Scope of Citizenship Studies

The study of migrant illegality and of the corollary effects of deportability and detainability has broadened the scope of citizenship studies in three particularly integral ways. The first is through destabilizations of taken-for-granted discursive and legal categories, such as citizen, non-citizen, migrant worker, illegal migrant, refugee, deportee, alien, and others, categories that are often left un-problematized within citizenship studies. The second notable way that the study of migrant illegality has further developed understandings of inclusion and exclusion is through examining processes of racialization and the ways in which racialization intersects with processes of illegalization. A third key contribution that the study of migrant illegality brings to citizenship studies is an examination of inclusion and exclusion beyond their binary representation. In other words, the study of migrant illegality in the context of citizenship and the nation-state opens up questions of exclusionary inclusions and inclusionary exclusions, more specifically through global apartheid, demonstrating a blurring of boundaries that allows scholars to simultaneously question the legitimacy of national sovereignty as well as the legitimation of exclusionary practices that national sovereignty provides.

The destabilization and denaturalization of unquestioned legal and discursive categories is integral to the study of migrant illegality. In his study of processes of illegalization in the context of Mexican migration to the US, De Genova aims to denaturalize migrant illegality as a taken-for-granted legal category (*Working* 227) and as an effect of discursive formation ("Migrant 'Illegality'" 431). Nathalie Peutz, in her call for an "anthropology of removal,"[4] argues that this area of scholarship provides an avenue from which to ethnographically interrogate the "'natural' order of things" (231). Her work also demonstrates a need for scholars of citizenship, transnationalism, and migration to focus "not only on the reversal of movements and rights but especially on the *transfer* of peoples by state/corporate, local/global actors" (Peutz 231). In particular, Peutz's article raises questions of the fixity of the division between the deportable and non-deportable, the citizen-alien divide, the shaping of the remaining social and political community through deportation practices, gendered and racialized practices, and new subjectivities (231). Bosniak notes that many scholars of citizenship tend to hold nationalist presumptions as both current fact and conceptual necessity. She critiques these theorists for treating national territory and boundedness as pre-satisfied conditions for the study of citizenship (*Citizen and Alien* 5). As Bosniak argues, these presumptions narrow rather than broaden studies of citizenship, wherein scholars simply focus on the requirements of citizenship in terms of satisfying substantive needs within pre-given boundaries (*Citizen and Alien* 5). She writes, "The result [of formal citizenship in liberal democratic states] is a model of bounded solidarity in which compatriot insiders 'take priority' over non-national others and in which the territorial border encircling compatriots is policed against penetration by those others" (*Citizen and Alien* 125). Taking account of illegality compels theorists of citizenship to challenge taken-for-granted assumptions of national belonging, territory, and of the nation-state system itself.

As Stasiulis and Bakan note, the activism of non-citizen actors plays an integral role in redefining and expanding the notion of citizenship and belonging beyond the conceptual boundaries of the nation-state (141). Contemporary examples in Toronto include the aforementioned "Don't Ask, Don't Tell" campaign (explained above) and No One Is Illegal. No One Is Illegal-Toronto is a group of immigrants, refugees, and allies who work towards justice for all migrants. This group contests immigration systems that divide migrants into categories of those deserving and undeserving of permanent residency and formal citizenship. To make sure that *everyone* has equal and equitable access to all rights and entitlements they argue that *no human being is illegal*. Discrimination between people on all bases is rejected and justice is demanded for all migrants and Indigenous peoples. Central demands include an end to detention and deportation, access to services for all residents, a full and inclusive regularization program, and the recognition of Indigenous sovereignty, among others (see http://toronto.nooneisillegal.org/ for a full list of demands).

The study of migrant illegality also challenges us to engage with "often unacknowledged normative commitments," in which compatriots take priority over national and territorial outsiders (Bosniak, *Citizen and Alien* 134–35). It also allows scholars to question hegemonic understandings of the liberal democratic state as simply based upon fairness, equality, and inclusiveness. Instead, scholars can examine and challenge the ways in which exclusionary citizenship practices enforce and legitimate social and political inequalities within liberal democratic states (37).

A second contribution of the study of migrant illegality to the examination of citizenship in liberal democratic states is the tendency for scholars (see above Ong, *Neoliberalism*; Stasiulis and Bakan; Sharma; De Genova, *Working*) to engage with a corollary issue of migrant illegality—racialization—and its intersections with gendered, classed, ableist, and other forms of repressive and marginalizing practices. For example, De Genova argues that the spatialized social condition of migrant illegality cannot be separated from the racialization of Mexican migrants as "illegal aliens" in that US Mexican migrants are racialized in opposition to "American-ness," which is discursively produced as white (De Genova, *Working* 8). As De Genova writes:

> *The boundaries of racial whiteness have been produced and policed within the social order of the nation-state, but the pervasive equation of whiteness within "American" national identity itself has also required that such racialized boundaries overlap with "national" frontiers and nation-state borders.* (Working 102)

The historical consolidation of white supremacy in the US is therefore inseparable from the ongoing history of colonization of the North American continent (De Genova, *Working* 102). Rather than taking Mexican migrants as his object of study, De Genova critically examines nationalism and racialization in the United States from the standpoint of Mexican migration (*Working* 18).

The third significant contribution of migrant illegality to studies of citizenship is an examination of inclusionary and exclusionary processes as blurred or interconnected. In other words, migrant illegality encourages us to look at the ways in which inclusions may be exclusionary and exclusions may be inclusionary. For example, Peutz's call for an "anthropology of removal" challenges anthropologists to "confront the tenacity of the state (even a 'failed' one) and the inevitable logic of its exclusionary practices" (218). These exclusionary practices demonstrate the eagerness of states to assert and perform their sovereignty in what Peutz calls an "age of terror" (218). Unfortunately, Peutz does not denaturalize the "age of terror" and the "terrorist threats" that she refers to; nor does she examine the ways in which discourses of terror legitimate the exclusionary practices that she is examining.

John Torpey argues that the notion of belonging that informs the concept of citizenship is challenged when people leave the spaces in which they "belong," enter spaces where they do not belong, and cross borders (245). Torpey notes that in monopolizing the legitimate means of movement, states and the international state systems must "define who belongs and who does not, who may come and go and who not, and to make these distinctions intelligible and enforceable" (249). Susan Bibler Coutin, Bill

Maurer, and Barbara Yngvesson point out that the legitimation work of globalization reconfigures national sovereignty in new ways, altering the ways in which people are ordered, included, and excluded through global processes (801). As De Genova argues, the presence of illegal non-citizens within the nation-state works to "[subvert] the integrity of 'the nation' and its sovereignty from *within* the space of the US nation-state" (De Genova, *Working* 215). The study of migrant illegality, then, opens up key questions about the complicated nature of global processes of inclusion and exclusion in contemporary globalized times.

In this section I have looked at some of the varying ways in which scholars of citizenship have addressed the issue of migrant illegality within their work. As Antoinette Burton asks, "Who writes—who even sees—the histories of subjects exiled from the 'national body'?" (238). In engaging with migrant illegality and the intertwined processes of exclusion and inclusion, scholars of citizenship can open up answers to this question.

▸ The question of migrant illegality, often unaddressed or addressed in problematic ways in citizenship studies, can broaden the scope of this field of study, and expand the ways in which scholars engage with global processes of inclusion and exclusion. Traditionally, studies of citizenship have conceptually privileged status (legal) non-citizens to the exclusion of non-status (illegal) non-citizens, mimicking hegemonic discourses of social marginalization and exclusion. In what ways has this conceptual blind spot produced a body of literature that may too quickly accept the decentralization of the nation-state in the processes that make and unmake citizenship? How can the study of local and everyday processes that produce migrant illegality broaden understandings of emergent forms of citizenship? The study of illegality in the context of citizenship and the nation-state can open up questions of exclusionary inclusions and inclusionary exclusions, which demonstrates a blurring of boundaries that allows scholars to simultaneously question the legitimacy of national sovereignty as well as the legitimation of exclusionary practices that national sovereignty and the globalized nation-state system provide.

Although few Canadian studies have focused on processes of migrant illegalization, there are notable Canadian, American, and European studies that have laid significant groundwork on citizenship and migrant illegality. Non-status immigrants in Canada face significant risks including detention, deportation, and surveillance.[5] The day-to-day difficulties of people without full legal status include the lack of access to public services, such as legal support, education, health care, social services, and basic personal security.[6] Economic exploitation through underpaid wage labour and mistreatment at the hands of employers is widely experienced by non-status immigrants.[7] De Genova has pointed out that the social space of illegality sets into play an erasure of legal personhood that enforces invisibility and exclusion ("Migrant 'Illegality'" 427). Nyers has demonstrated that the emergence of non-status immigrants as political activists in Canada and elsewhere has provoked important questions about the nature of politics and who is able to become political.

A critical examination of processes of migrant illegalization, grounded in lived experiences of non-citizens, opens up traditional anthropological concerns with citizenship, sovereignty, and the nation-state in new ways. In particular, three key contributions of the study of migrant illegality in the examination of global processes of inclusion and exclusion are identified in this chapter: first, the destabilizing of taken-for-granted discursive and legal categories; second, the examination of racialization and its interconnection with other exclusionary processes such as illegalization; and lastly, the blurred and complicated ways in which processes of inclusion and exclusion may operate through simultaneously inclusionary and exclusionary practices.

For example, in my own research I develop an understanding of migrant illegalization within service provision as sites of governmentalized borders. In doing so, I explore the potential of Toronto's Sanctuary City movement to challenge these borders that emerge when people with precarious status attempt to access or simply avoid social and community services. Toronto's Sanctuary City movement aims to make communities safer spaces for all inhabitants of the city, regardless of immigration status. Specifically, the movement is interested in developing accessible social and community services, including education, health care, food banks, shelters and affordable housing, and ensuring that immigration enforcement is not welcome in community spaces. Thus, the movement opens up possibilities for new modes of governance to emerge, one that is not based upon the differentiation of people into categories of deserving and undeserving, and one in which all members of the city can engage in forms of civic participation. Toronto's Sanctuary City movement has the potential to unmake the gendered and racialized production of migrant illegality and thereby develop new modes of belonging that are not based upon formal citizenship, thus posing a challenge to the sovereign power of the nation-state.

NOTES

1. The intent of this chapter is not to outline in great detail the varied and complex experiences of people with precarious immigration status, although my doctoral research addresses these concerns. Instead, I aim to address the conceptual blindspot within the particular academic context of contemporary citizenship studies with respect to the issue of migrant illegality and to highlight the potential of this issue to broaden the study of citizenship. However, everyday lived experiences of migrant illegality are important, and I recommend the following for further reading: Nicholas De Genova's *Working the Boundaries* (2005), Cecilia Menjívar's *Fragmented Ties* (2000), and Aihwa Ong's *Buddha is Hiding* (2003).
2. No One Is Illegal-Toronto is a group of immigrants, refugees, and allies who work towards justice for all migrants. "No One Is Illegal" is a phrase that is used worldwide by migrant justice organizations, including in Canada, the UK, and New Zealand. There are also No One Is Illegal groups across Canada,

including Vancouver, Montreal, Ottawa, and Toronto. Each group is completely autonomous and there is no overarching leadership or organizational structure. For more information, see http://toronto.nooneisillegal.org/.

3. Permanent residency can also become precarious in situations where a permanent resident is convicted of a crime that has a maximum sentence of ten years or more. In this case, permanent residency can be revoked. People with precarious immigration status are often referred to as non-status immigrants and undocumented or migrant workers by activists and advocates of migrant rights and as illegal migrants or aliens by government bodies and corporate news media in Canada and the United States.

4. By "anthropology of removal," Peutz refers to an anthropological investigation of deportation experiences and practices.

5. For further material on non-status immigrants in Canada, see Wright, "Moments of Emergence"; Lowry and Nyers, "No One Is Illegal"; Walters, "Deportation, Expulsion, and the International Police of Aliens"; and Welch, "The Immigration Crisis."

6. See Balibar, *We, The People of Europe?*; Bacon, "For an Immigration Policy Based on Human Rights"; and Tactaquin, "Illegal Immigrants are Treated Unfairly."

7. For further discussion, see Sharma, "Immigrant and Migrant Workers."

3

ISRAEL'S WALL, DISPLACEMENT, AND PALESTINIAN RESISTANCE IN THE WEST BANK

MAZEN MASRI

We managed to create a non-violent body to struggle and fight against the apartheid wall. This body is called the Ni'ilin Committee Against the Wall. It includes organizations and activists that decided to fight the wall in a peaceful and non-violent way. And when we say peaceful way we mean that we cannot fight the occupation with armed resistance because we know that they are stronger than us. But this non-violent struggle is a message to the world that we are refusing this wall and occupation, we refuse the Israeli plan that wants to kill us. We send a message that this wall is illegal, and we are saying it is an unfair apartheid system, and we are sure that it will not last forever. Sooner or later, there will come an age, if not in our day then for our kids, when we will be celebrating the victory of tearing down this wall.

—AYMAN NAFI, *Mayor of Ni'ilin, qtd. in "Nilin Village"*

THE CONSTRUCTION OF THE WALL by Israel in the West Bank is creating various problems. It has restricted the freedom of movement of Palestinians, affected their health, welfare, employment, and social fabric. It has also led to a wave of displacements, which this chapter will focus on. The issue of displacement has been a concern since the beginning of the construction of the wall. The International Court of Justice, in its 2004 *Advisory Opinion, Legal Consequences of the Construction of a Wall in the Occupied Palestinian Territory*, voiced its concern about the many people it has displaced. The court stated:

> *Since a significant number of Palestinians have already been compelled by the construction of the wall and its associated regime to depart from certain areas, a process that will continue as more of the wall is built, that construction, coupled with the establishment of the Israeli settlements...is tending to alter the demographic composition of the Occupied Palestinian Territory. (International Court of Justice para. 133)*

Although displacement as a result of the wall has always been a concern, monitoring the movement of people from certain areas as a result of coercion is somewhat understudied. The first study to tackle this issue was published in 2006 as a joint project by Badil Resource Center for Palestinian Residency and Refugee Rights and the Internal Displacement Monitoring Group. This project, however, was only a pilot study focusing solely on the Jerusalem area. Other studies have been also published, but most of them are small in scale and scope and focused on specific areas. To date, there has been no comprehensive study to detail trends of movement with reliable up-to-date data. Also, there is no monitoring mechanism in place to monitor and document displacement. In 2007, a group of organizations, including human rights organizations and some UN agencies, formed the Permanent Working Group on Forced Displacement to monitor and collect data about people who have been displaced in the Occupied Palestinian Territory. But this group has made no significant contribution to researching and monitoring the ongoing displacement.

Given the human rights violations that are inherent in the construction of the wall, which come in addition to other human rights violations that Palestinians have been suffering from since the mass population transfer of 1948,[1] the wall and all of its effects were met with resistance by Palestinian society. The continuous state of oppression and deprivation of human rights is in essence a denial of humanity. Resistance is one of the ways through which Palestinians reassert their humanity. Resistance takes different shapes and forms, and, in the case of the Palestinians directly affected by the wall, the very fact that they are adamantly insisting on staying on their lands is seen by many Palestinians as an act of resistance in and of itself.

Because of the scarcity of reliable sources, this chapter focuses less on facts and figures of displacement and more on trends and patterns of displacement as well as resistance to it. The chapter begins, in the next section, by situating the current displacement in the context of the way in which the wall has been rationalized in Israeli political thought, especially the prevailing Zionist notion of the legitimacy of *transfer*. The third section provides specific details about the wall as well as an overview of the political rationale for the wall. The fourth section focuses on the Palestinian experience of displacement and the impact of the wall in everyday life. Palestinian methods of resistance are the focus of the fifth section, and the final section offers concluding remarks.

Historical and Political Context

Since the late nineteenth century, the Zionist project of creating a settler colonial state in Palestine has had a huge impact on the indigenous population.[2] One of the main effects of this colonization process is displacement. This displacement is not a mere by-product of the colonization process. In essence, the transfer of the Palestinians was a condition for the Zionist project to succeed. Zionism, as proclaimed by the First Zionist Congress, which convened in Basel in 1897, is a movement that "aims at the creation of a home for the Jewish people in Palestine to be secured by public law" (Basel Programme qtd. in Vital 368).[3] This creation of a new home could not have happened without two main processes: the mass immigration of a Jewish population to Palestine and the local population's agreement or acquiescence to the creation of the Jewish state. Theodor Herzl, the founder of political Zionism, did not seek the approval of the local population in the late nineteenth and early twentieth centuries. What mattered to him was the approval of the world's powers: their support for the Zionist movement would be needed. Dealing with the indigenous population was not a major issue as they were not seen by the Zionist movement as a people worth considering, a reflection of the influence of the notions of European supremacy on the Zionist movement (Masalha, *Expulsion* 6). Zionist political thought soon began to embrace the concept of transfer of the local Palestinian population as the solution of the problem of the local population, or what soon began to be known in the Zionist discourse as the "Arab Question."[4]

Since the late nineteenth century, *transfer* became a major part of mainstream Zionist political thought. It was thought that Jews were the only group that could be seen as a nation and that they had "a historic and natural right" over the area of Palestine (Masalha, *Expulsion* 17). This right, according to Zionist thought, was recognized internationally with the adoption of the Balfour Declaration in 1917 and the Declaration in the Deed of Mandate over Palestine in 1923. The Balfour Declaration and the Deed of Mandate were issued by European colonial powers. They did not take into consideration the interests of the original inhabitants. Nor were they accepted by the indigenous population (Morris 76). In fact, the indigenous population fought and resisted them by all means, starting from the early 1920s through strikes, petitions, delegations to the British government, and other forms of protest. This resistance continued until the creation of the State of Israel in 1948. But for the Zionist movement, it did not matter that the people who were most affected by these policies were never consulted, never gave their approval, and had even embarked on a large-scale and sometimes violent campaign to reassert their rights and prevent the demise of their nation. The same reasoning and processes that led the Zionist movement then still shape the policies of the state of Israel today: namely, Palestinians have lesser rights than the Jewish immigrants, and, therefore, geographically "transferring" them or implementing apartheid policies against them is seen as legitimate.[5] This set of beliefs was seen very clearly during the major wave of ethnic cleansing during the 1948 war and its aftermath (Pappe; Masalha, *Expulsion*). It was also seen, although at a slower pace, in the years after the creation of Israel, as well as during and after the 1967 war (Masalha, *A Land*).

In addition to transfer, segregation is a recurring and consistent theme in Zionist ideology. As early as the 1920s, Zionist parties and groups had encouraged Jewish-only organizations and urged the Jewish immigrants not to undertake joint Arab-Jewish initiatives. Even in the area of workers' unions, where one would expect workers to come together to have more power against the employers, the Zionist leadership encouraged separation by creating workers' unions that were organized along national/ethnic lines, as opposed to more inclusive unions (Teveth 92–117). It was thought that separation on all levels was needed to create an independent Jewish state. After the creation of the state, the policy continued, but became more acute; it turned into segregation.

The wall that Israel is in the process of building in the Occupied West Bank is yet another intensification of Israel's transfer and segregation policies.[6] It affects the lives of more than 2.6 million Palestinians and actively contributes to further displacement of Palestinians by creating severe conditions that force the affected communities to leave areas they have been living in for generations. The wall is contemplated as part of the segregation system that would stop any mixing between the Palestinian population in the Occupied West Bank and the mostly Jewish Israeli population in Israel. This is not an attempt to stop the flow of Israeli settlers to Israeli settlements in the West Bank, which, according to the International Court of Justice, are *illegal* under international law.[7] It is an attempt to consolidate a strong Jewish majority in Israel within the 1949 borders and to strengthen the separation policy. This, Israeli leaders hope, would prevent a situation whereby Palestinians would start an anti-apartheid struggle demanding full national and political rights under one state, as opposed to the current demands of the official leadership of the Palestinian people to independence in a sovereign Palestinian state.[8] From a contemporary Zionist perspective, a two-state solution that would create a Palestinian state alongside Israel is more desirable. The creation of such a state would be used by Israel as a way to avoid the responsibility for the expulsion of the Palestinian refugees in 1948 and to maintain a Jewish majority in Israel. This would come mainly at the expense of Palestinian refugees and the Palestinians living inside Israel who do not enjoy full civil and political rights.

To prevent the struggle from shifting to a "one-person, one-vote" struggle, Israel has three options. The first is to control the growth rate of the Palestinian population. The second is to physically expel large numbers of them to other areas. Both of these options are not very likely today, which leaves Israel with a third option: giving up Israeli civilian presence in areas that are heavily populated with Palestinians such as Gaza and parts of the West Bank where, according to the two-state solution, a future Palestinian state would be established. Areas in the West Bank, which Israel sees as strategic, but that are not heavily populated with Palestinians, would remain under Israeli control. The possible fate of Palestinians who live in such areas of the West Bank—areas marked by Israel to remain under Israeli control—has not been determined. Because Israel sees Palestinians as a demographic threat, it is conceivable that Israel will not grant them Israeli citizenship. Still, they will be in areas that Israel will treat as part of Israel proper, with very few, if any, rights. Those communities are the most vulnerable communities under Israel's displacement policy because their location is an obstacle to Israeli strategic interests. The displacement of those communities has already started.

The Wall: History, Form, and Details

While the idea of creating a barrier in the West Bank can be traced back to the late 1990s, the idea for the construction of a combination of an eight-metre-high wall, razor wires, sniper towers, trenches, military roads, electronic surveillance devices, and buffer zones began to be implemented in 2002. This system is now about 760 kilometres long, and it cuts through and surrounds Palestinian villages and towns. Vast tracts of the land on which the wall is built are private property that was expropriated by Israel's military authorities. In some places, the buffer zone is up to 100 metres wide, adding more to the misery of the local population. The construction of the wall is a huge project: from the beginning of construction until December 2006, it entailed digging up and moving 38.7 million cubic metres of earth, using one million cubic metres of concrete to create the slabs that form the wall, and paving 2.25 million square kilometres of asphalted military roads. More than fifty-three contractors were hired to carry out the construction of the wall, using plans created by sixty planning and architecture offices ("Israel's Security Fence").

The wall deviates significantly from the 1949 armistice line (also known as the Green Line), which sets the borders between the Occupied Palestinian Territories, occupied in 1967, and areas under Israeli sovereignty, which have been controlled by Israel since 1948.[9] These deviations make the wall twice the length of the Green Line. If the construction is completed according to the projected route, 87 per cent of the wall will be inside the West Bank, isolating approximately 10 per cent of the areas in the West Bank. In a number of areas, such as the area south west of Nablus, the wall deviates about twenty-two kilometres, creating what is called the "Ariel Finger" because it encircles the illegal settlement of Ariel. In the vicinity of the Ariel settlement in the northern West Bank and the areas around Jerusalem, the deviation is very significant and it encompasses dozens of villages and thousands of people.

In a report released in July 2008 by the United Nations Office of the Coordination of Humanitarian Affairs (OCHA) for the Occupied Palestinian Territory, the UN paints a bleak picture of the humanitarian situation. About 285,000 Palestinians will be trapped in the area between the wall and the Green Line, about 250,000 of them in the Jerusalem area. Twenty-eight Palestinian villages, where 128,000 people live, will be surrounded by the wall on three sides. About 26,000 people living in eight communities will be totally surrounded by the wall on four sides. These communities will be connected to the rest of the West Bank through a tunnel or an access road (OCHA, "Humanitarian Impact of the Barrier" 6).

To understand the actual situation on the ground, we also need to understand the regime of gates, checkpoints, tunnels, bridges, and bypass roads associated with the wall. This is a sophisticated system that, together with the wall, aims to control and restrict Palestinian presence and traffic in the West Bank. It creates "Israeli-only roads" for the Israeli settlers in the West Bank that forbid Palestinian commuters. A system of tunnels, bridges, and checkpoints separate Palestinian traffic from that of Israeli settlers. The entire system is designed to isolate Palestinian cities, towns, and villages. Essentially, this system dissects the West Bank into four main areas: the northern West Bank, from Jenin to south of Nablus; the central area, which includes Ramallah and the surrounding villages; the southern West Bank, including Hebron, Bethlehem, and surrounding villages; and the Jordan Valley, which, because of its location and topography, is very easy to isolate. This process has been referred to by Palestinians as the "Bantustanization of the West Bank," associating it with the infamous attempt by South Africa during the apartheid era to create political entities for the native African population that would be presented as independent states, although they were totally dominated by South Africa (Farsakh).

The system of segregation, of which the wall is the most dramatic manifestation, did not develop and evolve as a matter of mere coincidence or as a result of security needs. Security is always cited by Israel and its supporters as the only justification for the wall. This has been the case in almost all of the propaganda of the Israeli government and in the submissions of the Israeli government before the Supreme Court of Israel in petitions filed against the construction of the wall.[10] Yet, a deeper analysis of the situation, a more thorough understanding of how the Israeli political system operates, and a closer look at the statements issued by Israeli officials show otherwise. Even the International Court of Justice in its *Advisory Opinion* on the wall was not convinced that the route of the wall was chosen to attain security objectives (para. 137).

Since 2001, the Israeli political system has been undergoing a shift in strategy. Israeli leadership, mainly under former Israeli Prime Minister Ariel Sharon, came to grips with the fact that the state of prolonged occupation of the West Bank and the Gaza Strip and the apartheid situation there is not tenable in the long run. Demographic pressure and international censure would turn the whole area of historic Palestine into a single state where Israelis and Palestinians would have equal rights, as opposed to the situation since 1967, whereby in the same geographical unit one national/ethnic group has monopoly over power and resources.

The situation of prolonged occupation and the apartheid reality has also increased the tension inside Israel. Israel defines itself as a Jewish and democratic state. This statement by itself is contradictory. Critics say that the way Israel defines the Jewishness of the state is not compatible with democracy (Bishara). On the one hand, a democratic state should allow political participation of all its subjects; on the other hand, in order for a state to be "a Jewish state," it has to have a significant Jewish majority among its citizens. The current situation whereby millions of disenfranchised Palestinians are under Israeli control intensifies the contradiction and the tension in this definition. It brings the situation closer to a critical point where one of the two elements of the definition should be dropped—either an undemocratic Jewish state or a non-Jewish democracy. The analysis and understanding of this situation could be seen clearly in the platform of the Kadima party, which was the ruling party of Israel from 2003 to 2009. Their platform highlights the assertion that the Jewish people have "national and historic rights" over all of *Eretz Yesra'el* (all of historic Palestine, not only Israel) and emphasizes the importance of Jewish sovereignty and Jewish majority; it then adds, "Giving up a part of the *Eretz Yesra'el* is not giving up ideology, but it is exercising the ideology that aims at securing the existence of a Jewish and democratic state in the Land of Israel" ("Political Action Plan"). In essence, the platform recognizes that maintaining effective control over the Palestinian population is a threat to the Jewish majority, and in order to maintain the Jewish majority, it is important to give up parts of *Eretz Yesra'el* that constitute a threat to that majority—that is, areas that are heavily populated by Palestinians.

Faced with this prospect, the Sharon government embarked on a plan to "separate" from the Palestinians. The plan was first called the "Separation Plan" but was then changed to the "Disengagement Plan" because of the negative connotations of the apartheid philosophy that accompany the term "separation." The underlying assumptions for the plan were that Palestinians do not seem to be going anywhere in the near future; also, the prospects of achieving a peace treaty with them are not good. There was a need, therefore, for a way to minimize the Israeli presence in the Occupied Territory and, at the same time, keep the areas that Israel is interested in either because of their strategic value or because of their resources (mainly water). This strategy would separate the Palestinian and the Israeli populations, prevent the creation of a single bi-national state, and allow Israel to maintain control of the areas its settlers withdraw from, as well as to continue to exploit resources, such as water. This strategy was also needed to maintain a Jewish majority in Israel, so that it would continue to be a Jewish state. The plan had two major steps. The first step was to initiate, plan, and start working on the construction of the wall and the associated regime of controlled roads, gates, and checkpoints in the West Bank. The second step was to pull the Israeli settlers and military facilities from the Gaza Strip, which was already surrounded by a fence, and to control it from outside.

The wall, therefore, is part of a bigger segregation plan. Although security was cited as the reason for its construction, in reality, the wall is a strong tool for consolidating Israeli control and seizing Palestinian land. These purposes are reaffirmed in statements by Israeli leaders, who state time and again that the route of the wall will be the border between Israel and the future Palestinian state. This walled state will be a Palestinian state according to Israeli design. This confined state is seen today as a vital Israeli interest because it will help reduce the tensions between the democratic component and the Jewish component in Israeli self-definition.

Impact on the Palestinian Population and Modes of Displacement

No matter where Palestinians live in the West Bank, the wall affects them in one way or another. It affects all aspects of life, including access to land, employment, health care, education, and livelihood. It affects family life, social relations, and other vital needs. This section focuses on the effect of displacement and not all of the other human rights effects, even though they are interrelated: the violation of human rights usually triggers displacement.

How the wall affects Palestinians and causes displacement varies from one area to another, depending on the immensity of human rights violations and the way the wall affects the different areas. In this section, I consider two kinds of displacement caused by the wall: direct displacement and indirect displacement.

Direct Displacement

Situations of direct displacement mainly affect population centres that are completely surrounded by the wall or very close to the wall. The intensity of the effects of the wall varies. In some places, houses and property have been destroyed and expropriated to build the wall. For example, in the case of Nazlet Issa in the northern West Bank, the Israeli military authorities demolished a number of residential and commercial buildings to clear the route for the wall. Displacement also occurs through proposals to relocate entire communities outright to accommodate the new political geography created by the wall. For example, two Bedouin communities, Arab Aramadin and Arab Abu Farada, which are both trapped in a closed zone near Qalqilya, have been explicitly proposed for dislocation (Hass). This mode of displacement seems to affect mostly villages and population centres that are trapped in the areas where the wall deviates from the Green Line. Such displacement means that these villages are west of the wall, on the "Israeli" side. Although the wall's route was designed to include those villages on the "Israeli" side of the wall, essentially annexing them to Israel, Israel is only interested in annexing the land—not the people living on it. Residents of these areas still hold Palestinian Authority (PA) issued identity cards and are seen as PA residents. They will not be entitled to any of the rights that Israeli citizens, or even residents, enjoy.

Closed Zones

The situation in isolated areas, where about 10,000 people live in the north section of the West Bank alone and which Israel usually refers to as "closed areas," is inhumane. Because their homes are now on the "Israeli" side of the wall, residents of the closed areas, aged sixteen and above, are required to obtain "permanent resident" permits, and must renew them every six months to be able to continue to live in their homes. These permits are not always granted. A 2007 study conducted by OCHA and the United Nations Relief and Works Agency for Palestine Refugees in the Near East (UNRWA) counted the number of people in fourteen of the fifteen communities in the closed areas in the northern West Bank who could not obtain permits. The study reported that twenty-six men, eighty-one women, and four children were not able to get "permanent resident" permits (OCHA, "The Barrier Gate" 6). The denial of permits means that these people will not be able to leave their homes under any condition because, if they do, they risk not being able to get back to them. They are essentially confined to their villages. As mentioned, the numbers here only refer to the northern West Bank, and the available data is not comprehensive. It is mostly based on information received from the community officials. A deeper and more methodical survey is likely to show that the number of those who cannot risk leaving their villages is actually higher.

Furthermore, the wall in these closed areas has separated the residents from most essential services. The residents there rely on the bigger urban centres of the West Bank, located east of the wall, for their health care, education, and daily supplies. Because of the wall, the residents can only access that area through gates. These gates are only open during specific hours and do not allow twenty-four-hour access. This means that people who come back late from work, for example, outside the closed area are not allowed to return to their homes. Worse, it also means that no ambulances are able to access those communities when the gates are closed. This is a serious problem given that most of those communities have no local health care facilities. In fact, nowadays it is common practice for expectant mothers to leave the closed areas weeks before the expected day of delivery because there is no guarantee that when their labour begins they will be able to leave the closed zone.

The wall in the closed areas also has a huge effect on social relations. Any person who wishes to enter the closed area is required to get a visitor permit from the Israeli Civil Administration. These permits are required for any person who is attending a wedding, funeral, or any other social event. In some cases, marriages are affected by this system of permits. Even for those who hold valid permits to pass through the gates, treatment at the gates is often violent and humiliating, and entails waiting for long hours.

All of these hardships and restrictions are difficult to cope with. While there is still no study of the psychological effects on the population in that area, which essentially lives in an open-air prison, some surveys addressing the issue of displacement have been conducted. The OCHA-UNRWA study from 2007 reports that 3 per cent of the population surveyed have left their area of residence as a result of the wall. Although it is not the publically stated policy of the Israeli government, there is very little doubt that this is the actual objective. Add all these conditions to the legitimacy of the idea of transfer in the Zionist and Israeli political thought and one is left with almost no doubt about the real goals of the wall and the Israeli policy.

If displacement as a policy objective is a matter of inference and prediction in the case of some closed areas, the Israeli authorities eliminated any reason for doubt in the case of the villages Arab Aramadin and Arab Abu Farada. Both are small villages: Arab Aramadin has a population of 270 and Arab Abu Farada has a population of 120. They were founded in the 1950s by Bedouin refugees who were expelled as part of the ethnic cleansing that took place in 1948.[11] The villages are located in the closed zone near the Palestinian town of Qalqilya, which is itself completely surrounded by the wall. Representatives from the villages have submitted a number of complaints to the Israeli army challenging the route of the wall. In a response letter to the residents' complaints, the representatives of the Israeli army have plainly stated that the army is contemplating the idea of offering the residents of both villages the option to move to another location east of the wall.[12]

While displacement is a constant threat that looms over residents of Arab Aramadin and Arab Abu Farada, forcible displacement was the fate of the residents of Khirbet Qasa, a small village of about 270 people in the Hebron area in the southern West Bank. This village was located in an area that is east of the Green Line, but west of the wall—an area that Israel wants to annex. On October 25, 2007, the whole village was razed to the ground. The residents were not even given enough time to gather their belongings. Although the residents lived in that area since they were expelled from what is now Israel in 1948, the army said that those houses and huts were built without permits and therefore should be demolished. This was the excuse that the Israeli authorities used for destroying a whole village that existed before Israel occupied the area ("Army Demolishes").

Indirect Displacement
The wall and its associated regime cause displacement even in areas that are not totally surrounded by the wall. In many villages along the wall's route, the wall stands between the residential areas of the villages and their agricultural areas. Although in some areas Israel has allowed the passage of farmers to their agricultural land through special gates, the gate system fails to address the problem. The army only allows farmers who hold special permits to access their lands through the gates. The permits are usually given for a period of three months only, and the allocation of those permits is usually done in an arbitrary manner. For example, in 2003, the Israeli authorities distributed 630 permits only in the village of Jayyus, located in the Qalqilya district in the northern West Bank where the wall cuts through 8,600 dunums (one dunum equals 1,000 square metres) of agricultural lands. Among those who got the permits were deceased, emigrants, and minors. More than

100 landowners were denied permits. In 2004, the Israeli authorities changed their policy and made the criteria for permit renewal stricter. Applicants were required to prove that they own land west of the wall by submitting a map of the land in question, a land deed, and proof that the land has not been sold. Because of the nature of the land laws in the area and because of bureaucratic complications, satisfying all of those demands is a very difficult, and oftentimes, impossible task. In addition, current policies limit the number of agriculture workers who do not own land from getting permits (OCHA, "The Humanitarian Impact" 14–16).

The statistics about Jayyus demonstrate how the gate system does not provide reasonable access to agricultural land. The number of permit holders in Jayyus has dropped from 630 in 2003 to 250 in 2007. In 2008, only 168 people were granted a permit (OCHA, "The Humanitarian Impact" 16). This leaves most of the residents of those villages, who rely heavily on agriculture for their livelihood, with limited areas of land to cultivate. As a result, the unemployment rates in the villages have risen considerably, and the residents, mainly the youth, are forced to start looking for alternative forms of employment, usually in urban areas such as Ramallah. Because the wall's associated regime of checkpoints, bridges, and tunnels imposes severe restrictions on the movement of Palestinians, villagers seeking employment in the urban centres are forced to move. In Jayyus, for example, the level of unemployment has reached about 70 per cent, and residents, especially the young and the educated, have begun to leave the village (OCHA, "The Humanitarian Impact" 18–19).

While agricultural areas where the wall passes are drastically affected, the wall has also affected urban areas. A study conducted in 2006 by Badil Resource Center for Palestinian Residency and Refugee Rights and Internal Displacement Monitoring Centre reveals that in the Jerusalem area, 17 per cent of the Palestinians who have changed their previous residence (that is, 32.9 per cent of Jerusalemites) did so as a direct result of the wall. The survey also shows that 63.8 per cent of Palestinians in Jerusalem are considering changing their place of residence within Jerusalem and its suburbs because of the movement restrictions caused by the wall. The major factor that led to displacement at this scale was the way restriction of movement made it impossible to achieve an adequate standard of living. The wall also had negative effects on the social fabric. According to the survey, 21.4 per cent of all Palestinian households in Jerusalem have been split and are separated from their relatives. The wall also figures as an important factor in the choice of spouses (Badil 27–31).

The best way to sum up indirect displacement is to quote paragraph 134 of the *Advisory Opinion* of the International Court of Justice. In describing the effect of the wall on the local population, the court said:

> *The construction of the wall and its associated regime impede the liberty of movement of the inhabitants of the Occupied Palestinian Territory (with the exception of Israeli citizens and those assimilated thereto) as guaranteed under Article 12, paragraph 1, of the International Covenant on Civil and Political Rights. They also impede the exercise by the persons concerned of the right to work, to health, to education and to an adequate standard of living as proclaimed in the International Covenant on Economic, Social and Cultural Rights and in the United Nations Convention on the Rights of the Child.*

Resisting the Wall

Palestinians have resisted the colonization of their land since the early twentieth century. The resistance took different forms and had different targets. During the period of the British Mandate, for example, the Palestinians were aware of the growing numbers of Jewish immigrants from Europe and their plans to create a Jewish state in Palestine. Palestinians found different methods to organize themselves to counter the threatened loss of their homeland.

These methods ranged from petitions and delegations lobbying the British authorities to armed struggle. Most prominent of these acts of resistance was the six-month strike in 1936 protesting the policies of the British Mandate and the revolt, known as the "Arab Revolt," which started in 1936 and lasted until 1939 (Morris 128). The latter swept all parts of Mandatory Palestine, and the British troops were able to suppress the revolt only after using extremely brutal tactics (Morris 150). The creation of the Palestine Liberation Organization (PLO) in 1964, which was recognized as the official representative of the Palestinian people, and its subsequent takeover by Palestinian factions were acts of organizing and resistance carried out mostly by refugees who had been displaced in 1948. Return to the towns and villages from which they were displaced, which is usually one of the demands of displaced people, was one of the main goals of the PLO.

Already accustomed to organizing against Israeli pressures, Palestinians reacted immediately to the construction of the wall in different ways. Although the wall is an act of the state, and an apartheid state to be more precise, against a civilian, local population, the Palestinians did not take the construction of the wall as a *fait accompli*, but resisted its completion with different strategies. Most Palestinians involved in this resistance also know, from different episodes in their struggle, that the power of the state is difficult to challenge and that the deeds of the state are hard to reverse. Even knowing that the balance of power leans overwhelmingly against them, they still do not accept the new reality, at least not without a fight. Of course, because the Israeli army is one of the strongest in the world and Israel is the most powerful state in the region, the resistance is mainly civilian and mostly non-violent.

One form of resistance, which seems to be the most effective, is popular organizing. Another form of resistance is formal legal action. Despite achieving some success on the international level, legal action has largely been a failure. In addition, the construction of the wall, and the UN's failure to intervene to stop it, was one of the main triggers for a campaign of "Boycott, Divestment, and Sanctions" against Israel (see below for more discussion of the BDS).

Popular Organizing

As early as 2002, a campaign called the "Anti-Apartheid Wall Campaign" was launched to mobilize against the wall on three different levels. The first level was the local communities, where people on the ground organized popular committees. As of 2008, more than fifty popular local committees have been formed. The second level is the national level, which coordinates the activities of the different local committees. The third level is the global one, which identifies the campaign against the wall as part of the global struggle against racism and colonialism.

The campaign is highly focused on grassroots organizing. The people who are directly affected by the wall are the best-suited and positioned to lead the struggle against it. Also, the fact that those committees are comprised of people who know their regions very well makes compiling reliable information possible. The high level of participation among women and the youth is remarkable. For example, in Salfit and in Tulkarem, two women's committees were formed to mobilize women against the wall ("Stop The Wall").

Providing activists worldwide with reliable and up-to-date information about the situation on the ground is one of the most important activities of the campaign. With all of the maps, confiscation orders, court decisions, and government resolutions, getting a reliable and clear picture of what is happening on the ground becomes vital. The campaign devotes a lot of resources to research and documentation and to disseminating information to a wide public, both local and worldwide in various languages.

A good example of popular resistance to the wall is the village of Bil'in, west of Ramallah, where the wall has annexed 60 per cent of its land. Since 2005, the Bil'in popular resistance committee against the wall has been organizing peaceful demonstrations on a weekly basis. Palestinians and international solidarity activists, in addition to some Israeli activists, join forces to resist the wall. These demonstrations are often confronted violently by the Israeli army. The army usually uses tear gas and rubber-coated bullets to disperse the non-violent demonstrators, often leaving some demonstrators wounded. On a number of occasions, demonstrators have been killed by the Israeli army. Recently, the Israeli army began to experiment with new kinds of weapons and equipment that emit strong smells or make unendurable noise.

Due to the damage that this kind of resistance causes to the image of Israel internationally, and to the high level of participation of international solidarity activists, Israeli authorities have tried to stop the weekly protest at Bil'in. They try to do this in a number of ways, including blocking the access road and declaring the area a closed military zone to prevent the activists from getting to the village. Those means have not yielded much success and did not break the will of the protesters. Although the ongoing resistance campaign did not stop the construction of the wall, it was successful in delaying construction and raising the awareness about the wall and the human rights violations internationally.

Another village that has also been mounting a similar resistance and protest campaign is Ni'ilin. The organized resistance in this village was able to stop the construction of the wall a number of times by vandalizing the heavy equipment that the contractors use for doing the groundwork. At one stage, the protesters were able to vandalize two kilometres of barbed wire that was laid out there to stop them. This protest, however, did not come without retaliation from the Israeli authorities. In August 2008, two minors aged twelve and seventeen were killed by Israeli soldiers during the demonstrations. In July 2008, the Israeli authorities decided to put an end to the popular resistance of the people on Ni'ilin and started a vengeance campaign against the village. The village was put under curfew, and Israeli soldiers rampaged the village, destroying property and arresting the organizers of the popular resistance. The curfew was ended only after four days, after 400 people from the neighboring villages Budrus, Shuqba, Qibbiya, Deir Qaddis, Bil'in, Saffa, and Beit Ur marched to Ni'ilin and broke the siege and the curfew imposed on the village.

Resistance Through Legal Action

With the beginning of the construction of the wall, and after the first seizure orders were issued by the Israeli army, many Palestinians, desperate to save their lands and livelihood, tried to seek legal recourse through the Israeli legal system. Although the majority did not really have any great expectations from the Israeli courts, for some it looked like one of the few ways to stop the wall. Most Palestinians who sought legal remedies were not surprised when the remedies were denied, except in a small number of cases. Even in the cases that were not a total failure, the success was usually a small change in the route of the wall, which made the wall slightly less destructive. The overwhelming majority of Palestinian petitions to the Supreme Court of Israel were rejected. This was in line with the approach historically taken by the Court, which legalized Israeli settlements and other illegal activities in the Occupied Palestinian Territory (Sultany). Under the Supreme Court's oversight, a whole system of apartheid was created.

On the international level, though, the results were much better. As a result of discussions in the UN General Assembly, the question of the legality of the wall was referred to the International Court of Justice (ICJ). Although the ruling of the court would be an advisory opinion, given that Israel does not accept ICJ jurisdiction, the court's opinion still had an important effect. Even if it is not enforceable, an advisory opinion from the ICJ (the highest authority on international law) asserting that the wall is illegal would give much moral support and standing to the people resisting it. In July 2004, the ICJ ruled that the wall is illegal under international law and that it is a breach of international humanitarian law, the laws of occupation, and international human rights law. It also stated that by constructing the wall, Israel is impeding "the exercise by the Palestinian people of its right to self-determination" (para.122).

Although the legal action through the ICJ was successful in that it declared the wall illegal, it was not enforceable against Israel. Still, there was some room for further legal action under the ICJ *Advisory Opinion*, since the Court has ruled that some of the rules violated by Israel include certain obligations characterized as *erga omnes*, that is, obligations imposed on all states not to recognize the illegal situation resulting from the wall, and obligations not to provide aid and assistance in maintaining the situation created by the wall (para. 156–60).[13] Unfortunately, the Palestinian leadership has not used these openings and has not pursued any further legal action.

After making attempts with the Israeli legal system, the people of Bil'in decided to try other legal systems. The wall on Bil'in lands is meant to protect a settlement called Mod'in 'Illit. Two of the construction companies building the residential units in this settlement are registered in Canada, which gives Canadian courts jurisdiction over their action. In July 2008, Bil'in, represented by its mayor, filed a lawsuit in Canada against the two Canadian companies, seeking an injunction ordering them to cease the construction and return the land to its condition prior to the settlement construction. The claim, however, was dismissed on procedural basis without discussing it on its merits. The court declined jurisdiction, citing *forum non conveniens* doctrine—a doctrine that allows courts to deny jurisdiction even if the formal requirements are satisfied because of little or no connection between the forum (the court) and the action pursued and the existence of a different forum that has stronger connections (*Bil'in [Village Council] v. Green Park International Inc.*).

The Boycott, Divestment, and Sanctions Campaign

During the Second Intifada, which started in September 2000 (also known as Al-Aqsa Intifada), especially after the failure of the Camp David negotiations in July of that year, frustration among the Palestinians reached new heights. In addition to years of suffering, either from living as refugees or under military occupation, the Palestinians had to endure Israel's brutal policies in dealing with the Intifada, which reached an unprecedented level of violence, mostly against civilian populations. The West Bank and Gaza Strip became war zones that Israel attacked periodically using an arsenal of weapons that left destruction everywhere. Under these horrible conditions, Palestinians began formulating a new approach that focused on garnering international support and directing the solidarity efforts towards putting pressure on Israel using non-violent means. This idea started to gain momentum, and calls for a boycott campaign began to surface in 2002 and 2003. In 2004, there was an attempt to coordinate these efforts with a more structured approach to a boycott campaign. This led to the creation of the Palestinian Campaign for the Academic and Cultural Boycott of Israel (PACBI), which issued a call for boycott in 2004. This call was mostly by academics and intellectuals and directed mainly towards academics and intellectuals worldwide. It is also mainly focused on boycotting Israeli academic and cultural institutions (PACBI Call).

The construction of the wall, and the failure of international law and the international community to stop the construction of the wall despite the ICJ *Advisory Opinion* gave the boycott movement more momentum. One year after the ICJ *Advisory Opinion* was issued, 171 Palestinian civil society organizations issued a comprehensive call, calling "upon international civil society organizations and people of conscience all over the world to impose broad boycotts and implement divestment initiatives against Israel similar to those applied to South Africa in the apartheid era" ("Palestinian Call for Boycott"). The civil society organizations also appealed to pressure their "respective states to impose embargoes and sanctions against Israel" ("Palestinian Call for Boycott"). The impact of the wall on the Palestinians and the use of the boycotts, divestment, and sanctions (BDS) is clearly evident in the call. The "Palestinian Call for Boycott, Divestment, and Sanctions Against Israel" begins with the sentence, "One year after the historic Advisory Opinion of the International Court of Justice (ICJ) which found Israel's Wall built on occupied Palestinian territory to be illegal; Israel continues its construction of the colonial Wall with total disregard to the Court's decision." It then goes on to describe Israel's activities in the West Bank, stating that Israel "has unilaterally annexed occupied East Jerusalem and the Golan Heights and is now de facto annexing large parts of the West Bank by means of the Wall." Dismantling the wall was also one of the demands of the call for boycott, together with ending the occupation and colonization of all Arab lands, recognizing the fundamental right of Palestinians in Israel to equality, and recognizing the right of return of the Palestinian refugees.

The inclusion of the dismantling of the wall in the call for the boycott shows that resisting the wall became one of the uniting elements of Palestinian people everywhere. The 2005 call for boycott was endorsed by Palestinian civil society organizations, including organizations based in the West Bank and the Gaza Strip, Israel, and Palestinian refugee organizations and committees worldwide. Response to this call was swift. Many groups worldwide, including workers unions and students unions, responded to the boycott call. A lot of responses came in the form of supportive resolutions that were adopted by unions and organizations; other responses came in the form of action. In February 2009, for example, dock workers belonging to the South African Transport and Allied Workers Union decided not to offload a ship carrying Israeli goods as part of their BDS activities ("Press Release: Victory for Worker Solidarity").

Since 2005, the number of Palestinians and Palestinian organizations who support BDS as a means of struggle to achieve their rights has been rising steadily. The campaign has been gaining momentum, and it has begun to crystallize into a mass movement that operates on two levels: 1) a local level that utilizes popular education about the boycott as a means of resistance and urges Palestinians not to buy Israeli goods; and 2) an international level, whereby Palestinian civil society provides guidance to solidarity organizations who wish to conduct solidarity activities in the form of BDS. In November 2007, during the first BDS conference, which was held in Ramallah, the civil society organizations who called for the BDS campaign formed a committee called "The Boycott, Divestment, and Sanctions Campaign National Committee" to better coordinate the BDS campaign.

If the South African boycott campaign, which contributed to the fall of the apartheid system, is adopted as a benchmark to judge the success of the Palestinian campaign, the Palestinian campaign seems to be very successful. In less than four years it has achieved what took the African National Congress (ANC) years to achieve in terms of awareness raising and participation. Of course, this success could be attributed to a number of factors, most important of which is the progress in communications technology that has led to the faster dissemination of the Palestinian call for boycott. Although the success of the Palestinian BDS movement is inspiring, it lacks the support of the PLO. As of 2011, the PLO has been unwilling to adopt the BDS campaign as an official policy, as opposed to the situation in South Africa where the ANC—the major political organization in the struggle against apartheid—adopted boycotts as part of its platform. This failure of the PLO makes work around the demand for sanctions harder because campaigns for sanctions are targeted at governments who have the power to impose sanctions, as opposed to boycotts and divestment, which could be implemented by individuals, corporations, and other groups. Notwithstanding the hardships, the BDS campaign is one of the main contemporary Palestinian grassroots movements that resisting the wall helped crystallize.

▶ The construction of the wall epitomizes the crimes that Israel has committed against the Palestinian people. It represents the ugly face of occupation, colonialism, and apartheid. These are regimes that, as John Dugard (the former United Nations Special Rapporteur on the Situation of Human Rights in the Palestinian Territories Occupied Since 1967) has put it, were identified by the international community as inimical to human rights. All of the practices and the violations that are part of the wall and the occupation are violations that should be addressed by international law, and yet, international law and the international community have failed to stop or reverse these violations. This failure has been repeated in Palestine since 1948, and it seems that its effect goes beyond the effects of other human rights violations. As Dugard has said:

> *In 1994, apartheid came to an end and Palestine became the only developing country in the world under the subjugation of a Western-affiliated regime. Herein lies its significance to the future of human rights. There are other regimes, particularly in the developing world, that suppress human rights, but there is no other case of a Western-affiliated regime that denies self-determination and human rights to a developing people and that has done so for so long. This explains why the OPT [Occupied Palestinian Territories] has become a test for the West, a test by which its commitment to human rights is to be judged. (para. 63)*

He further adds:

> *If the West, which has hitherto led the promotion of human rights throughout the world, cannot demonstrate a real commitment to the human rights of the Palestinian people, the international human rights movement, which can claim to be the greatest achievement of the international community of the past sixty years, will be endangered and placed in jeopardy. (para. 63)*

The Palestinians, suffering under the brunt of occupation and apartheid, have tried all of the means available for them to resist. They are still resisting. From international campaigns such as "Stop the Wall" to Bi'lin and Ni'ilin villagers who organize against the wall, Palestinian people and their allies are determined to stop the bulldozers that are destroying their homes and lands. The BDS movement, organized under the banner of the 2005 BDS call, which is led by organizations representing workers, students, women, artists, and refugees, shows the level of determination and commitment of the Palestinians not to resign themselves to the miserable fate resulting from Israeli practices. It is a decision to take their fate into their hands and to reassert their humanity by demanding that Israel and the world respect their human rights. While the level of success of the resistance efforts are hard to measure at this time, one should bear in mind that the fight here is against a state with the fourth strongest army in the world, and that the resistance is one episode of a century-long struggle.

NOTES

1. The mass population transfer of 1948 is also known as *Nakbah* or *Nakbe* in Arabic, which means "catastrophe."
2. This chapter adopts an approach that views the Israeli-Palestinian conflict as a conflict between a settler society (Jewish Israelis, migrating from Europe and elsewhere) and an indigenous population (Palestinians), which is mainly comprised of Arabs (Christian, Muslim, Druze, and Jewish) but also includes other ethnicities. See Rodinson, Zureik, Said, Shafir, Bishara.
3. It should be noted that there are different streams within the Zionist movement, such as labour Zionism, revisionist Zionism, religious Zionism, and others. The definition in the accompanying text above refers to political Zionism, which we can consider mainstream Zionism.
4. The term "the Arab Question" emerged in the 1920s. It was used to describe the issue of how the Zionist movement should deal with the indigenous Palestinian population in Palestine (Teveth). In a way, it is a reflection of how Europe saw the presence of Jews in its territory as the "Jewish Question."

5. For a more detailed analysis of the applicability of the crime of apartheid to Israeli policies, see Tilley, "Occupation, Colonialism, Apartheid?" See also MacAllister.
6. The West Bank is the area inside the 1949 armistice line, which outlines the western, northern, and southern borders, and the River Jordan and the Dead Sea, which form the eastern border. It was occupied by Israel during the 1967 war, together with the Egyptian controlled Gaza Strip and the Egyptian Sinai Peninsula and the Syrian Golan Heights.
7. The Israeli settlements in the West Bank were found to be illegal under international law by a number of bodies, including the International Court of Justice.
8. In an interview with an Israeli newspaper, Israeli Prime Minsiter, Ehud Olemert said, "If the day comes when the two-state solution collapses, and we face a South African-style struggle for equal voting rights [for the Palestinians in the territories], then, as soon as that happens, the State of Israel is finished" (qtd. in Ben).
9. Although Israel does not recognize the Green Line as the border line, there is international consensus that this line marks the borders between the Occupied Territories and Israel.
10. See for example the wall's website http://www.securityfence.mod.gov.il/Pages/ENG/default.htm.
11. For information about the ethnic cleansing of 1948, see Pappe.
12. Parts of this letter were quoted in the petition submitted to the Supreme Court of Israel in HCJ 10714/06 *Mara'ba v. The Government of Israel*. The petition was dismissed.
13. For accuracy's sake, I am following the wording of the court ruling here. My interpretation of the ruling is that other states need not submit themselves to Israel's demands that they overlook the illegal situation and not provide assistance.

4

THEATRICALITY AND THE EXPOSURE OF EXCLUSION

Théâtre du Public and Theater for Everybody's Les Murs Tombent, Les Mots Restent (Walls Fall, Words Live On)

CATHERINE GRAHAM

AS AN ART FORM that demands that we quite literally make space in a public arena for a variety of bodies and voices, theatre has a particular contribution to make to public discussions of the problems of displacement and mobility in the contemporary world. By bringing human bodies and discourses together to define the concrete material circumstances in which a public voice can be developed, international collaborations like the Théâtre du Public and Theater for Everybody's production of *Les Murs Tombent, Les Mots Restent (Walls Fall, Words Live On)* help us to consider what circumstances must exist in order for us to be able to hear the concerns of others. Created for the 2006 Festival du Théâtre Action, an itinerant festival that toured activist productions throughout the French-speaking part of Belgium over a two month period, *Les Murs Tombent, Les Mots Restent* demonstrates how the use of a body-centred public medium like theatre can lead to new ways of thinking about the problems of creating public spaces where the stories of displaced and marginalized groups can be heard.

To tell the story of how *Les Murs Tombent, Les Mots Restent* created a public space for discussion of the current situation in Palestine, I cannot start with the first moment of the performance; instead, I must look back to the struggles of three groups of theatre artists to come together across international borders. The particular living and working situation of the Palestinian artists associated with Theater for Everybody defined much of the working process, as did the choice by the Théâtre du Public to work with them in creating a play about Palestine for European audiences (Dumoulin).[1] Each group—in this case two actors in Gaza, two in the West Bank and an actor and director in Belgium—created a story that they thought would help European audiences engage in public dialogue about the problems caused by the walls the Israeli government has constructed to isolate Palestinians within the West Bank and Gaza. The plan was for the Belgians to travel to Palestine to meet with their Palestinian counterparts, then for each group to develop their own work in preparation for a one-month creation period in Belgium, during which the stories would be combined and adapted for European performance. It was a simple enough plan, but the political realities of the Middle East repeatedly intervened to complicate its execution. As we shall see, the artists' determination to engage with each other despite all the obstacles these realities posed for them ultimately determined both the thematic and formal structures of the play.

From beginning to end, the creation of *Les Murs Tombent, Les Mots Restent* was marked by the difficulties of moving into, out of, and between the two parts of the divided Palestinian territories, the West Bank, and Gaza. When Philippe Dumoulin and Soufian El Boubsi, both Belgian-born artists associated with the Théâtre du Public, first travelled to the West Bank to meet their Palestinian counterparts in 2005, they were held for ten hours at the Tel Aviv airport, apparently because of El Boubsi's surname. During subsequent visits to the Wall in the West Bank they were stopped numerous times by Israeli patrols, clearly because of El Boubsi's appearance. In Belgium this form of racial profiling is known as "le délit de la sale gueule," which literally means "the crime of Having an Ugly Mug," but in this case might best be rendered in English as "Travelling while Arab." (All translations from the French are my own.) El Boubsi had never set foot in Palestine before, but within days had developed a very personal sense of what it meant to appear to be a young Arab man in relationships[2] with Israeli authorities (Dumoulin).

Work within the Palestinian territories was further complicated by the difficulties of moving between the West Bank, where two of the Palestinian actors lived and worked, and Gaza, the home of the other two and headquarters of Theater for Everybody. It was, in fact, impossible for the Palestinian actors to work together within Palestine and even Dumoulin and El Boubsi were unable to get into Gaza. Fortunately, one member of Theater for Everybody from Gaza was ultimately able to meet the others in Ramallah, in the West Bank, but much of the work of putting the performance together could only be done in Belgium during the final period of creation. Even this period, however, was cut short when one of the young Palestinian actors was held for a full week in a Cairo airport transit zone reserved for young residents of Gaza exiting the country through Egypt. What had been planned as a month long creation and rehearsal period was now reduced to three weeks! While many of the stories in the play were developed from stories the creators had heard from others, the experience of these difficulties very much marked the group's approach to telling the story of the Wall to European audiences. In Dumoulin's words, "One good visit to Palestine is much more instructive than all the video reporting in the world."

Dumoulin's assertion points to one of the things we rapidly discover in trying to make theatre in any circumstances: the ways in which displaced and marginalized groups are excluded from public space configures that space in ways that affect us all. It is this feature of theatrical creation, in which bodies must share the space of performance to tell their story, that not only allowed but required the creators of *Les Murs Tombent, Les Mots Restent* to engage in something more than a discussion of principles or an evocation of political and geographic landscapes. According to a pamphlet describing the play, its goal was not only to relay information about the problems caused by the "security" wall Israel has erected around the Palestinian territories, but to question the cultural values that lead us to build walls and close ourselves off from others, not just on the level of nations but in our personal relationships. The core story of the play is that of a couple who are trying to get their child to medical help in the middle of the night, but whose car breaks down in the no man's land between Palestine and Israel, leading to an argument about the previous choices each has made that have led them to this situation. A parallel story of a European journalist who is reporting on the situation in the territories and of the translator who tries to get him to see what is really going on asks us not only to think about the difficulties of living in a situation where one is blocked at every turn, but to question "our European view of this distant conflict" (Théâtre du Public, Publicity Pamphlet).

This shift of attention from political values and socioeconomic facts to culturally determined human interactions is an important part of the communication strategy that both the Théâtre du Public and Theater for Everybody regularly employ, but it is not determined only by the needs of theatrical practice. Their emphasis on how cultural values underlie the ways in which people succeed (or don't) in living in the same space point to the same kind of argument about "the primacy of practice" that Kwame Anthony Appiah puts forward in his recent book *Cosmopolitanism*. "When it comes to change," Appiah says, "what moves people is often not an argument from a principle, not a long discussion of values, but just a gradually acquired new way of seeing things" (73). Appiah goes on to point to art as an example of how this might take place.

> *Conversations across boundaries of identity—whether national, religious, or something else—begin with the sort of imaginative engagement you get when you read a novel or watch a movie or attend to a work of art that speaks from some place other than your own. So I'm using the word "conversation" not only for literal talk but also as a metaphor for engagement with the experience and ideas of others. And I stress the role of the imagination here because the encounters, properly conducted, are valuable in themselves. Conversation doesn't have to lead to consensus about anything, especially not values; it's enough that it helps people get used to one another. (85)*

It was to create the opportunities for this kind of engagement that the creators of *Les Murs Tombent, Les Mots Restent* decided not simply to show the situation of the Palestinians, but to include the story of the European journalist in the staging of this particular conversation.

The decision was based on an acute awareness of the position of the European audience who would watch the story unfold on stage. To simply recreate stories of individual Palestinians who confront the problems of living in overcrowded and under-resourced areas that are under constant military surveillance would have left the European audience in a similar position to the one they find themselves in as they watch television news: they would assume the role of "outside observers" without ever really considering their own relationship to a distant conflict and the people trapped in it. According to Dumoulin, the creators of *Les Murs Tombent, Les Mots Restent* hoped that the role of the European journalist would create an imaginative opening within the theatre space for the point of view of European audiences. By experiencing the ways in which the journalist sees the conflict differently as he spends more time with Palestinian civilians, they hoped European audiences might experience a parallel evolution in their own ways of understanding both stories about Palestine and the people who tell them (Dumoulin). This choice effectively invited European audiences to join the conversation these theatre artists had chosen to engage in when they started to work together.

To invite audiences to join in a conversation was a radical step in that it proposed a direct alternative to the professionalized and managed public discourse that dominates much of Western political news coverage. The problem with this professionalized public discourse is that it makes it increasingly difficult to get the concerns of ordinary citizens onto the public agenda at all. Arguably, the growing popularity of films and television shows that humourously counter government and corporate "spin" point to an increasing pubic awareness of, and irritation with, this restriction of real public debate. These critiques, however, often seem based on a positivist approach to knowledge, presupposing that some ultimate truth is waiting to be discovered once the particular "spin" of powerful institutions is erased from the picture. As a result, while these critiques undermine the credibility of the "spin" they address, they often do little to help us understand how a preoccupation with "facts" may itself inhibit the public life of a democracy.

As Dorothy Smith pointed out twenty years ago in her book, *Conceptual Practices of Power*, facts themselves are constructed in a way that is designed to exclude unwanted knowledge from particular arenas of debate. In Smith's words, a demand for a particular kind of fact in the training of professionals is often little more than a demand for a blind adherence to a "virtual reality vested in texts" that ensures its efficacy by "cutting social science off from the actual relations and organization of people's lives" (45). The core activity that makes this particular "virtual reality" possible, Smith argues, is the objectification of knowledge as *fact*. "Facts," she says, "are neither the statements themselves, nor the actualities those statements refer to. They are an organization of practices of inscribing an actuality into a text, of reading, hearing, or talking about what is there, what actually happened, and so forth" (71). The proof of professionalism in such a system, and consequently the authorization to speak publicly, is not only the adherence to authorized procedures and concepts but also the separation of the professional from the environment on which s/he is exercising her profession. "As professionals," Smith says, "we know how to practice and preserve the rupture between the actual, local, historically situated experience of subjects and a systematically developed consciousness of society. If we are to claim full and proper membership in our discipline, we must be competent performers of this severance" (52).

The net result of this fact-making machinery is both the deliberate erasure of the source of knowledge, the subject who *knows*, and the exclusion from professional discourse of all those who cannot be counted on to know in a way that is guaranteed to produce the appropriate facts. When public debate is dominated by such professional discourses in the form of "expert opinion," this exclusion can be generalized to the population as a whole, since an inability to produce the kind of "fact packages" our expert political discourse expects effectively excludes us from public conversation.

Faced with such exclusions, artistic practices like those that led to *Les Murs Tombent, Les Mots Restent* suggest that we need to start asking not only about the "facts" of particular situations but about what is lost when we reject all knowledge that does not come in the "fact packages" our political culture has led us to expect. One of those things, I would suggest, is the broad sense of public agency that is crucial to democratic governance. If we view those who do not present their experiences and concerns to us in the "fact packages" that we expect as being simply inadequate interlocutors, we narrow the range of public discourse that is available in our communities. Members of displaced or marginalized groups can then be seen not as our fellow citizens, but, at best, as "problems" we feel called upon to help find solutions for. When we reduce our interaction with members of these groups to encouraging a greater personal effort to "succeed" or to making available the services of professional agencies to help people "adapt," we miss out on the possibility of creating and maintaining the kind of public spaces necessary for a truly vibrant democracy.

But what would it take to change this? Numerous feminist political thinkers have suggested over the years that the problem of developing vibrant public debate cannot be solved only on the level of policy, but must also be tackled as a cultural problem. As Nancy Fraser puts it: "in stratified societies, unequally empowered social groups tend to develop unequally valued cultural styles. The result is the development of powerful informal pressures that marginalize the contributions of members of subordinated groups both in everyday life contexts and in official public spheres" (79). Fraser suggests that the solution to this problem is not that we agree to pretend that differences of status and cultural style do not exist, but that we overtly thematize cultural differences and thus encourage the development of "alternative publics," since in her view, the "proliferation of subaltern counterpublics means a widening of discursive contestation, a good thing in stratified societies" (15). If we accept Fraser's suggestion that the overt thematization of the cultural styles that are habitually excluded from public arenas is critical to undoing the exclusion of marginalized groups from public discourse, it starts to become clear why artists can play such an important role in revitalizing public debate.

When engaged in a project like the creation of *Les Murs Tombent, Les Mots Restent*, I would suggest that the work of the artist is to create public interventions that call attention not just to the social effects of particular practices and policies, but more importantly to the cultural styles that allow us to consider some of these effects as questions of public concern and others as unworthy of public attention. This strong sense of the term "artist" can clearly be applied to artists working in all media, but I would further suggest that, because of the nature of most practices of exclusion in Western democracies, the theatre artist can play a particularly important role in focusing attention on the informal, and largely unconscious, social pressures that create these exclusions.

I make this claim for theatre because these informal pressures are largely carried in the body, in the form of what French sociologist Pierre Bourdieu calls "habitus." Habitus, says Bourdieu, function in ways similar to conscious strategies, in the sense that they are organized and deployed in such a way as to induce others to carry out desired actions, but they cannot really be considered strategies because the bodies that carry them out never consciously choose them as one possible strategy among others (175). This apparent lack of strategy in the enactment of moves that are intended to obtain particular results can be attributed, in Bourdieu's view, to the embodiment and consequent "naturalization" for a particular culture or social group of socially-defined narratives. While different habitus feel "natural" to those educated in the culture that created them, they are not inherent biological structures, but histories (or stories) that have been incorporated into individual bodies as ways of enacting social worlds. Effectively, habitus reiterate existing social structures by replaying historical relations of power on an everyday level. As long as these histories remain unconscious, they can continue to be acted out as social processes of exclusion with no one being held accountable for either their existence or their effects.

Theatrical creation, however, as an art form whose main medium of thought and communication is the interaction of human bodies, can open a road to making these unconscious processes of exclusion conscious and so demonstrating that they can be changed. In creating theatre, it is difficult to create believable characters or situations without paying attention to the embodied histories that play out as social relationships between particular bodies in particular environments. So, the artistic skills involved in creating theatre can offer important opportunities to draw public attention to precisely those elements of culture that allow some concerns and perceptions to be seen as appropriate topics for public debate while others are viewed as simply below the threshold of public significance.

When Rami Albanna, Georgina Asfour, Kamel Basha, Philippe Dumoulin, and Naim Hamdan took to the stage for the performance of *Les Murs Tombent, Les Mots Restent*,[3] it was clear that their artistic choices worked to emphasize how human interactions can create the public spaces necessary for a truly participatory democracy. The performance took place on a bare stage, with very minimal props and only a few chairs and a coat rack as set pieces. Scene-change music and a few sound effects were played over the theatre's loudspeaker system, but much of the music used in the play consisted of vocal performances by the actors themselves. While all these choices were undoubtedly dictated, at least in part, by the demands of touring to small communities and the restrictions of a short rehearsal period—itself a result of the travel restrictions facing Palestinian participants—the effect was an important one. It was clear to anyone in the audience that the world we were seeing was created by the actions of the human beings who chose to pay attention to certain things and not others. Nothing in the performance appeared to be inevitable or beyond human control because everything we could see or hear was clearly created by the artists themselves. This was itself an important use of theatricality to draw attention to the fact that the transmission of information, the telling of our stories and the act of listening to the stories of others, always involves a choice about what is worthy of attention and what is not.

To illustrate how this worked, I would like to look in some detail here at the theatricality of the third scene of *Les Murs Tombent, Les Mots Restent*, which presents a particularly interesting example of how theatre allows us to produce the kind of overt thematization of cultural styles that Fraser suggests is so critical to an attempt to widen access to the public spheres of healthy democracies. In this scene a European journalist (played by Phillippe Dumoulin) passes through an Israeli checkpoint to enter the Palestinian territories, where he meets the translator (played by Georgina Asfour) who will assist him in his work. Audience members must, however, figure out the context of the scene as it is performed, since no identifying information is given to them. The scene opens with four performers entering the empty stage and forming a line at the back of the performance area, facing the audience. The initial part of the scene is played without words, as one of the actors distractedly sings to himself in a wordless tune with strongly marked rhythms (Théâtre, *Les Murs*). In this segment, the only information the audience has about the situation is conveyed to them by the action and interaction of performers' bodies, thus focusing attention not on the discursive justifications for Israeli security practices or Palestinian and European reactions to them, but on the ways in which we make cultural sense of these practices by relating them to other experiences we have had of getting past someone who tries to block our progress by making unreasonable demands. As the scene progresses it becomes clear that the European journalist is trying very hard to fit in to this new world, but that his cultural style of reacting to the situation is quite different than that of the Palestinian men he finds himself with.

In the opening moments of this scene the audience cannot help but grasp who is the outsider. While the three Palestinian men wear only loose pale-coloured shirts and pants, the European journalist also wears a leather vest and carries bulky camera equipment over each shoulder. We see in his interaction with the Palestinians, brief and wordless, just what Appiah describes as the first task of intercultural communication: people getting used to one another (85). The Palestinians are clearly familiar with the situation they find themselves in; they face the audience looking out casually for some unseen observer who appears to be slightly above and behind us. The journalist does not know where to look, glancing first at the audience, then at the Palestinians on either side of him, trying to see what they are focusing on. As they start checking their pockets, the journalist starts to repeatedly tap the camera equipment he carries on both sides of his body, ignoring the rhythm of the background song and looking back and forth at the men on either side of him, who look from him to each other, apparently bemused by this stranger's odd actions (Théâtre, *Les Murs*).

The net effect of this sequence is both to establish the European journalist as the one whose cultural style does not match the others and at the same time to get the audience to view this character as central to the action of the scene. The fact that only this performer makes eye contact with us certainly invites the audience to view the scene from his viewpoint, but the structure of the scene is also a powerful driver in that direction. At this point, the audience is essentially in the same position as the fictional journalist: we are in the presence of people who seem to understand what is happening and we are called upon to use our powers of observation to figure out what is likely to come next so we can react appropriately. In focusing on the journalist, we imaginatively enter into the position of the ones who are not "in the know," who will not be able to join in the conversation of this public space because we do not know how to match the cultural styles of those who are used to functioning in this situation.

The core of the scene then depicts what the men must do to get official approval to pass through the Israeli checkpoint, and focuses on the efforts each of them makes to resist the objectification inherent in the inspection process. The exclusion they risk here is important not only on the level of the narrative, in which the need to pass Israeli checkpoints is central to the plot, but also in terms of any ability to build solidarity between the characters and between performers and audience. In the first case, the need to assert an identity as a social agent and not just an object of someone else's gaze is a crucial point. In the latter case, however, the different cultural styles that can be brought into play to achieve this and, ultimately, the social conditions that have fostered these styles are important foci for audience attention.

As if on some signal, of which we in the audience are not aware, the men look up, focus their attention on the imagined observer, and start to sing more loudly. Since this wordless tune, sung in unison, doesn't focus attention on individual performances, the music effectively produces a kind of soundscape for the scene more than expressing any personal or collective agency through song. The European again looks at the others as he has done in the opening segment of the scene, then, matching his action to theirs, walks to the front of the stage to the rhythm of the music. On reaching the front of the stage, the Palestinians start emptying their pockets, looking straight ahead as if at an outside observer, removing watches and the contents of their pockets and tossing them on the stage floor two feet ahead of them (Théâtre, *Les Murs*). The audience is in an awkward position here, and it will only become more difficult as the scene continues. We feel a sense of attachment to the men on stage since they are our only source of information about what is going on, but are physically on the side of the observer who clearly treats these men not as potential interlocutors, but as objects to be examined. Suddenly, our conventional role as a theatre audience, silently analyzing and judging the actions of the fictional characters onstage without fear of being called to account for our own reactions, starts to become elided with the role of the checkpoint officials, who will inspect the men without ever entering into conversation with them. Throughout this part of the scene, the European journalist, whom we have been encouraged to view as the central character, does not look at us, but watches his companions for clues about what he must do. By observing his companions and bringing his movement in line with theirs he learns, as do we, what is expected of those who want to pass through the checkpoint. His actions, however, mark him as only incidentally included in this group. He is initially more clumsy than the Palestinians he tries to communicate with, an image created theatrically by the amount of baggage he carries; it is more awkward and takes longer for the journalist to pull the straps of camera bags over his shoulders, remove his vest and deposit them on the floor. In fact, he barely manages to complete the process in time to join the others as they turn to march back upstage, where they take their places and turn to face the observer once more (Théâtre, *Les Murs*).

Almost immediately, another order seems to come from the unseen observer and the men, looking above and behind the audience, again march forward, this time unbuttoning their shirts, which they remove and toss on the ground at the front of the stage. Though all move downstage and sing in unison, each has a particular reaction to this demand to remove clothing. One of the Palestinians (Naim Hamdan) removes his shirt as simply as possible and throws it to the floor in front of him, calling little attention to his action. The youngest of the group (Rami Albanna) untucks his shirt, pulls it over his head, then pulls out his undershirt to cover the top of his trousers while wiping his eye with one hand. The third (Kamel Basha) humourously confronts the official, removing his shirt and twirling it around provocatively before dropping it on the floor and, for a brief moment, standing with arms akimbo looking up at the official defiantly. By now our European friend seems to feel used to the practices of the checkpoint and, while he is again slower to remove his shirt than the Palestinians are, he moves with an assurance that indicates a new-found confidence in his ability to move appropriately within this world. When he turns with the others to march back up stage, he produces a kind of semi-danced swagger, swinging his arms with elbows held high and moving his head to the rhythm of the music. We too, as an audience, relax a little, as we now understand that we are watching some kind of inspection procedure and the repetitive rhythm of the move to the front and return to the back of the stage offers a certain reassurance about how to watch this action (Théâtre, *Les Murs*).

Our relief is short-lived however, because a new order clearly unsettles the group. One of the Palestinians and the European journalist gesture to the top of their trousers, looking questioningly at the silent observer, as if asking if they will really be required to remove them. This pause in the rhythmic action of moving to the fore-stage and returning upstage gives many in the audience time to feel awkward about witnessing what now promises to be a ritual of humiliation, a feeling that is reinforced when the Palestinian who appears to be the youngest of the group, puts one hand over his face and begins to wail. Despite the awkwardness, all four men do what is demanded of them: they again walk to the front of the stage and begin to remove their shoes and trousers. The performance now focuses, however, on acts of resistance to the humiliation of objectification, as the characters assert what little agency they can under the circumstances. The Palestinians on either side of the European journalist stomp downstage, remove their shoes and throw them to the floor in a loud expression of anger, during which the young man continues to hide his face and wail. The third Palestinian stares straight at the position of the unseen observer and does a kind of striptease gesture of coyly removing his trousers to reveal long underwear, then twirling the trousers provocatively, just as he had done with his shirt, before throwing them to the ground (Théâtre, *Les Murs*). The gesture calls attention to the voyeuristic stance of those who observe the actions of the objectified inspectees, including both the checkpoint officials and, potentially, some of the audience members who witness the inspection. The journalist appears to take his cue from this action, gesturing to the others as if taking up a dare as they move forward, then looking at them smiling as he removes his trousers as if this were all just good fun. His cultural style, however, is subtly different from the others,' focusing attention not on the position of the observers but on his own insistence on mastering the situation. As all four return upstage, he amplifies this gesture by pulling up the bottom of his undershirt to reveal his undershorts in a gesture reminiscent of "mooning" the officials (Théâtre, *Les Murs*).

Whatever relief we may feel from observing this cheeky assertion of personal agency is seriously undercut in the same moment by the gestures of the young Palestinian next to him, who continues to wail as he covers his face with one hand and pulls down his undershirt with the other hand in an attempt to cover his genitals. On the night I saw the performance, audience anxiety was only increased, and much nervous laughter resulted, when the journalist winked at the audience then started pulling on the waistband of his undershorts, staring at the unseen observer then glancing at the audience as if to ask, "will I take these off too?" (Théâtre, *Les Murs*). In the audience, we do not know what will actually happen next, and, especially given the taboo on male frontal nudity in Western performance culture, the prospect of observing what amounts to a strip search is not a comfortable one. This is further amplified by the knowledge of the importance of personal modesty and the prohibition on exposing the body in many Muslim cultures, which is making this situation positively traumatic for at least one of the Palestinian men. While the performer playing the European journalist may elicit laughter through what is essentially a cheeky threat, we cannot but be aware of how painful it might be for the young Palestinian beside him to be forced to follow him in carrying out the threatened action. Again the performers march to the front of the stage, with the audience now waiting apprehensively for what might come next. This time they remove their undershirts, show them to the observer, drop them to ground, then turn and abruptly stop singing. Only now do we see the word CHECKED stamped diagonally on their flesh, in a manner reminiscent of an inspection stamp on a side of beef (Théâtre, *Les Murs*). The night I saw this performance, the audience laughed loudly at being presented with this commentary on the nature of checkpoint appraisals, a laughter that was perhaps amplified by our relief at not being presented with the highly taboo image of male nudity in a live theatrical setting.

Before I move on to discuss the rest of this scene, it is worth taking a moment to consider how the theatricality of the presentation directs audience attention in ways that not only produce tension and provide relief, but that start to make us conscious of our own positioning in relation to this action. The tension in the initial part of the scene comes largely from the audience's inability to identify the appropriate habitus within the scene. While we as audience members are not called upon to deploy a habitus in a way that will induce the characters on stage to carry out a specific action, in order to visually follow the action of the scene we need to figure out what kind of a scene we are watching. Because we do not at first know what kind of narrative this is, we quite literally do not know where to look or what to look for. As it becomes clear that the scene is showing us an inspection procedure, we relax a little in our role as audience members, simply because the rhythmic pattern of this action guides us as to how to watch it. Directing the attention of this primarily European audience to the European journalist as a central point in the scene also makes us more comfortable given that, being based on the kind of historical patterns of action with which most of us are familiar, his ways of reacting to the action inevitably seem more "natural" to us. While all four characters on stage struggle to assert some degree of agency in the face of the objectifying nature of the inspection process, we feel free to enjoy the European journalist's light-hearted reaction of responding to the demand to take off his clothing as if this were some kind of a children's game, like "truth or dare." We are almost grateful to him for lightening the atmosphere since we can comfortably recognize his schoolboy strategy of responding to a dare by asserting that he will not be humiliated by a challenge, but will go even further than the person throwing out the challenge demands. We hardly notice that there might be a reason why the other three men only assert themselves when they are facing the inspector, but never do so when their backs are turned to him.

Theirs is not a habitus that we are familiar with, and so we don't take much note of it because it does not seem particularly important. The next part of the scene, however, jerks us out of our new confidence and perhaps makes us start to notice what we had been taking for granted and what we are not paying attention to at all.

Even before our appreciative laughter and applause dies down at the performed joke of having the word CHECKED actually stamped across the actors' backs, the scene becomes frantic and takes on a dangerous edge as all four men whirl to face us. The journalist now looks to the imagined observer the men have been facing, and to others who apparently surround him from above, and starts to shout, "Don't shoot! Don't shoot!" While the Palestinians scramble to pick up their belongings and exit the stage, we hear a representation of gunfire in the form of a drum roll on what sounds like a small snare drum. Again, the journalist is marked as different by his different reaction to the situation: while the others simply pick up their things and rush out of the area, the journalist tries to communicate directly with the imagined Israeli soldiers while pulling on his shirt (Théâtre, *Les Murs*). We immediately understand one of the major reasons for the differences in the reactions of the Palestinians and the European journalist in the earlier scene: the Palestinians know the soldiers might shoot, while the European journalist apparently does not. It is only here that we begin to understand that the differences we observed in the characters' actions in the previous scene were not simply the result of different individual temperaments. What we witnessed were the expressions of distinct habitus, social histories built up through long experience within particular relationships of power and almost automatically deployed by individual bodies who instinctively play their part in the enactment of a historically defined world. At this moment we start to recognize that the journalist, who seemed to give us a privileged understanding of what was going on in this scene, was not the best source of information about the realities of the inspection procedure. He was simply more comfortable for us to watch because we could relate more easily to his cultural style and engage more readily with the habitus he acted out.

What is perhaps most striking about the journalist's reaction to the unexpected gunfire however, aside from his obvious panic, is his assertion of his professional status. Immediately after crying out "Don't shoot!" in both French and English, he identifies himself as a journalist, a reporter, again in both French and English. "Don't shoot!" he shouts again, raising one arm in the air as he tries to pull on his trousers with the other, "I've got a press card." The character who barely a minute ago was taking up a dare like an errant schoolboy is now, unlike the Palestinians who accompanied him, trying to dress himself before leaving the inspection area, and invoking his professional status as a reason why he should not be considered to really be part of the situation in which he finds himself (Théâtre, *Les Murs*). He tries to ensure his personal safety by invoking his ability to practice the crucial professional rupture Smith describes between "the actual, local, historically situated experience of subjects and a systematically developed consciousness of society" (52). While the tone of his voice is pure panic as he starts to pull on his trousers and cries, "Press Card! OK? OK? OK?," his almost instantaneous reaction is to attempt to establish himself as a potential interlocutor; he instinctively appeals to his professional status as a reason he should not be treated as an object, but should be allowed into a dialogue with the authority figures who watch him from outside the situation. "I am here," he seems to say, "but I am not really of this situation," and his habitus would certainly point to that being true (Théâtre, *Les Murs*).

It is interesting that the profession the theatre artists have chosen for this European who joins the Palestinians at the checkpoint and in the territories, all the while asserting his difference from them, is that of a journalist. He could have been a nurse, a humanitarian aid worker, a teacher, or even a theatre artist, but he is not; instead, he is associated with a profession that is known primarily for its ethic of objectivity, its concern with "facts." In trying to save himself when the guns come out, he does not assert his national or civil status, but his reliability as a professional with a press card, a man who is certified as one who can be counted on to produce the kind of "fact packages" that will make him an appropriate interlocutor. At the same time, because the medium in which he is introduced to us is theatrical, our attention is focused on the difference between the professional cultural style of cool objectivity he tries to lay claim to and the panicked body. In the audience, our expectations of professionalism are shaken as our attention is focused on the frantic body that turns in circles, half dressed and desperate in its attempts to redefine itself as more than an inarticulate object that may or may not be allowed to move from one space to another. In the theatre, as in life, there can be no social status and no social world that is not defined by the interactions of individual bodies. As a consequence, the live performance of the "fact finder" who struggles to produce an appropriate professional rupture between his own body and emotions and the social standing he wants to claim, calls on us to pay attention to this connection between this vulnerable and emotional body and the world his actions help create.

In the end, the Israeli guards never respond to the journalist's calls, which peter out as he recognizes he will not be answered. Instead, a woman (Georgina Asfour), dressed in a long loose skirt and jacket, appears on stage right. There is a pause as the journalist takes in her presence. "Can I help you?" she asks. The journalist is at first taken aback and then recovers enough to recognize that she is likely the translator who is supposed to meet him. The two stand facing each other, almost on opposite sides of the stage, as this is verified; then the journalist, remembering the appropriate gesture for the situation, moves towards her, one hand extended and the other holding the pant leg he has not yet succeeded in getting into. Not surprisingly, the female translator declines the handshake of this half-naked man, averting her gaze and indicating that he should move away and dress himself, which he rushes to do, hurriedly getting his second leg into his trousers (Théâtre, *Les Murs*). The moment is pure carnivalesque inversion. Whereas the journalist's behaviour during the inspection asserted mastery by challenging the threat of humiliation, he is now clearly in the vulnerable position, diminished socially by his lack of clothing and his inappropriate reaction to both the gunfire and the female translator.

This theatrical image is not, however, simply a cheap joke at his expense. The questions the translator proceeds to ask him make clear that there are real political stakes in getting the journalist to pay attention to all the information available to him and to recognize that he does not stand outside the politics of the situation he has come to observe. The remainder of this sequence repeats the pattern of movement we saw in the beginning of the scene, but in a much more informal mode. The journalist now moves to the front of the stage to retrieve the rest of his clothing as the translator asks why he is in such a state of undress. After explaining that the soldiers at the checkpoint did not want to let him through, he assures the translator, in response to her question, that he has a press card. He scrambles to deliver it to her, limping upstage with one shoe on and one shoe off and assures her that it was issued by the "Israeli Government Press Office," then returns downstage, doing up his belt as he goes. There is another pause as the translator examines the press card. She does not take this document as certification of his standing as a relatively anonymous social actor who will reliably do an impersonal task predefined by his professional status. Instead she asks, "In exchange for what?" The journalist, facing the audience with his back to the translator as he does up his belt and collects his belongings, looks back at her in silence, then claims not to understand what she is asking him. In face of her silence, he finally admits, while putting on his vest, that they made him sign a paper. He is again prompted by the translator and, after a brief pause, says that the paper confirmed that he would not hold the Israeli government responsible for injuries incurred in the exercise of his profession. The translator's only response is: "And? That's all?" The journalist, now putting on his other shoe and a watch, reluctantly admits that he must also submit any article discussing security or defense to military censors. "And that's why they let you pass," she declares, still observing him from behind. There is a brief silence and then the journalist abruptly turns and walks towards her to snatch the press pass from her extended hand, before returning downstage to pick up his camera equipment (Théâtre, *Les Murs*).

Much of the rest of the scene takes place as a series of verbal confrontations between the journalist's and translator's versions of the situation. The translator refers to the eight-metre-high imagined object they stand side by side and stare at as a "wall," whereas the journalist calls it a "barrier" because that is what he has heard it called in Israel. Faced with the contemptuous tone in which the translator tells him of the differences between the Israeli and Palestinian views of the Wall, the journalist reminds her that he has chosen to come to the territories because he wanted to hear another point of view. Through the action that follows, the journalist and translator move horizontally across the stage area, sometimes looking each other straight in the face, sometimes turning their backs on each other. At first, the journalist moves downstage to capture better pictures of the Wall, as he continues to speak to the translator, who is now behind at centre stage. While the journalist is ostensibly the observer here, the translator is observing him and audience members are asked to pay attention to both modes of observation. Watching the journalist's fascination with the Wall, the translator asks if he has never seen this wall before and he tells her that he has not, since he is based in Tel Aviv, where his colleagues who come to report on the conflict always stay, but which is far from the Palestinian territories. The translator notes that Tel Aviv's beaches and nightclubs are very attractive to foreign journalists and provide a much different way of life than that in the Palestinian territories they report on.

As she tells him more about that life, the journalist moves upstage in a large horizontal arc to return to her side as he takes in the critique. Suddenly a good subject for his reporting occurs to her: the ways in which deteriorating access to resources in the territories is leading to malnutrition in children. She goes so far as to happily touch his arm as she suggests this. The journalist takes a step back, and refers directly to the constraints of his particular form of public discourse: "Yes, yes," he says, "it's a good subject, but you know I need images. Without images…" She is disappointed, and turns her back on him to move horizontally across the stage, but he keeps the conversation going by quickly suggesting that he has heard of soldiers shooting into a crowd at another checkpoint. The translator turns to face him from the other side of the stage and explains that things got out of hand when water trucks could not get through to the village. He responds that they must have provoked the soldiers somehow, that soldiers do not shoot for the pleasure of doing so. She holds her position and responds very quietly that this must, of course, be the case, because the soldiers are only doing their job, protecting public order. She then walks directly towards him and asks: "Stopping children from going to school, patients from going to the hospital, farmers from going to the fields; how is that protecting public order? Who is provoking whom?" The journalist is now apparently sympathetic, his tone conciliatory: "I understand. It's normal that someone in your position would say that." The translator's response, as the journalist turns his back to walk away from her while he finishes speaking, is telling: "And in your position, is this normal?" The scene ends as she relents and tells him to come with her because they have a long day ahead of them. As he turns to follow the translator across the stage, gunfire and shouting are again heard. The journalist immediately moves behind his slightly shorter female companion, who stares in the direction of the imaginary observers and, as the scene ends, says only: "Your friends, I think. You must have provoked them" (Théâtre, *Les Murs*).

This last sequence is perhaps the most crucial in the scene, as its staging draws our attention to the concrete changes in individual behaviour that must take place if new voices are to be admitted into public discourse. While the verbal discourse of the scene is structured as a series of confrontations between different points of view, the physical movement of the scene marks it as different from what has gone before. Whereas movement in the first scene was forcibly controlled by an observer who stood outside the space we can see, the relationship of the translator and the journalist develops with each in full view of the other and of the audience. Further, as the scene progresses, the forced, mechanical movement that characterized the inspection process gives way to mutually constructed movement patterns, with each character changing position in response to the actions of the other. As a result, we in the audience learn to switch our focus from one point of view to the other as the action progresses. This learning is reinforced visually through a particular theatrical use of the stage space. While the initial part of the scene worked completely on the vertical plane of the stage and the inspection process forced a uniform style of the movement on the men on stage, movement in the sequences between the translator and the journalist gradually and repeatedly returns both parties to a conversation on the same horizontal plane. While they argue about facts and values, their movement demonstrates that they can inhabit the same space and thus enter into dialogue even if they have opposing views of the situation they discuss.

The way in which this movement develops is an important part of the message of the play itself. In the first moments where the journalist and translator meet, the translator holds her ground while the journalist responds to her questions and demands, but the stage picture is very different from that in the inspection sequence. The translator's physical stance on stage is one of firmly holding a position, which forces the journalist to move awkwardly between her and his gear, a stance that is not one of the professional observer. Unlike the soldiers in the first sequence, she does not insist on seeing without being seen and so does not erase the subject position from which she questions the journalist's assertions. What is more, she expects the same stance from the journalist and so does not acquiesce to his implied desire to look only at certain aspects of the situation and so to consider his relationship to the Israeli government as being a private matter, outside the purview of public discourse.

Given that the piece was created for a European audience, this insistence on having the translator hold to a fixed position on the stage while she enters into a discursive relationship with the journalist is an important theatrical choice. As the sequence reaches its climax, we learn that the assumptions behind the questions she poses from a fixed point on the stage are correct. The fact that she maintains her position helps to destabilize the dominant culture's tendency to see the excluded not as political subjects who have positions they may be justified in holding, but as problems whose position in social interaction should be eliminated by integrating them into an already existing pattern of action. Her style of questioning the journalist and the awkwardness he feels in responding to her is important not only for the thematic information about Israeli government policy that it brings out, but also for the way in which it demonstrates how a real discursive relationship between dominant and non-dominant cultural groups can develop. As audience members who must decide where to look in order to follow the action, we learn in observing this scene that we must pay more attention to the voice that is likely to be less familiar to us if we want to know what is likely to happen next.

The theatricality of the scene would seem to assert that real dialogue can take place only once the non-dominant cultural voice is accepted on its own terms and the dominant cultural voice is subject to the same kind of scrutiny that often faces an unfamiliar interlocutor. The comic treatment of the journalist calls attention to the difference between what he says he believes (that soldiers would not shoot unprovoked, for instance) and the way in which his body reacts to the situation (by hiding behind the translator when gunfire is heard). We are no longer asked to scrutinize the translator's social position while ignoring that of the journalist and so learn to question the kind of professional stance that refuses to be accountable for its own social positioning. As we learn to focus our attention differently in response to the action, the combination of verbal discourse and shifting physical stances show us that while each character is acting out a habitus learned within a particular set of power relations, these stances can change as people learn to move in relation to the positions and perceptions of others. While the verbal interaction between this journalist and translator is largely in the mode of confrontation, their physical actions show us the beginnings of a new and mutually understandable world in which they can function as equally valued interlocutors, thus demonstrating that, while habitus is a powerful driver of social interaction, it is not a destiny. By the end of the scene, the words of sociologist Arthur Frank might seem to apply to both the characters and the audience members who learn to successfully follow the action on stage. "People construct and use their bodies," says Frank, "though they do not use them in conditions of their own choosing, and their constructions are overlaid with ideologies. But these ideologies are not fixed; as they are reproduced in body techniques and practices, so they are modified" (47).

It is worth noting here too that the force of these scenes comes in part from the way they were created. Theatre artists who came from very different cultural and political positions in the world had to learn to work together in order to create the fictional world on the stage. Their task was not only to walk in the shoes of another but also to approach the other as other, finding ways of making their bodies work together to create a plausible fictional world. In the very process of creating a fictional world in which both their truths could be told, they were able to discover how the habitual actions of those who create a world must change to open space for new kinds of relationships. By calling attention to the ways in which their own patterns of action had to be adjusted to create a space of mutual respect and understanding, they call on us as audience members to change the ways in which we observe the world and to learn how to pay attention to all those who are involved in creating it. The promise that the theatre holds out to us is perhaps that, like these actors, we too can learn to build new worlds by learning to interact differently and not simply insist on pulling the Other into our familiar patterns of action.

Clearly, the importance of such a change of attention patterns cannot be restricted to our cultural life. As political philosopher Seyla Benhabib reminds us:

> To think from the standpoint of everyone else entails sharing a public culture such that everyone else can articulate indeed what they think and what their perspectives are. The cultivation of one's moral imagination flourishes in such a culture in which the self-centered perspective of the individual is constantly challenged by the multiplicity and diversity of perspectives that constitute public life.
> (Benhabib, Situating the Self 141)

The kind of theatricality we are discussing here may do more than help us "get used to each other" in Appiah's terms. It may also allow us to create public spaces in which we learn to be conscious of the danger that our patterns of information gathering and our habits of focus may exclude precisely the information we need to understand the kind of world we are engaged in building. If it succeeds in doing that, theatre might then become a space not only for individual and community self-expression but for the revitalization of the diminishing public spheres of contemporary Western democracies.

NOTES

1. The working method for creating the performance was one the two companies had successfully used two years before to create *L'Or Bleu* (*Blue Gold*), a play about water written collaboratively by the two companies as part of a larger collaboration with Indian and Rwandan theatre artists.
2. Instead of "relationship," which gives a more abstract sense of association, the plural "relationships" is used here to point to multiple events.
3. I saw this performance in the pre-festival showcase in Wépion, Belgium in September 2006.

5

MAPPING MANIPUR

PAVITHRA NARAYANAN

Forgive me.
I am obsessed with history
and always scratching for clues.
    —JOY KOGAWA, Woman in the Woods

Facing North-East

IN 2004, with a camera in hand, I visited Bangalore to capture the mood that enveloped the numerous baristas, pubs, and designer stores. When I set the camera at the end of M.G. Road, what the camera recorded was lives that did not intersect—youth with disposable incomes, street children who begged them to buy their wares, and a group of young boys and girls carrying banners. In stark contrast to the billboards on M.G. Road that defined Bangalore as the "City of Opportunities," "City of Gardens, "City of Lakes," and India as the place where you had the "freedom to have everything" because it was virtually connected, the banners read: "We want peace," "Indian Army go back," "Stop draconian rule," "We condemn the killing of Manorama," (see Figure 5.1), and "We

FIGURE 5.1: Manipuri students in Bangalore demand the withdrawal of the Armed Forces (Special Powers) Act, August 2004.

FIGURE 5.2: Manipuri students in Bangalore protest the killing of Manorama Devi, August 2004.

can no longer tolerate sexual abuses by security personnel" (see Figure 5.2). These images, alongside those of street children selling Indian flags and pins in anticipation of the Independence Day celebrations the following month, encapsulated the inequalities in India. Individual people with individual dreams within a geographical area certainly do not make a collective. As the camera panned these unequal lives, one of the boys from the march walked up to me and asked if I would make a film about the protest. He told me that they were students from Manipur protesting the killing of Manorama Devi. The Indian media was also there covering the march. Maybe, in his request, the student hoped that someone would see them as more than just news coverage. It was at this moment that my lens literally turned towards the North-East of India.

The North-East, for the government, the media, and the public, for the most part, has signified insurgency, unrest, and violence. Altogether omitted from public discussions of the region are the problems that have produced civil unrest or the violence caused by the Indian Army. However, in July 2004, the organized women-led movement of the Meira Paibis, in an unprecedented and tragic form of protest, made sure that the entire country would turn its attention towards the North-East. Enraged by the brutal rape and murder of Manorama Devi by army personnel, twelve of the forty women who had gathered stripped naked in front of the gates of the army headquarters in Imphal, the capital city of Manipur, and held up a sign that read "Indian Army Rape Us." The protest shocked the nation and catalyzed Manipuris across the country to protest Manorama's killing. The single demand of the protestors was the removal of the Armed Forces (Special Powers) Act (AFSPA) from Manipur.[1] The AFSPA grants the army unrestricted power and impunity to carry out military operations in order to maintain "law and order" and has been in effect in Manipur since 1972. The greater the demand to remove the armed forces, the greater the number of forces deployed, and for months after the Manorama protest, Manipur literally burned.

This study places the violence that engulfed the state after the courageous protest of the Meira Paibis within a historical framework of postcolonial struggles and sites of resistance that are often omitted from national histories. Starting with the role of the North-Eastern states of India in governance, democratic participation, and nation building, this chapter explores the political formation of the North-East, focusing on the State of Manipur. The merger of the frontier regions with the nation-state was not a smooth process and fueled multiple forms of resistance. The study examines India's experience in dealing with conflict, especially the implementation of the AFSPA, whose origins date back to the colonial era. The chapter then examines the collective action by the Meira Paibis, who, in the absence of protective governments and policies, have emerged as one of the most formidable women's organizations in history. Through their activism, these women have ensured that the atrocities against ordinary citizens like Manorama Devi will not go unnoticed. Their lives remind us that there are other narratives that run parallel to popular historical narratives and that it is imperative that the national history of India be interwoven with these alternative histories. The study concludes by looking at one of the major consequences of conflict zones—that of displacement. While most of the scholarship on conflict-induced displacements has largely focused on ethnic relocations, migrations of men and women within the state, and people housed in refugee camps, this chapter draws attention to the mass exodus of Manipuri youth who have left their home state in search of an education, jobs, and a future that does not hold the threat of violence. The position of this diasporic population, whose migration does not fit squarely within displacement studies as there is no data to record if their movements are forced or voluntary, reflects "the subtle interplay of contradicting nationalisms" (Phanjoubam, "Population Displacement" 39) inherent in

India. They are left homeless, not in the way Rey Chow describes diasporans who are in-transit between cultures as homeless (197); they are homeless because their home state and the nation-state remain a contested space. For these diasporans to have the option of relocating to their place of origin, the Indian government has to actively rethink its approach to the North-East and address the concerns of North-Eastern scholars, activists, administrators, and citizens. If the Indian government does not rethink its approach and address the problems in the North-East, we face the prospect of the historical narratives of postcolonial India frozen in time, or worse still, dispersed into memories of conflict and betrayal.

The Political Formation of the North-East in Postcolonial India

The North-East extends from Sikkim eastward to the Darjeeling Hills of West Bengal and is comprised of eight administrative units—Arunachal Pradesh, Assam, Manipur, Meghalaya, Mizoram, Nagaland, Tripura, and Sikkim. This region shares international borders with Bangladesh, Bhutan, China, Myanmar, and Tibet, and connects with India by only a thirty-seven-kilometre common border via the Siliguri Corridor known as "the chicken-neck"[2] (Baruah 17). The population, which consists of hill tribes, plains tribes, and non-tribal groups, accounts for 3 per cent of India's population, and occupies 8 per cent of the land (B.P. Singh 257). This region has 420 languages and dialects and a religious mixture of animism, Buddhism, Hinduism, Christianity, and Islam. Linguistically and culturally, the North-East has more similarities with South-East Asia and Tibet than with the other states of India. However, it is incorrect to think of the North-East as a homogenous unit because the multiethnic, multilingual, tribal, and non-tribal people of this region do not share similar politics or ideologies. Even their present regional identities are a recent phenomenon; it was only in 1972, after a complete reorganization of this region (Chaube, Munsi, and Guha 44), that it came to be known as the North East (Baruah 19).

The states of the North-East, "mostly independent before British annexation" (Roy), were added to political India during the British Raj. At the time of Indian independence, the regional composition of the North-East consisted of the Assam plains of the old Assam Province, the hill districts, the North-Eastern Frontier Tracts (NEFT) of the North-Eastern borderland and the two princely states of Manipur and Tripura that opted for merger with India in 1949 (Inoue 19–20). With geographical borders rather than linguistic and ethnic differences defining the new nation-state of India, the merger of Assam and the hill states with independent India was not a smooth process. The homogenous grouping of the North-East into a single unit occurred in 1956, when the states were reorganized in India and "only fourteen states were created based on language characteristics. In the North-East, only Assam State was approved" (Inoue 21). Long silent tribal and non-tribal linguistic groups of the hill districts, dissatisfied with the outcome of the reorganization, demanded not only autonomy from Assam but also freedom from India. To them, the reorganization was "a negation of their ethnic identities" and a move "to institutionalize the hill people's subordination to the Assamese" (Inoue 21). However, India was not ready to remap the arbitrary borders drawn by the British and "the demands of minority groups for a Nagaland State to be created out of Assam and for separation of the Mizo areas from Assam were not met" (Inoue 21). The Indian government "feared that by conceding to such demands from any group it could lead to a chain reaction resulting in India's Balkanization. They were determined to prevent such a conclusion to their protracted and painful nationalist struggle" (Ali 31). The first Prime Minister of India, Jawaharlal Nehru, categorically told A.Z. Phizo, President of the Naga National Council, that Nagaland could have autonomy but not independence: "We can give you complete autonomy but never independence. You can never hope to be independent. No state, big or small, in India will be allowed to remain independent. We will use all our influence and power to suppress such tendencies" (qtd. in G. Singh 40). Nehru's words reflect what Partha Chatterjee calls the "narrative of anticolonial nationalism," where alternative paths were suppressed and marks of resistance erased (156).

When dealing with dissent, especially in the North-East, nationalism acquired an aggressively imperial flavour, and the protagonists of the freedom struggle responded to the rebellion of the ethnic groups exactly as Britain had to the Indian nationalists—with military force. Viewing the issue as a law and order problem, India deployed armed forces. In January 1956, the entire Naga Hills district was declared a "disturbed region" and an iron-fisted military regime took over (Ali 32). The resistance to military oppression took the shape of the Naga Nation Army (NNA). Equipped with weapons left behind by the British and Japanese and those taken from ambushed soldiers of the Assam Rifles, the NNA combatted the Indian Army, and in the next two years 1,400 Nagas and 162 soldiers were killed (Ali 33). In 1958, the Armed Forces (Special Powers) Act was passed (Baruah 12), which not only empowered law enforcement personnel to shoot and kill any person for the maintenance of law and order, but also granted them immunity for their actions (Government of India 1958).[3] The act only intensified the resistance. When peace talks failed, Delhi was urged to grant Nagaland statehood in 1963 (Ali 34).

In Mizoram, a similar quest for independence led to violence. Localized political control seemed to be the answer and statehood or autonomy was granted to different ethnic groups "to meet local and language demands" (Dasgupta 363). In 1969, a part of Assam was organized as Meghalaya and granted autonomy (Dasgupta 363). The Mizo hills area, known as the Lushai Hills District, was renamed the Mizo Hills District of Assam in 1954, and when it became a Union Territory in 1972, the area was named Mizoram. With the North-Eastern Areas (Reorganization) Act of 1971, Meghalaya, Tripura, and Manipur were granted statehood in 1972, and Arunachal Pradesh was made a Union territory.

Only Arunachal Pradesh made a peaceful shift to statehood in 1982, as it was the initiative of the central government (Inoue 26). Mizoram attained statehood in 1987. In 2003, Sikkim was added to this region. It was granted statehood in 1973 (Baruah 17), after the state assembly dissolved the treaty that India signed with Sikkim allowing it to retain a special status as a protectorate of India. "Responsible Indian officials," observes Sanjib Baruah, recognize that this North-Eastern "transformation of non-state spaces into state controlled spaces" (9) was "primarily in support of an agenda driven by national security and not, as in other parts of India, in response to popular sentiments seeking recognition for historical regions or their fiscal viability" (19).

With the exception of Assam, the other North-Eastern states had neither participated in nor been influenced by the Indian national movement. Yet, there was an assumption that a shared history of anti-imperialism would suffice to infuse a sense of pan-Indian consciousness. In the process of nation building, the nationalists had mapped the North-East into what Benedict Anderson calls their "imagined community." In Anderson's definition, a nation is "an imagined political community—and imagined as both inherently limited and sovereign. It is *imagined* because the members of even the smallest nation will never know most of their fellow-members, meet them, or even hear of them, yet in the minds of each lives the image of their communion" (6). It was inconceivable in the minds of the Indian nationalists, a sentiment echoed by many "mainland"[4] Indians today, that the imagined space of the North-East could be remapped, that it could conflict with their own imagined community, or that these non-national communities might be entitled to the right to self-determination. This refusal to redefine the nation outside of colonial constructs, Chatterjee says, is the tragedy of postcolonial India.

> *The autonomous forms of imagination of the community were, and continue to be, overwhelmed and swamped by the history of the*

> *postcolonial state.* Here lies the root of postcolonial misery; not in our inability to think out new forms of the modern community but in our surrender to the old forms of the modern state. *If the nation is an imagined community and if nations must also take the forms of states, then our theoretical language must allow us to talk about community and state at the same time. I do not think our present theoretical language allows us to do this. (11, emphasis added)*

There is no denying that the multicultural, multiethnic, and multilingual makeup of the different regions made the process of nation building a complex and formidable task in postcolonial India. But while the leaders of the nationalist movement had a clear-cut vision of an India rid of colonial power, the direction that this new nation should take was less clear. Though the nation that was imagined was not colonial, it had inherited the institutionalized structures of the colony. M.V. Pylee, the constitutional historian, writes, "India inherited the British system of government and administration in its original form. The framers of the new Constitution *could not think* of an altogether new system" (qtd. in Chatterjee 15). What this also meant was that India adopted the repressive state model that uses force to deal with dissent.

National integration in the North-East, Mahmud Ali explains, "became synonymous with state control" (8). If the fate of these frontier regions depended earlier on the British, it now lay in the hands of the new nation-state. Indian nationalists sought to maintain the British concept of "fixed boundaries" (Ali 8). In the attempt to secure "the empire's frontiers along defined, and defensible borders, treaties were signed, broken, negotiated and renegotiated, and punitive military action was alternated with subsidies and material incentives" (Ali 8). Once again, the North-Eastern regions were engaged in warfare—this time, with the new empire. Resistance soon came to be interpreted as insurgency, and since the 1950s there have been military and paramilitary forces in this region engaging in what the government calls counterinsurgency operations. If the policy of resorting to military force was to restore law and order and bring peace, then it is clearly a policy that is ineffective. For the past six decades, what the people of the North-Eastern states have witnessed is a violent display of masculine military privilege. What they have been left with is a war zone of armed men, some sanctioned by the government and some not. The pervasive military presence has only led to an alarming increase in the number of armed underground groups.[5] According to the South Asia Terrorism Portal (SATP), Manipur has thirty-nine underground groups; Assam has thirty-nine as well; Meghalaya has four; Tripura has thirty; Mizoram has two; Nagaland has three; and Arunachal Pradesh has one. Baruah notes that the groups are classified as active or inactive as if to suggest "that insurgencies in the region do not end: they only become temporarily inactive" (20). It is important to note that the different underground groups are far from unified and have distinctly divergent agendas. In fact, there is little support, if any, for some of the groups from the civilian population. With the prolonged conflict between the state and the underground groups being the major news item about this region, North-East Indian history has become a picture of constant insurgence and violence.

A Colonial Hangover: The Armed Forces (Special Powers) Act (AFSPA)

Along with the institutions of law and order, bureaucracy, civil services, and the army, India also inherited the colonial judicial system. Much legislation, including the current one dealing with insurgency in postcolonial India, can be traced to the British introduction of preventive detention in 1793. In his analysis of the origins of "anti-terrorist" legislations, Manas Mohapatra[6] notes that although this law "was understood as harsh...the framers (of the Indian Constitution) believed that preventive detention was the only way to save 'the infant nation from being engulfed by communal riots and social unrest'" (326). One of the first pieces of legislation that independent India enacted was the AFSPA, which is "based on the British colonial ordinance, called the Armed Forces (Special Powers) Ordinance promulgated in 1942 to assist in suppressing the 'Quit India Movement'" ("License to Kill" 5).[7] The Indian Parliament passed the Armed Forces Special Powers Ordinance in September 1958 to counter the resistance by the Nagas, who orchestrated a rebellion known as the "mother of all insurgencies"[8] (Baruah 9). The act, which authorized the governor of Assam and the chief commissioner of Manipur to declare the entire or any part of Assam and Manipur to be "disturbed areas," empowered security personnel in such "disturbed areas" to arrest any person without a warrant and to shoot or kill "for the maintenance of public order" ("AFSPA"). Under this act, "no prosecution, suit or other legal proceeding ...[could] be instituted against any person in respect of anything done or purported to be done in exercise of the powers conferred by this Act" (Government of India 1958). Though the act was ostensibly to remain in force for only a year, it was extended every year. In 1972, it was amended to confer the governor of a state, the administrator of a union territory, the Central Government with the power to declare an area "disturbed"[9] (Amnesty International, "India: Briefing, 1958" 3). From declaring Assam and parts of Manipur as "disturbed areas" in 1958, the notification gradually extended to other North-Eastern regions, and within two decades the entire North-East was declared "disturbed" (Baruah 13). The "armed forces" of the act are the army and paramilitary forces such as the Border Security Force, Assam Rifles,[10] Rashtriya Rifles, Sikh Regiment, National Security Guards, and others (Amnesty International, "India: Briefing, 1958" 3). The "others" include the police and "unidentified gunmen," the latter being militants who "surrender" but are then made to assist state agencies in counterinsurgency operations (Baruah 25).

Authoritarian in structure, the AFSPA enables security personnel to violate civil liberties of citizens. Regardless of the rights granted to them by the constitution, suspects are detained for days and months without due process: "the arresting forces are not required to communicate the grounds of the arrest, and no advisory board is empowered to review the arrests under AFSPA" (Mohapatra 328). As early as 1958, when the bill to implement the act was introduced by the Home Minister, Mr. G.B. Pant, as a necessary course of action "for the protection of the people" ("License to Kill" 7), Mr. Laishram Achaw Singh, a member of parliament from the Inner Manipur Parliamentary Constituency, who was one of the few who objected to the bill, warned that it would be misused.

> *This piece of legislation is an anti-democratic measure and also a reactionary one. Instead of helping to keep the law and order position in these areas, if they declare some areas as disturbed areas, it would cause more repression, more misunderstanding and more unnecessary persecutions in the tribal areas....This is also an act of provocation on the part of the Government. How can we imagine that these military officers should be allowed to shoot to kill and without warrant arrest and search? This is a lawless law. There are various provisions in the Indian Penal Code and in the Criminal Procedure Code and they can easily deal with the law and order situation in these parts. I am afraid that this measure will only sever the right of the people and harass innocent folk and deteriorate the situation. (qtd. in "License to Kill" 8)*

The objections were overruled, and as of 2011, the justification of the AFSPA is that it is the only law that can counter insurgency. It is a common perception, and particularly so in a post-9/11 world, that "rights" have to be compromised for "security," and legislations like the AFSPA are imperative to deal with conflict and resistance. However, this point of view puts the blame of conflict entirely on underground groups and completely ignores the conditions that triggered the conflict and the violence caused by security personnel. This "state-centric view of security," says Baruah, also makes a person "blind to the insecurities of citizens during armed civil conflicts as well as counterinsurgency operations" (25). The militarization of the North-East has rendered the lives of Manipur's civilians less secure on every level. Far from enhancing the security of Manipur's civilian population, it has introduced a world of new hazards and they are caught in the line of fire between armed underground groups and security forces. For decades now, scholars, activists, and civilians of the North-East have demanded the removal of the AFSPA, but the government has made no move to repeal this act. To the outsider, the demands of the people of the North-Eastern region are not a central issue. Viewing their problems primarily as encounters between militants and the state, the permanent counter-insurgency operation in the North-East, the manner in which these operations are conducted and the violence by the armed forces have been ignored. It took twelve middle-aged women to strip naked in order for the country to finally take notice of the atrocities of the AFSPA and to turn its attention towards the North-East and towards Manipur in particular.

Manipur

For the visitor, the first glimpse of Manipur from the plane is picturesque—a green valley lined by hills. A different reality sets in as you near the Silchar Airport in Imphal, the capital city. Truckloads of armed personnel loom, giving the airport the air of a war zone. After witnessing an India where cities have changed dramatically with technology and infrastructure due to the influence of multinational corporations and trade policies, where "going global" is the key phrase, one experiences a sense of shock at the realization that the capital of Manipur has not been part of this change. Scholars call attention to the fact that Manipur, like other North-Eastern regions, did not receive the same treatment as the rest of country by the Indian government. India had inherited "the legacy of a century of imperial neglect and isolation" (Chaube, Munsi, and Guha 44). In its two hundred years of colonial rule, Britain's contribution to economic development in India was certainly meager, and the extreme inter-and intra-regional disparity in economic growth is one of Britain's many legacies. Concentrating chiefly on the presidency towns, Britain left huge tracts undeveloped, and the peripheral zones of India were among the regions that were ignored. Tea plantations and petroleum attracted attention to the North-East, but the region's rugged topography and relatively greater hostility towards the British meant the area was isolated (Chaube, Munsi, and Guha 41–43). The isolation increased when the region became landlocked after Indian independence and the partition of what was then called East Pakistan. In the wake of conflict, the Indian government failed to implement constructive development policies in most of the North-Eastern regions.

India, like Britain, primarily invested in and developed mineral, oil, and tea production only in Assam, while industrial production for the rest of the North-Eastern region has hardly been explored. Gulshan Sachdeva explains that it is the economic policy framework that "has created an unbalanced and unsustainable economy and destroyed the basis for institutions of a modern market economy in the region." With the exception of the North-East Frontier Railway and National Highway 34 running close along the railway, there is no land route connecting the frontier regions to the rest of India. Agriculture also remains underdeveloped, though it is the chief economy of the area (Chaube, Munsi, and Guha 45). In his report on the industrial development in Assam, K.K. Sen, the director of Economics and Statistics of Assam, wrote, "The entire North-Eastern region has been suffering from imbalance in industrial development which resulted in a widening gap between per capita income of the region and the country as a whole." While a look at the allocation of funds for the North-East by the central government might dispute the claim that the North-East has been neglected,[11] the fact is, the financial flow has not been directed towards establishing industrial development or networking the North-East with the rest of India.[12] In Imphal, the non-investment in development is apparent in the lack of basic infrastructure, such as roads, telecommunication, electricity, and hotels. The dusty crowded roads in the daytime transform into dark, lonely stretches at night, as there are few streetlights. A 6 P.M. curfew ensures little or no activity on the streets, and the few who venture out run the risk of being stopped by security forces. Education, health care, and basic amenities are secondary to security measures. Indian policy makers' oversights have led to a disintegration of the economy and compounded the problems in Manipur. The lack of employment opportunities has led not only to displacement—there has been a mass exodus of the youth in search of jobs—but has also contributed to the growing number of underground groups—"fewer economic alternatives make it easier to recruit young men to the life of a guerilla" (Baruah 27). Sachdeva argues that the existing policy framework is "one of the important factors that has contributed to the emergence and continuance of insurgency in the region." As the scholars point out, the policies that have resulted in unequal development of the North-East have created the sense of being ignored and isolated, leaving individuals to imagine solutions for themselves.

Establishing a stable economy is imperative in the creation of a democratic society. However, the process of economic planning would be fruitless without an institutional change towards the North-East and policies regarding "security." In 1980, the entire state of Manipur was declared "disturbed" and no part has since been "de-notified." Since the 1960s, the AFSPA has engendered an environment of abuse of power by security forces. With numerous incidents of arbitrary detention, torture, rape, and killing,[13] the men in uniform pose an enormous threat to civilians.[14] India's policy of implementing the AFSPA has taken away from the citizens the very thing that it used as a justification for conducting counter-insurgency operations at the expense of civil rights—security. The institutions of law and order have failed the citizens of Manipur. They remain caught in the midst of violence by the armed forces and underground groups, a corrupt state government, an authoritative central government, and a straggling economy. And yet, this bleak picture, which is often the only picture that outsiders see, is only part of the narrative of Manipur. The people in the other half of the story are the activists, alternative media groups, the Meira Paibis, and ordinary civilians like Manorama Devi. Their lives remind us that there are other narratives and that the narrative of the national history of India has to be interwoven with alternative histories.

Contemporary Manipuri society is a heterogeneous mix of different ethnic groups including the Meiteis, Kukis, and Nagas. The Meiteis consist of two-thirds of the population and live in the plains of the valley, while the Kukis and Nagas, who are animists or former animists now converted to Christianity, occupy the hills (Parratt 906). The Meiteis, who are 90 per cent Hindu and 10 per cent Muslim, have a closer affinity to Indian culture than the other ethnic groups. It is their language—Meiteilon (also known as Manipuri)—that is the lingua franca of the state. The transformation to its present structure occurred over 2,000 years. The history and literature of Manipur, recorded from AD 33, shows that the society was initially ruled by different tribes of the valley and the hills. For most of its history, the region was an independent kingdom and enjoyed a sovereign status. Tracing the emergence of Manipur as a political entity, Bhagat Oinam suggests that around the eleventh century there was a shift in the political structure, and the society moved towards a feudal system (68). The major transformation occurred in the eighteenth century when King Garib Niwaz declared Hinduism as the state religion (Oinam 72). The next shift happened in 1891, when the British defeated Manipur, and it became part of the empire (Oinam 68). Manipur, like other North-Eastern regions, did not join India's freedom struggle, and they fought their own wars against the British. The independent kingdom entered into a formal relationship with the British when King Jai Singh signed a treaty with the East India Company in 1762 to seek Britain's help against attacks by Burma (Thingnam 96–97). For the British, this alliance was motivated by "political and commercial considerations"—Manipur served as a strategic location for trade with China, a buffer zone between Burma and British India, and an ally "to control the North Eastern Frontier" (Thingnam 97). However, the relationship between the two countries soured with the growing power, influence, and interference of the office of the British Political Agent, established in 1835 to function as a medium of communication and foster trade between Manipur and Britain (Thingnam 98–99). This tension led the Anglo-Manipuri war of 1891, and Manipur's subsequent defeat against the British ended the land's sovereignty (Oinam 68). With Indian independence, Manipur merged with the Indian dominion as a Part–C state, and for a brief period between August 15, 1947 and October 15, 1949, it regained its status as a sovereign nation (Oinam 69). It became a Central Government Administrative Agency after it joined India in 1949 and Manipur was given the status of a Union Territory. In 1972, it was granted statehood (Inoue 26), and in 1992, the Meitei language was recognized as an official Indian language.

Origins of the Present-day Conflict in Manipur
It was alongside anti-colonial struggles that a dual Manipuri consciousness seemed to emerge—the first was a Manipuri national consciousness, linked to a Meitei identity, and the second was a socialist consciousness, driven by a Marxist-Leninist ideology. As Ali points out, it was a challenge for Delhi that "Manipuri revolutionaries sought to create a sense of Manipuri nationalism that was independent of wider Indian nationalism, and (that) they struggled to establish a primary set of power relations independent of India" (44). Manipuri nationalists sought to create a

socialist state and they rejected the structural framework offered by India. Suspicious that the Manipur Merger Agreement, which resulted in the merger of the kingdom with India in 1949, was not entirely legitimate, they questioned the status of Manipur in an independent India. The idea of secession, says R. Upadhyay, started when a group of Meitei youths, headed by Hijam Irabot, demanded the freedom of Manipur from "Indian occupation." It was this group that evolved into the United National Liberation Front (UNLF) in 1964, under the leadership of Arambam Somorendra Singh (Upadhyay). The UNLF, the oldest underground group in Manipur, started as a social organization, but in the 1990s it took up arms and formed an armed wing called the Manipur People's Army. They have the same objective as Irabot's group: "to establish an independent socialist Manipur" (South Asia Terrorism Portal, "United National"). However, their demand for a nation-state of Manipur is exclusively about Meiteis. The hill tribes feel that they are forced to assimilate into a monolithic Manipuri identity, and this has led to internal conflict between Meiteis and other ethnic groups. The People's Revolutionary Government of Kungleipak, another Meitei underground group, like the UNLF, is based on socialist ideas, but, as Ali points out, in spite of their Marxist leanings, these revolutionary groups failed to "incorporate the interests of all working people irrespective of their ethnic origin or affiliations" (45). The demand of the Nagas of Manipur to remap the hills of Manipur to be part of Nagalim, further intensified the inter-ethnic group conflict. There seems no solution to redrawing boundaries because "unclear land ownership patterns and lack of properly demarcated village boundaries have been the root of the conflict" (R. Goswami 10). The Indian government's arbitrary and disparate responses to the demands of the Meiteis, Kukis, and Nagas have added to the tension. Ali postulates that the reason the Indian government negotiates with the Naga and Mizo groups and not the Meiteis is because the Meitei revolutionaries "are led by hardened Marxist-Leninists intent not only on separation but also on the revolutionary transformation of their homeland" (47). Delhi's attitude, he adds, has left the Manipuris with "no alternatives but to continue to fight" (Ali 47–48). Given its historical background, "several disenchanting voices visualizing Manipur as a 'nation-state' continue to be heard" (Oinam 69).

In the absence of protective governments and policies and caught in the same confining space as underground groups and armed forces, the people of Manipur have witnessed a scale of violence unimaginable to most Indians. Through rallies and alternative media, Manipuris have demanded that the central government pay more than just military attention to the conflict in the state. However, the response of the government has not gone beyond an occasional increase of central funding or working out cease-fire agreements with underground groups. In spite of the protest by the Meira Paibis, which was a desperate call for protection of civil liberties, no solutions were sought. Manipuris view Manomohan Singh's first visit to Manipur in November 2004 as nothing more than a symbolic gesture. During his visit, the prime minister officially handed over the historic Kangla Fort to the Manipur state government (it had been the headquarters of the paramilitary force, the Assam Rifles, since 1915), upgraded Manipur University into a Central University, and laid the foundation stone for a 97.9-kilometre-long, Jiribam-Imphal, broad gauge rail line project, which ends at Tupul, twenty-five kilometres away from Imphal (Kumar). Regarding the repeal of the AFSPA, Singh said the government would set up a committee to review it so that it could be replaced with a "more humane law that takes into account legitimate aspirations and national security concerns" (Kumar).

The committee, headed by the former Supreme Court Judge B.P. Jeevan Reddy, clearly recommended that the AFSPA be withdrawn, among other suggestions on how to address the situation in Manipur. The committee report read: "It is highly desirable and advisable to repeal the Act altogether, without, of course, losing sight of the overwhelming desire of an overwhelming majority of the [North-East] region that the Army should remain (though the Act should go)" (Varadarajan, "Repeal Armed Forces Act").[15]

However, the prime minister's promise to make changes to the AFSPA turned out to be yet more empty rhetoric, and the report, like many other investigations, remains a futile effort. It was never even made public until *The Hindu* obtained a copy and published it.[16] Bibhu Prasad Routray, commenting about Manmohan Singh's visit, expressed the sentiments of many Manipuri people: "The Prime Minister's visit remained an immensely forgettable affair, as far as North-Eastern hopes and aspirations are concerned." Baruah rightly points out that "the fate of the AFSPA underscores an impasse in Indian policy toward the North-East" (16), an impasse that could not be broken even when twelve women stripped naked. The Meira Paibis still remain the strongest visible collective force in Manipur confronting the armed forces on charges of violations of civil rights.[17]

The Meira Paibis

The struggles of the grassroots women's organization, the Meira Paibis—The Bearers of the Torch—against the Indian government today, are often compared to the Nupi Lan or Women's War in Manipur[18] (see Figure 5.3). The Nupi Lan movement is one of India's significant anti-colonial movements. In fact, the first two major wars against the British by the Manipuris, in 1904 and 1939, were organized and led by women.

> *The first war was a revolt against punitive labour levies or civil rights violation, and the second was a protest against British interference in the rice trade. The British attempted to strengthen their colonial economic position by destroying the self-sufficiency of the village economy. As they tried to take over an economy that was traditionally controlled by women, the colonial rulers had to face an extremely tough and at times violent opposition from the women. The*

> *movement gathered momentum as different issues got embroiled and more and more women joined in. Eventually, the nature of the movement shifted from the export policy of the colonial government to the freedom movement. (R. Goswami 11–12)*

The movement was sustained by the women until the new political movement of Hijam Irabot and his followers took it over in 1940 (Longjam). Scholars unanimously agree that Nupi Lan is an important landmark in the history of Manipur because it brought about constitutional, political, and economic reforms in the state. "The firmness of conviction and unity of women cannot be undermined," says Ibotombi Longjam, because the Nupi Lan occurred "without any male participation or leadership." Nupi Lan is also significant because it marks a time when different ethnic groups supported each other in their fight against a common enemy, and the movement established a pattern of women confronting administrations that fail the people.

Collective action by women is part of Manipur's history, where a Habermascian marketplace has been the facilitating space for activism. Indeed, it is from this market space that the Nupi Lan broke out (R. Goswami 11; see Figure 5.4). Since 1786, the market in Manipur has been controlled by women. Known as the Nupi Keithel or women's market,[19] this space is particularly significant not only because it established the dominant role women played in the economy but also because it became the location for interactions, dialogues, and collective decision making (R. Goswami 11). It is from this tradition of collective action against imperial forces that the Meira Paibis emerged.

The movement of the Meira Paibis started in the 1970s as the All Manipur Women Social Reformation and Development Samaj (Nupi Samaj), a grassroots movement by village women who sought to battle the increasing abuse of drugs and alcohol (Mentschel, "Armed Conflict" 20). A few years later, they took on the issue of domestic violence. According to a North-East Network

FIGURE 5.3: *Meira Paibis (Bearers of the Torch): The grassroots organization of Meitei women from the Manipur Valley have emerged as one of the most formidable forces challenging the atrocities against civilians by army personnel in Manipur.*

FIGURE 5.4: *Nupi Keithel (Women's Market in Manipur): A Habermascian public sphere that has been the facilitating space for activism by Manipuri women of the valley.*

report, they resemble the traditional Meitei women's courts known as Paja, where women heard cases of domestic violence and dispensed justice (R. Goswami 12). Nitin Bahuguna reports that, "in areas patrolled by the Meira Paibis, drug use patterns changed substantially, with decline in riotous behaviour and greater safety for women at night." Their incessant campaign against alcohol resulted in Manipur being declared a "dry" state in 1991 (Thokchom). For a society that for decades has been protected and transformed by women, it came as no surprise that it was women who once again emerged in the 1980s as the formidable force challenging the armed forces.

Keisam Taruni, a Meira Paibi, recalls that the first encounter of the Meira Paibis with the Armed Forces was on December 29, 1980, when a young boy named Lourenbam Ibomcha was charged with planting a bomb and arrested by the army. On hearing of the arrest, the president of the organization, Ima Ramani, along with two other women volunteers, Ima Chaobi and Ima Momon, went to the army camp and demanded the release of the boy. They were asked to wait, and after an hour, Ibomcha was released. While the release surprised them, what shocked them was the sight of the brutally tortured boy. It was at this moment that the Meira Paibis or the Bearers of the Torch were born (Taruni). The women vowed to protect civilians against the Armed Forces and they took to patrolling the streets with "meiras" to "save Manipur [from being a land of blood and tears]" (Mentschel, "Narrative"). The "meira," Paula Banerjee explains, is "an improvised bamboo torch." It has become a "symbol of their movement, and thus the name 'Meira Paibi Uprising' (Uprising of women who hold *meira*)." Having decided to patrol the streets at night, the women required a place to stay, and they constructed small sheds, "now popularly known as *Meira Shang*. Today, all the localities have Meira Paibi organizations, and almost every locality has their own *Meira Shang*" (Banerjee).

Ever since December 29, 1980 these guardian angels of Manipur walk the streets at night carrying torches, with no weapons of defense, or they keep vigil in the Meira Shang after they have finished their day's chores. On an average, says Homen Thangjam, "a Meira Paibi spends three to four hours daily with her group in keeping vigil over the leikai. All the while they are exposed to dangers—to the bullets of the conflicting parties, sexual and physical harassment, as well as to the elements of weather." It is important to note here that the women who volunteer to be part of this organization, who play multiple roles as homemakers, protectors, and peacekeepers, are simply village women who have taken it upon themselves to restore some form of protection for both the men and women of Manipur. They defy simple classifications as gender or political activists. Their participation in activism is a direct outcome of a system that has failed its civilians. Outlining the cause of the organization, the leader of the Meira Paibis, Ima Ramani says, their aim "is to protect the people caught in the crossfire between militants and security forces. We are neither protecting militants nor fighting the security forces. Our only concern is the safety of our children. Our fight is to protect human rights which are being misused under the AFSPA" (Thokchom). In their role as Meira Paibis, the women have been successful in securing the release of many civilians who have been falsely accused and arrested by the army. But the arrests and killing of civilians, and rape of women by the army, says Taruni, have increased in frequency. The proverbial last straw was the midnight arrest of Manorama Devi by the army, her brutal murder and rape, and the discovery of her bullet-ridden body thrown callously in the fields at daybreak. Shocked at the brutality of the crime, the Meira Paibis organized the historic protest at the Kangla Fort, which stunned the country and left Manipur burning for days.

On July 15, 2004 twelve Meira Paibis stripped naked in front of the gates of the Assam Rifles Battalion, carrying the banner—"Indian Army Rape Us." This expression of anger against the army, said Ramani, "was the bursting of the bottled-up anger and hurt sentiment caused by a series of atrocities on Manipuri women by security forces, armed with the AFSPA" (qtd. in Thokchom). It was their "last resort" for justice: "We called out to the army personnel to come out and kill us, because we could not bear what we saw" (Taruni). The villagers who found Manorama's body reported that "there were scratch marks from fingers all over her body, a deep gashing knife wound on her right thigh, signs of bruises on her breasts, deep cut marks on her inner thighs, and genitals, and several bullet wounds" ("Merciless Killing"). The protest made headlines in 2004, and the image of the naked women carrying the banner resulted in the conflict in Manipur and discussions about the removal of the AFSPA to become centre page news. However, five years later the protest is no more than a distant memory to most Indians. As Neerja Chowdhury states, the Meira Paibis really remained unheard.

> *India failed to reach out to Manipur's women. On that day, the prime minister should have rushed to Imphal. Sonia Gandhi could have gone, or the home minister or defense minister. A visit by a senior person would have expressed an understanding of the women's anguish and shown the Centre cared, even if it could not find immediate solutions. But the government chose to wait and watch.*

The AFSPA is still in effect, and the media mentions Manipur only when a violent incident is reported. The Meira Paibis, along with the rest of Manipur, continue to be in the line of fire of both the Armed Forces and the underground groups. As for Manorama Devi, she is even less remembered.

Manorama Devi

Who was Manorama Devi? She was a thirty-two-year-old daughter, sister, and the only income earner of her family. She wove cloth and made just enough money to take care of her widowed mother and school-going seventeen-year-old brother.

At 12:30 A.M. on July 11, 2004 armed personnel of the 17th Battalion of the Assam Rifles dragged Manorama Devi from her home. A few hours later, her bullet-ridden body was found in an open field close to the garrison where the men from the Assam Rifles were stationed. The army, under whose command the Assam Rifles men operate, explained that she was shot while escaping from custody (Varadarajan, "Anybody remember Manipur?"). It was the standard army response for every person who died in military custody, and Manorama might have been yet another victim of this violence, if not for the arrest memo that her brother, Thonjum Dolendru, asked for and was granted before the soldiers took his sister away (Dolendru). The arrest memo is the first and only piece of legal evidence against the army. The memo stated that no property in any form had been recovered at the time of Manorama's arrest and that she was being charged on the suspicion that she had links with an underground group, the People's Liberation Army (PLA).[20] Later, the 17th Assam Rifles issued a statement alleging that Manorama, a corporal of the PLA, was an expert in explosives and that a radio set, a hand grenade, an AK-47 rifle, and some documents were found in her possession. The document also stated that Manorama resisted arrest and was shot when attempting to escape (Biswas, par. 12). However, army officials or politicians have given no explanation as to why she was dead within four hours of being taken into custody by the Armed Forces.

The autopsy of Manorama Devi's body was conducted at the Regional Institute of Medical Sciences Hospital after the Irilbung police picked up the body, even before family members could identify her. The results of the report were not released to the public. Since her family refused to take back the body, instead demanding an inquiry into the murder, the state authorities cremated her body and categorized it as "unidentified" ("Merciless Killing"). It was only after four years, in July 2008, that her family performed the last rites. They had waited, hoping for justice to be served. But the High Court has yet to look into the case. Inside Manorama

FIGURE 5.5: *The brutal death of Manorama Devi while in the custody of the Assam Rifles personnel triggered a wave of protests by Manipuris across the country against the Armed Forces (Special Powers) Act (2004).*

Devi's home all that is left of her are memories, her bed, and her photographs. Outside, the Meira Paibis continue to hold a vigil in the Meira Shang (see Figure 5.5).

Conflict-Induced Displacements

As Manipuris continue their quest for justice and peace the question is, what future does Manipur offer for the youth? Analysis of the conflict in Manipur that has carried on for decades reveals that functional systems have broken down, industrial development is not happening, and the process of democratization has been replaced by militarization. Describing his home state, Bunta Singh at the Manipur Network of Positive People describes Manipur as "a salad of so many things; no economic growth, no basic infrastructure, no electricity, no telephone facilities; we in Manipur have nothing to fall back upon except government jobs. It is either a government job or nothing" (qtd. in Rasheeda Bhagat). The threat of kidnapping and extortion from underground groups, the danger of being "picked up" by the Armed Forces, a lagging economy, the lack of infrastructure in the region to respond to globalization, and the limited opportunities to pursue higher education or seek employment, have all resulted in a significant migration of the youth from Manipur either to mainland India or overseas. According to Oinam Anand, "The law and order problem which comes out of the Conflict Situation in Manipur is one of the main reasons for parents to send out their children from the state. If the present trend continues for another decade then there will be schools without students." However, most of the literature on internal displacement due to conflict in Manipur focuses on ethnic relocations, migrations of men and women within the state, and people housed in refugee camps. The mass exodus of Manipuri youth in search of education and jobs is yet to draw attention.

Across the world, people migrate for higher education and jobs. In fact, as Ram Bhagat states, migration "has been a force to the democratization of society....In the Indian context, it paved the way for the lower caste groups to free themselves from the oppression and subjugation of traditional caste system if they moved to the urban areas" (2). Although spatial movements contribute to cultural changes and might enhance the socio-economic-political fabric of societies, they are not always voluntary processes. Sometimes people are forced to move due to caste structures, industrial development, and conflict in the region, but they are not defined as "displaced" people. In the *Guiding Principles on Internal Displacement*, Walter Kälin defines the internally displaced as "persons or groups of persons who have been forced or obliged to flee or to leave their homes or places of habitual residence, in particular as a result of or in order to avoid the effects of armed conflict, situations of generalized violence, violations of human rights, or natural or human-made disasters, and who have not crossed an internationally recognized State border" (18). Based on this definition, students who move out of the North-East for education or employment could technically be seen as internally displaced persons (IDPs), but because there is no way to pinpoint whether this movement is forced or voluntary, their movement remains outside the purview of IDP studies. Moreover, the Indian census only has records of the place of origin and the place of last residence of an individual and has no standard source of data to record whether migration is voluntary or forced. This kind of data results in "very important reasons for migration such as riots, terrorism, persistent ethnic conflict threatening the security of persons at the place of origin [being] ignored" (Ram Bhagat 15).

In recent research on the mobility of contemporary Indian youth, the growing numbers of North-Eastern students in Bangalore and Delhi has been seen as a positive trend. Raghu Karnad reports, "Young, hip North-Easterners are suddenly all the rage....The ever-morphing face of the Indian metropolis has, in the last five years, begun to be transformed by thousands of confident young faces from the North-East." However, the "ethnic typing," which Karnad observes "lends them a cosmopolitan edge," has also led to racial discrimination. Gin Gangte, a freelance writer, highlights the bigotry that these students face from their peers: "They have a hard time convincing their fellow Indians that they are also the citizens of the same country. Often north-eastern students are mistaken to be from China, Japan, Thailand, Vietnam or Bhutan because of their typical looks." In his report on displacement in Manipur, Pradip Phanjoubam calls attention to this "subtle interplay of contradicting nationalisms" inherent in India. While the discriminations against Muslim immigrants "are based on religious nationalisms," the xenophobia of the North-East, he says, "is more on linguistic and ethnic nationalisms" ("Population Displacement" 39). U.A. Shimray, a North-Eastern student who attended Delhi's prestigious Jawaharlal Nehru University in the early 1990s, narrates these experiences in his essay, "Youth on the Move." Life in the metropolitan cities is not easy for North-Eastern students who face culture shock and prejudice, he says, but the greater tragedy is that the options to return to Manipur, his home state, are limited. It compels him to make yet another move to Bangalore for a job, after his twelve-year stint in Delhi.

Shimray, like hundreds of other Manipuri youth, joins the dispersed or displaced population known as the diaspora. As Benzi Zhang notes, the term diaspora indicates not only a condition of "out-of-country" displacement, but also the mishmash "out-of-culture," "out-of-language," and "out-of-oneself" experiences (104). An integral aspect to this term is the sense of "home." Contemporary studies on modern diaspora expand the definition of home from a particular location to nation, so encounters with others become encounters with nation-states (S. Ahmed 340). Another problem that Manipuri youth who have relocated outside of their home state face is that, unlike diasporans who seek cultural reconnections with their place of origin and do not return because they have re-homed in transnational locations (Zhang 113), conflict-induced displaced people remain culturally connected to their home states but do not return to their place of origin because they cannot. To contribute to the cultural, social, and political evolution of a society, migration has to be a two-way flow. If all we witness is only the ebb of people in Manipur, we face the prospect of the history of the region being frozen into a single memory of conflict.

▶ Irom Sharmila's indefinite fast since 2000 is one among the several non-violent methods adopted by Manipuris demanding that the AFSPA be repealed. Every report on the act categorically states that the law is abusive and should be abolished. There is also no dearth of recommendations by North-Eastern scholars, activists, judges, NGOs, and civilians on how the Indian government could and should address the political problems in Manipur. But Manmohan Singh is yet to follow up even on the promise he made, when he stepped into office as prime minister in 2004, to "review and, if necessary, replace" the controversial act "with a more humane law that would seek to address the concerns of national security as well as rights of citizens," or act upon the AFSPA Review Committee's 2005 recommendation to withdraw the act ("Review of Armed Forces Act Will be Considered: Manmohan"). At the end of 2005 alone, the Manipur State Human Rights Commission (MHRC) had registered more than 120 human rights violations cases ("India Human Rights Report 2007"). In his customary Independence Day speech in 2008, Singh assured the country that the government would examine the committee's report. However, it was a sad moment of betrayal when the prime minister, while acknowledging the service of the Armed Forces, called the atrocities that they had committed against civilians "accidents."

> In the country, we still have regions such as Jammu and Kashmir and the North-East where complete peace and tranquility does not exist. The people in these regions are the victims of violence and terrorism. Wherever conditions deteriorate, we take the assistance of our Armed Forces. Wherever we have taken their assistance, they have shown patience and perseverance. Many of them have lost their lives. In order to ensure that the children of soldiers who have laid down their lives in the service of the nation get good education, we are starting a Prime Minister's Scholarship Scheme. Each year, 5,000 children would be provided scholarships for college education.
>
> However, accidents *do happen once in a while*. Keeping this in mind and with a view to protecting human rights, the Government had set up a Committee to look into the provisions of the Armed Forces (Special Powers) Act. The Report of this Committee is being examined in detail and we will take all necessary steps so that there are no violations of human rights under this Act. (Manmohan Singh, emphasis added)

To offer no apology and instead refer to Manorama Devi and hundreds like her, killed and tortured by the Armed Forces, as "accidents" is a tragic betrayal of justice and the loss of yet another opportunity to make the anniversary of the birth of a nation mean more than a mere political formation.

On the sixty-fourth anniversary of Indian independence, it was not the speech from the Red Fort, but an editorial from Imphal, that gently reminded the nation that its citizens did not have equal rights.

> *On the eve of the India's Independence Day, Imphal is acquiring the look of a war front. The scenario is not too different in other townships in Manipur as indeed in much of the Northeast. It has almost become a ritual every year. Various militant organisations would call for a boycott of the celebration of what is arguably the biggest and most important day in the country's history and in response the provincial governments would virtually stage flag marches to demonstrate the power of the establishment and push its way without being deterred by any threat whatsoever. Uniformed gun totting security personnel are on every corner of the streets frisking people, stopping motorists, checking their vehicles, questioning them etc. As expected, even a week before the big day approached, Imphal already began wearing a deserted look, especially after sunset. People return home early so as not to be accosted by security men and go through the humiliation of being made to stand on the side of the roads to be frisked and questioned like potential troublemakers. The ordinary people are supposed to be mere bystanders in this war game, but every time tensions escalate in moments like this, they have no choice than to be prepared to be the undeserved casualties, and sometimes become statistics of "collateral damage," the well known sugarcoating aimed at making civilian killing and harassment seem like necessary and pardonable fallout of a conflict. (Phanjoubam, "State of independence")*

The rights that people have and the quality of life they enjoy is a mark of the progress by which a nation should be measured. Constitutions, governments, and legislations are, at best, only logical foundations to ensure that this progress is achieved. However, the contemporary political rhetoric of the "war on terror" has reduced these structures to a single zero sum game between national security and civil rights. Ironically, it is in countries like India and the United States, which constantly reiterate that they are democratic nations, that we are witnessing the very antithesis of democracy—leaders justifying the creation of Orwellian police states, instead of building nations where justice, equality, and civil liberties are unassailable rights, not discriminatory privileges.

At the end of my interview with Thonjum Dolendru, the seventeen-year-old brother of Manorama Devi, I asked him, "Why did you speak with me? What do you think I can accomplish?" He replied, "Maybe there will be justice. Maybe the interviews I give might result in justice." Justice. That might be the response to Ella Shohat's question: "When exactly…does…'postcolonial' begin?" (103). When there's justice.

NOTES

1. The AFSPA is a legislation passed by the Indian Parliament that gives enormous power to security forces to carry out military operations in "disturbed areas." A detailed analysis follows later. The act will hereafter be referred to as AFSPA.
2. Pradip Phanjoubam points out that "the chicken-neck" exposes the isolation of the North-East from the rest of India and is a result of "a residual fallout of colonial politics and administration, rather than a given, natural, physical feature" ("Population Displacement" 22).
3. Aside from academic sources, it is important to consult official government documents, reports by non-government organizations, newspapers, and online sources to understand the politics of the past and present in North-East India. With limited access to Manipur, due to government restrictions

on travel, a lot of current information is available only through alternative media and unofficial sources.

4. Mainland India refers to the part of India on the other side of the Siliguri Corridor.

5. The government refers to the rebels as "insurgents." I will use the terms "Armed Forces" for the military and "underground groups" to refer to the armed rebels, "underground" implying that they are not the civilian resistance.

6. Mohapatra makes an excellent comparison between the USA PATRIOT Act of 2001 and India's AFSPA, the Terrorist and Disruptive Agencies (Prevention) Act of 1987 (TADA), and the Prevention of Terrorism Act (POTA) of 2001. His analysis shows that abuse of anti-terrorist legislations is not exclusive to India but is emerging in the United States also. It is important, he says, for countries like the United States to look to the histories of other countries so as to not repeat abuses and mistakes of the past.

7. Amnesty International provides a detailed briefing on the Armed Forces Special Powers Act.

8. Pradip Phanjoubam makes a great argument on how the coining of this phrase has produced an iconic image that has not only immortalized conflict but has also led to government policies on insurgency, in the sense that if they tackled the mother right, "all its supposed offspring will come under control" ("Population Displacement" 27). The fact is, he says, "At this moment, it is practically impossible to say which is the mother and which the child in the complex matrix of North-East insurgencies" ("Population Displacement" 27).

9. For government documents relating to the Disturbed Areas (Special Courts Act), 1976, and the Armed Forces (Special Powers) Act, 1958 Act 28 of 1958, September 11, 1958, refer to the South Asia Intelligence Review site: http://satp.org.

10. The Assam Rifles raised as Catchar Levy in 1835 is the oldest paramilitary force in the country. The force has forty-six battalions and has a dual role of maintaining internal security in the North-Eastern region and guarding the Indo-Myanmar Border (Government of India). Thirty-two battalions are deployed in the North-East.

11. See Sahni and George.

12. Rafiul Ahmed and Prasenjit Biswas's *Political Economy of Underdevelopment of North-East India* and Wasbir Hussain's "Contemporary North-East India: Problems and Prospects" demonstrate the economic under-development of India's North-East.

13. The Manipur State Human Rights Commission, headed by Justice W.A. Shishak, registered more than 120 human rights violations cases—these include seven cases of illegal detention and killing by the central security forces, twenty-seven cases of negligence or excess on the part of the state police, and fifteen cases of rape, including of minor girls (India Human Rights Report 2007).
14. The report, "Where 'Peacekeepers' Have Declared War," published by the National Campaign Committee Against Militarization and Repeal of Armed Forces (Special Powers) Act, gives a detailed account of the violations by security forces and in the North-East.
15. In spite of the report's stance towards repealing the act, Amnesty International is concerned that the committee's recommendation to replace AFSPA with the Unlawful Activities (Prevention) Act, 1967 (UAPA), merely transfers power from one group to another and does not address issues of human rights violations and abuse of power (Amnesty International, "India: Briefing...One Step Forward").
16. The Jeevan Reddy report is available on *The Hindu* website http://www.hinduonnet.com/nic/afa/.
17. Irom Sharmila, known today as the "iron" woman of Manipur, has been on a fast since 2000, demanding the repeal of the AFSPA.
18. Saroj Arambam Parratt and John Parratt show how the Nupi Lan set up the democratic platform that Manipur needed: "The women's war had succeeded in opening up to public debate issues which had previously been the concern of only the small emergent political elite" (916).
19. The Ima Keithel ("Mothers' market"), says Bhagat Oinam, is the most important market that evolved historically. By the 1881 census, out of the total number of 15,433 persons depending on trading and commerce, women accounted for 14,861 (96.29 per cent). Local markets run by women are a common feature of the North-Eastern states as well as countries of Southeast Asia like Myanmar, China, and Thailand (81).
20. Formed in 1978, the PLA is one of the dominant underground groups in Manipur. A list of the underground groups is available on the South Asian Terrorist Portal site.

6

THE REFUGEE AND THE GOVERNMENT

A Saga of Self-Rehabilitation in West Bengal

SUBHASRI GHOSH

THIS CHAPTER FOCUSES on how a particular category of forced migrants from East Bengal responded to inadequate state provisions for rebuilding their lives by using the principle of *jabardakhal*, or forcible seizure, and stubborn political engagement with a government that saw them as temporary visitors and therefore non-citizens. The context is a forty-year tussle between the government and migrants, called "squatters" in the local parlance, who refused to accept the apathy of the government and who carved out a niche for themselves in the somewhat alien setting of West Bengal.

The Partition of British India into two independent nations of India and Pakistan in 1947 resulted in the uprooting and forced migration of thousands of minorities in the Punjab and the Bengal sectors in India. In Punjab there was an exchange of population where an immigration of forty-nine *lakhs*[1] (almost five million people) from West Punjab and the adjoining areas in Pakistan was matched by an outflow of fifty-five *lakhs* (five and a half million

The Indian Union and Pakistan on 15 August 1947.

people) from East Punjab and the adjoining areas in India (*Daily Jugantor* 1955). However, in Bengal the movement was essentially unidirectional. The tide of migration flowed from the Pakistan province of East Pakistan to the Indian state of West Bengal.

The government estimates the volume of migration between the years 1947 and 1950, which witnessed the largest growth of squatter settlements, as follows:

TABLE 6.1

Period	Number of Fresh Arrivals
1947	4,063,474
1948	4,090,555
1949	3,026,211
1950	11,072,928

Source: Ministry of Relief and Rehabilitation. *Annual Report on Evacuation, Relief and Rehabilitation of Refugees* (September 1947 to August 1948). New Delhi, 1949.

This chapter is set against the backdrop of this massive influx of refugees from across the border. I intend to show how the squatters were exasperated by what they perceived as their humiliation by the government's insufficient rehabilitation schemes and how they therefore undertook measures to rebuild their lives through forcible seizures and political engagement. They squatted on fallow, marshy lands, often in the dead of night, constructed makeshift tenements, and put pressure on the state government to declare them the owners of the land. With only the banned Communist Party of India (CPI) to support them, the squatters took on the government machinery and fought it with grit and determination. Their prolonged struggle is the focus of this chapter.

Inundated by the flood of migrants from 1947 onward, the government tried its best to tackle the crisis. The basic problem arose when government action was predicated upon a faulty understanding of the situation; it harboured the mistaken notion that the influx in the east was a temporary one and that the refugees would return to their original homes across the border once the situation reverted to normal back in East Bengal. The government believed that the in-migration would be matched by an out-flow of at least the majority: "the policy of the Government has been to create conditions in East Pakistan itself to stop the exodus of refugees from there and also encourage those who have come to go back" (Constituent Assembly of India, hereafter referred to as CAI, 1949,

TABLE 6.2: EXPENDITURE ON DISPLACED PERSONS, 1947–1948 TO 1949–1950

(Figures in lakhs of rupees)

Year	Establishment			Grants		
	West Pak. D.P.s	East Pak. D.P.s	Total	West Pak. D.P.s	East Pak. D.P.s	Total
1947–48	5.78	--	5.78	272.09	--	272.09
1948–49	13.37	--	13.37	1,654.85	185.48	1,840.33
1949–50	16.15	--	16.15	1,627.45	148.49	1,775.94

Source: Ministry of Rehabilitation, *Annual Report: 1960–61*, New Delhi, 1961.

640). In this context, Prime Minister Jawaharlal Nehru wrote to the West Bengal Premier, Dr. B.C. Roy on August 25, 1948:[2]

> *I have been quite certain right from the beginning that everything should be done to prevent Hindus in East Bengal from migrating to West Bengal...Running away is never a solution to the problem.... To the last I would try to check migration even if there is war. (qtd. in Chakraborty 109)*

Such feeling was based on the fact that East Bengal was unscathed by large-scale communal riots in the years immediately following Partition. Unlike those from West Punjab, East Bengali Hindus more often fled to the other side of the border on the pretext of the "what if" syndrome rather than any actual persecution. Punjabi migrants, fleeing in the face of ghastly communal mayhem, received more aid than their East Bengali brethren, at least in the initial years. This is evident in Table 6.2.

West Bengal thus languished from neglect since the people at the helm of affairs at Delhi were unable to comprehend the gravity

	Loans except Housing & RFA			Housing			Total
	West Pak. D.P.s	East Pak. D.P.s	Total	West Pak. D.P.s	East Pak. D.P.s	Total	
	0.71	--	0.71	--	--	--	278.58
	478.23	--	478.23	577.78	--	577.78	2,909.71
	931.77	87.88	1,019.65	973.49	227.76	1,201.25	4,012.99

of the situation that led to this wave of migrants and thus dished out relief measures that were not backed up by a supplementary program of rehabilitation. The central government allotted money for specific purposes under various heads, like grants, aids, loans. When the money thus earmarked could not be spent within the financial year, the amount reverted to the central exchequer. Right from 1948 to 1949, the premier was crying for money from the central government—from the prime minister to every other ministry concerned with relief and rehabilitation—when he found that his state was not getting the same deal as those dealing with border migration from the west. The premier's exasperation was expressed to the prime minister in a letter dated December 1, 1949.

> You are under the impression that your Government gave us a "large grant" for the purpose of "relief" and rehabilitation. Do you realise that the total grant received for this purpose from your Government in the two years, 1948–49 and 1949–50 is a little over 3 crores, the rest about 5 crores was given in the form of a loan? Do you realise that this sum is "insignificant" compared to what has been spent for

> *refugees from West Bengal?...I do say that the "grant" so far given is insignificant for 16 lakhs displaced people because it works out at about Rs.20/- per capita spread over two years.*
> (qtd. in Chakraborty 140)

The common sentiment of those in power in Delhi is exemplified by the following remark made on the floor of the Constituent Assembly by the Minister of Rehabilitation: "The question of rehabilitation is being considered, but we always live in the hope that many of them may be able to go back" (CAI, 19 February 1949, 772).

Thus, the stress in the initial years of migration was more on relief, which involves provision of food, clothing, accommodation, rather than on rehabilitation, which involves permanent treatment, namely providing East Bengali Hindus with infrastructure to rebuild their lives in West Bengal. Rehabilitation would include grants, loans, and subsidies to build houses and start small-scale businesses; reserved seats in educational institutions; and the granting of citizenship. Instead, the government only focused on providing a system of dry doles such as *atta* (wheat flour) or rice, *dal*, vegetables, oil, salt, condiments, sugar, and cash doles of Rs.15 per month per adult and Rs.10 per child (Chakraborty 110). Mohan Lal Saksena, Minister of Relief and Rehabilitation in the Government of India, instructed the representatives of Tripura, Assam Bihar, Orissa, and West Bengal (the cluster of states in eastern India that bore the brunt of exodus) to restrict government work to relief (*trankarya*) rather than rehabilitation (*punarbashan*). That the central government focused mainly on ad hoc assistance is evident from Table 6.3, which shows government allocation under the two heads.

The distribution of doles in the relief camps was erratic. The inmates of the Belur Camp in Howrah district received no doles from October 15, 1949 to October 29, 1949 (*Amrita Bazar Patrika*). Consequently, some of them starved, and life in the camps became particularly difficult for children. The management of these camps

TABLE 6.3

Year	Relief (in Rs.)	Rehabilitation (in Rs.)
1947–48	4,008,929	Nil
1948–49	1,094,019,452	11,012,453
1949–50	1,061,087,750	31,013,535
Total	3,060,016,131	42,025,988

Source: Government of West Bengal, *Five Years of Independence, August 1947–August 1952*. Calcutta: Government of West Bengal, 1953.

left much to be desired as they became dens of vested interests for the officials in charge who usurped the relief materials, especially food grains. Officials would often only release the materials in exchange for payment. Sanitation was poor and living conditions were often unhygienic, which resulted in the outbreak of infectious diseases. One refugee recounts:

> *I live in a relief camp. Some inmates have been infected with cholera. A refugee child succumbed to the disease in the morning. I had received only a handful of puffed rice in the morning. That is all. I do not dare to go to the Relief babu [the man-in-charge]. He gets irritated if we request for anything. (Dakshinaranjan Basu 51)*

The Reliance Camp in north Calcutta was nothing more than a huge godown (a storage room, usually dingy, for stocking up goods) where a large number of families were cooped up without privacy (in the form of screens, for example) from each other. There were fifteen tuberculosis patients among the inmates. Out of the nine tubewells in the camp, five were in an unserviceable condition (Ministry of Rehabilitation, 1959–1960, 7). Insufficient financial assistance and the deplorable condition of the camps forced many young women to engage in flesh trade to feed their hungry dependents. Hasna Saha, who has worked with the Refugee and Rehabilitation Department, Government of West Bengal, could vividly recall the names of several women who would disappear for days from the camp and, when they returned, admitted to having sold their bodies for money for the sake of their children (Bagchi and Dasgupta 84).

The riot of 1950 woke the central government from its stupor. It was the first major riot to affect East Bengal after the Partition of 1947. Violence broke out on February 10, 1950 in Dacca, and the epicentre was the Secretariat Building. Muslim clerics convened in its compound after the *Jumma namaz* and later assembled into a procession.[3] Shouting anti-Hindu and anti-Indian slogans, they moved along the Nawabpur Road plundering and looting the Hindu shops on the way. In no time the violence spread to engulf the districts of Mymensingh, Comilla, Chittagong, Rajshahi, Khulna, Sylhet, and Noakhali. Perhaps the worst affected was the district of Barisal where the casualty list reached nearly 2,500. The total casualties of the East Bengal riots were approximately 10,000 (Chatterji 345). The riots' echoes were felt on the other side of the border in Calcutta and the industrial suburbs of Howrah and Hooghly. To dampen the raging fire, the Nehru-Liaquat Pact was signed on April 8, 1950 between the prime ministers of the two countries, with the avowed aim to facilitate the return of the minorities to their respective homes. They were promised complete equality of citizenship, irrespective of religion, a full sense of security in respect of life, culture, property, and personal honour throughout the territories. But the pact failed to win the confidence of the minorities and facilitate a two-way repatriation of the migrants—which was its expressed purpose. Only then did the reality sink in that the refugees were here to stay. Up to that point, the refugees languished in the hellish atmosphere of the camps or were left to rot on the platforms of the Sealdah station (commonly called "the Gateway to Hell") in disease, hunger, and pestilence, struggling to find some meaning for their wretched existence, abandoned by the government. Feeling betrayed and cheated, some of the refugees took action and began the process to establish themselves in squatter settlements.

They had reason to express their sense of betrayal, since these same politicians had promised to look after them if, due to persecution on account of their religious identity, they happened to cross over to West Bengal. Jawaharlal Nehru, in his Independence Day message to the countrymen on August 15, 1947 had said: "We think also of our brothers and sisters who have been cut off from us by political boundaries and who unhappily cannot share at present in the freedom that has come. They are of us and will remain of us" (Ministry of Information and Broadcasting 28). This was further emphasized when the prime minister promised the premier of West Bengal that, "If they [the East Bengali Hindus] come over to West Bengal, we must look after them" (qtd. in Chakraborty 106).

To many, the pain of leaving one's ancestral home was lessened by the hope of finding a safe haven on the other side of the Radcliffe Line. But their hopes were grossly belied. It is true that many were battered in mind and body, having lost the urge to live life to its fullest, but there were many enterprising enthusiasts who were determined not to remain mute spectators to their seemingly sealed fate. They realized that they themselves had to take up the means to script their own future and found agency in creating squatters' colonies.

People migrating from the same district in East Bengal, and clustered around the same locality in Calcutta, got together to form an ad hoc committee known as the colony committee, which prepared the blueprint for the foundation of the colony during meetings held clandestinely in the dead of the night. For example, the Bandhab Cooperative, a single colony committee, prepared the blueprint for the foundation of the Viveknagar Colony in the Jadavpur area of Calcutta (*Viveknagar Colony*). The formation of such colony committees preceded the foundation of the squatters' colonies. Such committees remained active even after the foundation of the squatters' colonies, staving off eviction efforts, masterminding the struggle for regularization, and facilitating the overall development of the colonies.

This process of collective takeover has been immortalized by the term *jabardakhal*—forcible seizure. At night individual plots were marked off and shacks erected, and hogla leaves were used to thatch makeshift roofs. The colony committee fixed the size of the plots. These areas were usually undeveloped, low lying, marshy jungle and forested lands, prone to monsoon flooding. The plots conformed to the UN's definition of squatter settlements.

> *Squatter settlements are mainly uncontrolled low-income residential areas with an ambiguous legal status regarding land occupation; they are to a large extent built by the inhabitants themselves using their own means and are poorly equipped with public utilities and community services. The usual image of a squatter settlement is of a poor, underserviced, overcrowded and dilapidated settlement consisting of make-shift, improvised housing areas. The land occupied by squatter settlements is...further from the city centre...the land is often occupied illegally. (United Nations Centre for Human Settlements 15)*

These squatter colonies mushroomed in and around Calcutta primarily between 1949 and 1950. One hundred and forty-nine squatters' colonies were set up during this period. The geographical distribution of the colonies was as shown in Table 6.4. As the table demonstrates, the fringe areas of Calcutta like Jadavpur in the south and Dum Dum in the north came to be infiltrated by the refugee settlements. The city of Calcutta attracted the bulk of refugees up to this phase because "those who [had] come belong[ed] to what may be called the middle classes," and they gravitated towards the city because it offered employment opportunities (CAI, 1949, 1099). The Census Report of 1951 states that roughly 40 per cent of the city's total inhabitants, at that point, were born in East Bengal (Mitra vii).

TABLE 6.4

Area	Number of Settlements
Jadavpur	58
Behala	4
Dum Dum	40
Belghoria	3
Baranangar	7
Noapara	4
Khardah	15
Naihati	3
Bijpur	4
Titagarh	1
Jagaddal	4
Habra	2
Srirampur	3
Bally	1
Total	149

Source: Anil Singha. *Jabardakhal Colony*. Calcutta: Self-published, 1979.

The foundation of the squatters' colonies resulted in severe law and order problems as they heralded the beginning of a three-pronged struggle between the government, the locals, and the refugees. The government swung like a pendulum between the two communities: one who never paid the cost of crossing and the other for whom the cost was perhaps too heavy. In their urgent need to have a roof above their heads the squatters made no discrimination between government and private lands. In response, the landlords, absentee in most cases, hired local goons to evict them. In the initial years, the government forces also threw their weight behind absentee landlords.

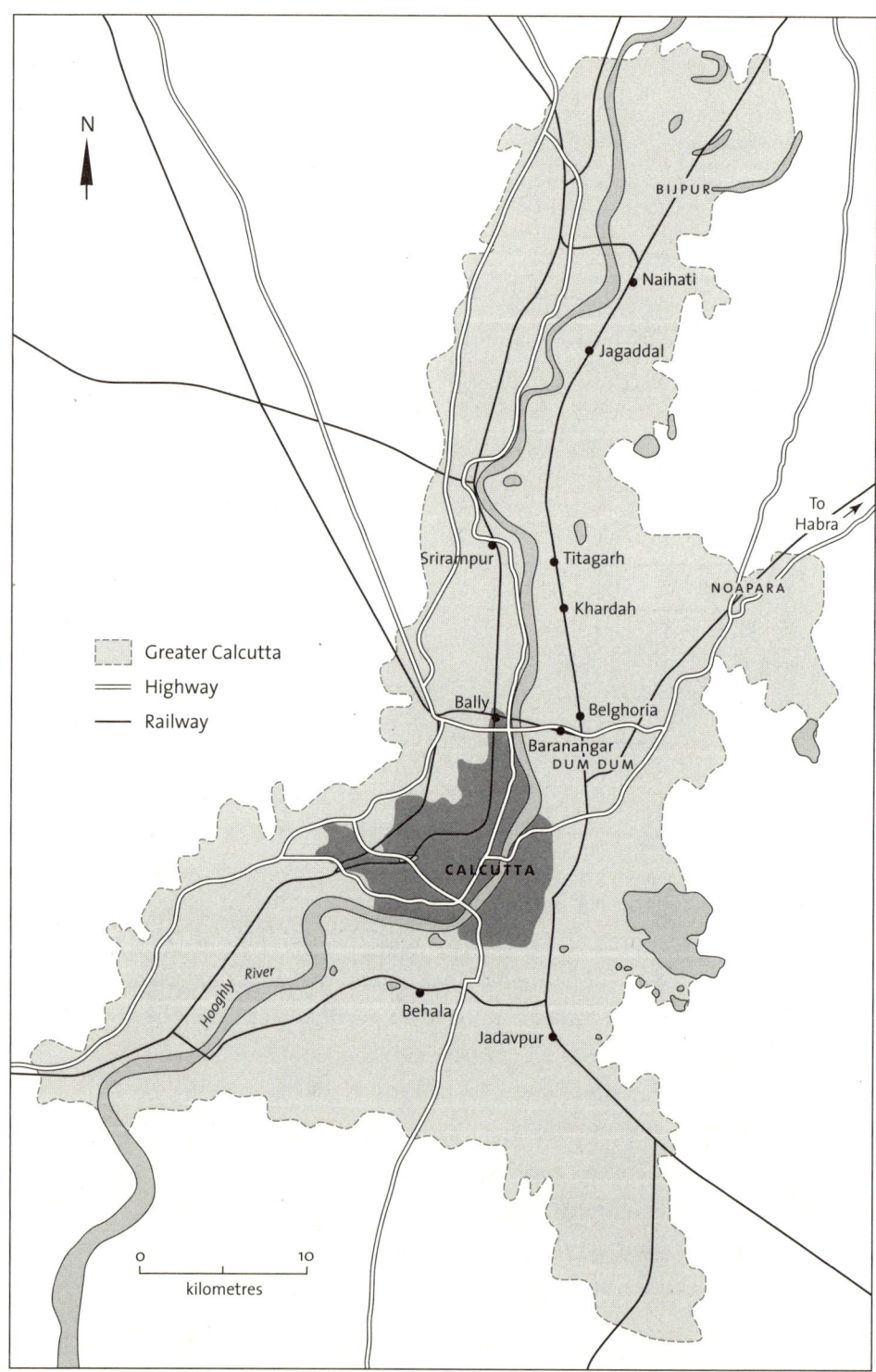

Map of Calcutta.

One can take the example of the Azadgarh colony, located in the Jadavpur area as a case study (Ganguly 141–48). In his memoir, Indubaran Ganguly, one of the founding fathers of the Azadgarh colony, pens a day-to-day account of the colony's foundation. A very interesting feature of this colony is that, instead of selecting the dead of night to divide plots, squatters worked in broad daylight—around nine or ten in the morning. Only those East Bengali refugees who possessed no land anywhere in West Bengal were eligible for a plot in the colony, for which they had to pay Rs.10. The size of a holding was roughly around three *cottahs*.[4] Again, the colony committee fixed the size of the plots and the eligibility criterion. By afternoon, the division was complete, and many of the plot holders started construction work.

For the next three years Ganguly led the life of a fugitive as nearly a dozen arrest warrants were issued in his name. The police went to extremes to arrest him—cordoned off his residence, barged into his house at odd hours—but to no avail. He managed to dodge them. Meanwhile, the original owner of the land, Debiprasad Chattopadhyay, did not sit quietly as his land was being illegally encroached upon. He arrived at the site with two armed bodyguards in tow at about 4 A.M. on January 25, 1950 and started his demolition drive in ward no. 3 of the colony. When challenged by the colony residents, the owner defiantly replied, "The government has set up refugee camps…why don't you go and take shelter there? Why encroach upon my land illegally?" (qtd. in Ganguly 70). An equally defiant group of squatters led by Ganguly answered back, "Yes, we will break the law. Do what you can. We will not budge" (Ganguly 70). Another group laid down on the ground to block Chattopadhyay's passage into the interior of the colony. In the face of stubborn resistance from the colony dwellers, he had to retreat hastily. This was the story of most of the squatter colonies. However, until mid-1950, there was no united forum of the squatters to spearhead the struggle for recognition.

Refugee movement was essentially fragmented and scattered, devoid of any united stand. In September 1948, the All Bengal Refugee Conference was convened by refugee congressmen, who were also at loggerheads with their West Bengal counterparts in power. Out of this conference emerged the all Bengal Refugee Council of Action, better known as *Nikhil Banga Bastuhara Karma Parishad* (NBBKP). It was made up of a mishmash combination of dissident congressmen as well as Communist Party members. The organization was instrumental in spearheading the foundation of squatters' colonies like Deshabandhunagar and Poddarnagar in north Calcutta.

At the southern fringe of the city, the *Dakshin Kalikata Sahartali Bastuhara Samhati* (DKSBS) was active amongst the squatters. Coupled with these organizations, numerous other small bodies were involved in venting refugee ire. Thus, the stage was already set for the emergence of a centralized, coordinating body. The devastating riot of 1950 proved to be the cementing factor. The onrush of migrants caught the government on the wrong foot and presented the opportune moment for the emergence of a centralized body for airing the migrants' grievances. The workers of the then-banned Communist Party of India (CPI), like Ambika Chakrabarti and Anil Sinha, rallied to support the formation of such a body. Their efforts bore fruit when, on June 4, 1950, at a conference held at the Commercial Museum Hall in Calcutta, the United Central Refugee Council (UCRC) was born.

From then on, it was the UCRC that took up the cause of the migrants. They fostered the regularization of the squatters' colonies, opposed the deportation of the refugees outside West Bengal in the name of rehabilitation, and protested against the arbitrary stoppage of doles to the camp inmates. For the squatters, the UCRC won a major victory when the Calcutta High Court, in reply to a writ petition filed on behalf of the squatters by the UCRC, passed a landmark judgment in late 1950 that, in case of continuous residence in a plot for three months, no criminal proceedings could be initiated. Only civil suits could be filed; but the very nature of the civil suit itself was a great deterrent.

The government now stepped in to play the role of the mediator and, in 1951, passed the Eviction of Persons in Unauthorised Occupation of Land Bill. The bill stipulated that any landlord, upon payment of a nominal court fee of fifty *paise*, could lodge a complaint with the competent authority for the eviction of the unauthorized occupiers.[5] This was an opportunity for landowners to be compensated for the period of unauthorized occupation. But at the same time, in order to protect the interests of the refugees, the bill sought to legalize their occupation in certain cases. The disputed areas were divided into high priced and low priced areas. Section 5 of the bill empowered the government to secure land offered by the owner for sale. But such a policy would be valid only in cases of low priced lands. It was highly unlikely that the owners would offer the high priced areas for sale, and the government itself was not willing to buy those lands at exorbitant prices. The bill called for the refugees to vacate those lands. At the same time it also provided for alternative accommodation as near as possible to the occupied land.

The central government declared in the Parliament:

Wherever we can acquire the land on which these persons are squatting at a reasonable rate, we acquire that land and we rationalise the present occupants in the sense that a man keeping too much of land is given a smaller plot and a man who has got an insufficient plot is given more land. Then we straighten the roads; we make provision for water and drainage etc., and settle these people on the land which they are squatting after acquiring it. Wherever the cost of the land was out of proportion, that is very expensive, we have to shift or remove them to another place. (House of the People 474)

The price ceiling was fixed at the 1946 price of Rs.1,250/*bigha* (1,600 square yards) in compliance with section 4(1) of the 1948

West Bengal Land Development and Planning Act. But the UCRC refused to accept the bill and was determined to oppose its passage in the Assembly, as chances of eviction still remained very much a reality. Its strategy was twofold: to oppose the passage of the bill on the floor of the House through sympathetic members and to organize the refugees for the defense of their newly-acquired homes, drawing them out into the streets for a bitter struggle.

In the face of stiff opposition, the government now presented an amended version of the bill: Rehabilitation of Displaced Persons and Eviction of Persons in Unauthorised Occupation of Land Act, 1951. In the amended act, unauthorized occupation was defined in Section 2(6) as "occupation of any land or part thereof without being authorised in writing by the owner" (Chakrabarti 465).[6] In case of such "unauthorised occupation," the owner could send an application to the competent authority, which would make relevant enquiries and issue notice asking the unauthorized occupant to furnish an explanation within thirty days of the service of the notice. If the authority was not satisfied with the reply as to why the unauthorized occupier would not vacate the land and pay the owner compensation for unauthorized occupation, the competent authority by order would direct this person to vacate the land within thirty days from the date of the issue of the order and fix the amount of compensation to be paid. The aggrieved party could appeal to a tribunal appointed by the state government, which was empowered to quash, modify, or uphold the order of the competent authority. The orders of the tribunal would be final and could not be challenged in any higher court, tribunal, or authority.

The act failed to settle the problems of eviction and occupation amicably as the question of eviction, the UCRC complained, still loomed large. Between 1951 and 1954 the competent authority issued many such notices; but under the directive of the UCRC the so-called illegal occupants ignored them and resisted any effort at eviction. One of the heroic acts of resistance worth recounting here was carried out in the Netajinagar Colony. Armed policemen surrounded the colony, blocking the main passage. Under the aegis of the UCRC, nearly four hundred residents of the nearby squatter colonies in the locality, namely, Azadgarh, Nehru Colony, Ashoknagar, marched into the Netajinagar Colony and encircled the police brigade. The air was rife with slogans: "We will not tolerate the demolition of the colonies; We will sacrifice our lives but not the colonies" (Ganguly 75). The police force, somewhat taken aback and perhaps unprepared to face such a huge mob, withdrew from the site. However, the respite proved brief. The very next day the police returned to the site armed with tear gas shells, and they started hurling them without any provocation. The agitated residents put up a road blockade under the leadership of the UCRC. Ultimately, the impasse ended with the assurance of the local congress leaders that, for the time being, no demolition drive would be carried out.

One of the hallmarks of these resistance movements was the participation of women. One of the present residents of Sahidnagar Colony recollects:

> Using ordinary kitchen utensils like ladle[s and] chopper[s] as weapons, the womenfolk staged defiant battles. Our leader was one Sandhya Banerjee. She used to drive the women out of their homes and organized protest marches. Under her instructions, we organized many agitations and withstood tear gas and brutal assault by the police. (Bagchi and Dasgupta 148)

In 1954, the central government appointed a Committee of Ministers, which recommended in its report the legalization and regularization of 149 squatter colonies set up before December 31, 1950. In addition, the Committee of Ministers advised the government to modify its stand regarding the fixation of the upper price ceiling, since the Supreme Court had already ruled as null and void the provision of fixing land prices at a 1946 rate. The government, however, did not modify its policy.

There thus ensued a tussle over the process of regularization. The UCRC argued that since the faulty policy of the government vis-à-vis the refugee issue had resulted in the birth of the squatters' colonies, it was the moral duty of the government to acquire these lands on behalf of the settlers and bestow the ownership over their holdings. The government, on the other hand, envisioned the process of regularization in a different manner. Between 1952 and 1957, Renuka Ray was the Minister of State for Rehabilitation. Instead of acquiring the lands on behalf of the refugees, she handed out *arpanpatras* by which each squatter was entitled to two and a half *cottahs* (approximately 167 square metres) of land. However, at the same time, each plot holder would have to pay Rs.1,875.50 to the owner of the land in installments as stipulated by the government (West Bengal Legislative Assembly, hereafter WBLA, 1960, 354). If anyone were found to be in possession of more than the prescribed area, they would have to pay an additional amount to be determined by the government. But such regularization did not bestow title deeds to the squatters and this was unacceptable to the UCRC. Ray's provision only made them authorized occupants of the land or tenants. But the government did not take any further step towards fulfilling the UCRC's demand of making the squatters the actual owners of the lands.

Moreover, the process of regularization was a cumbersome one. Preliminary steps, like enumeration and measurement, took much time. On the completion of the process, the government issued *arpanpatras* to the families who had occupied land before December 31, 1950, on production of proof of their refugee status. All the occupants were not bonafide refugees. Hence it took time to establish and select the eligible applicants and to hand out the *arpanpatras*.

Some of the colonies thus could be partially regularized—Jatindas Nagar, Deshapriyanagar of Barrackpore, Prafullanagar of Belghoria, and Bejoynagar of Naihati. Out of all the pre-1950 squatters' colonies, investigations were carried on in 120 colonies.

Twenty colonies were completely regularized while twenty-one colonies were partially regularized by 1956 (WBLA, 1956, 151). By 1957, sixty-five colonies in and around Calcutta were regularized (WBLA, 1957, 276). All in all, of the 149 squatter colonies, 136 were shortlisted for regularization, of which only eighty-seven could be regularized by 1958 (WBLA, 1958, 131–44). By the end of 1960, ninety-five had been regularized in full and thirteen in part (*Daily Jugantor*, 1960).

Moreover, from 1958 onward, the state government started levying corporation taxes on the squatter colonies of the Tollygunge-Jadavpur-Dhakuria belt. In the first phase, notices were issued for the payment from April–June 1958. Fresh notices were issued in January 1960 for recovering taxes from July–September 1960. The irony is that most of the colonies of this belt were not or could not be regularized at the time of the issue of the notifications because the government lacked a clear policy as to the mode of screening and identifying the bona fide refugees. One of the indicators was a "refugee slip," which was issued to those crossing the borders at Banpur (through Darshana-Gede) and Bongaon (for those following the Benapole-Petrapole route). But not everybody possessed this refugee slip. Those crossing the border at other points or coming directly to Calcutta by train could not acquire such slips. Hence establishing "eligible" refugee identities posed a problem, and the government could not come up with any foolproof screening process. As a result, regularization of many of these colonies remained elusive (*Daily Jugantor* 1960).[7] Although the UCRC continued to press the government to bestow ownership of plots, the government turned a deaf ear and carried on its previous programme of regularization through authorizing the occupation in return for deferred payments.

Thus, by 1960, when the government was basking in the glory of "satisfactorily" dealing with the refugee problem and declared the Ministry of Rehabilitation had served its purpose, consensual settlement of the regularization of the squatters' colonies still eluded both the parties. For the squatters, rehabilitation was far from complete because they faced an uncertain future; the roof above their heads could be snatched away any moment. But the government refused to acknowledge the intensity of the crisis and gave little cognizance to the grievances of the squatters. This proved costly to the Congress Party.

Bogged down by the growing discontent amongst the refugee population, the ruling party failed to win a majority in the assembly elections in 1967. The percentage of votes polled by the Congress party dropped from 47.29 per cent in 1962 to 41.13 per cent in 1967 (Franda 153). A coalition of fourteen parties, including both the communist parties (the CPI had split up in 1964 into the CPI and the Communist Party of India-Marxist) and ten independent candidates, forged a coalition named the United Front (UF) to assume power.[8]

The Rehabilitation Minister of the new coalition government, Niranjan Sen, handed out "entitlement deeds" that enabled their holders to obtain title deeds of the occupied lands whenever a decision to this effect would be taken in the future by the central government in New Delhi. Between 1967 and 1974, no concrete step was taken in this direction (United Central Refugee Council, hereafter UCRC, 46). This was also a period of intense political unrest in Bengal, with frequent mid-term polls, the imposition of the President's rule, and another huge wave of migration from across the border on the eve of the birth of Bangladesh.[9]

In 1974, when the Congress regained power in the state, Chief Minister Siddhartha Shankar Ray, with the approval of Prime Minister Indira Gandhi, decided to issue lease deeds for ninety-nine years to the squatters, without any payment in lieu. However, certain clauses were attached to the leases. At the expiry of the lease, the decision for renewal would rest entirely on the state government. Moreover, without the approval of the government, the land could not be transferred, and the occupant, if found guilty of any anti-government activities, would be evicted (UCRC 52).

This too was unacceptable to the UCRC. With the change of guard in the state in the 1977 election, the Left Front Government, a coalition of leftist parties, having come to power by drawing rich dividends from the refugee vote bank, changed the complexion of the situation and took up the cause of the refugees in right earnest. Chief Minister Jyoti Basu, in a letter to Prime Minister Indira Gandhi dated October 7, 1980, requested the right to bestow the gift of ownership of plots to the occupants. But in her reply, dated November 25, 1980, Gandhi turned down the request.

Undaunted, the state government was determined to have its say. In 1982, it decided to grant lease deeds of 999 years to the colonies situated in government-owned lands. But under the pressure of the central government, it was forced to revert to its original policy of ninety-nine years. In a letter written to Prime Minister Rajiv Gandhi dated March 21, 1985, the chief minister requested that he reconsider the central government's decision. The central government was unflinching. The state government was, however, determined to go ahead with its plan, and on November 12, 1986, Chief Minister Jyoti Basu handed over title deeds to 404 families of Netaji Colony in Baranagar. On December 5, 1986, through a written communication, the central government minister Buta Singh empowered the state government to bestow ownership to the occupants. Accordingly, the state government issued a proclamation on January 29, 1987 declaring that all plot holders of the squatter colonies would be given ownership rights.

The never-say-die attitude finally bore fruit. After years of struggle, with the baton passing from the first generation of protestors to a second generation, refugees from East Bengal could finally manage to erase the derogatory tag of "squatters" to emerge as proud owners of land over which they had built their homes with blood and sweat. Moreover, this process manifested a dynamic relationship between borders, identity, and government. Refugee-settlers could assume rights to land before being adopted by the state in the role of citizen and could even affect the popularity of government parties. Ethnic, religious, material, and class borders interacted with each other in complex ways to debunk the notion that government sets fixed borders based on various vectors of identity and is able to organize humans around these. Here humans were able to contest and redefine these borders.

Who does the land rightfully belong to? This cardinal question, which the squatters' movement brought to the fore in post-independence Bengal, still resonates and remains unanswered. From 2006 onward, eviction from land in the name of development has triggered fiery debates in West Bengal. There was widespread protest by the civil society against the police atrocities at Nandigram on March 14, 2007 where police shot and killed fourteen villagers who were protesting against the government's proposed land acquisition. The opposition cried foul and people took to the streets. Ironically, the same Left Front leaders who had been in the forefront of the squatters' struggle for recognition, who had waged prolonged battles, had withstood brickbats, gunshots, and arrests, were themselves now being accused of committing the same "crime" of employing government forces to grab land in various parts of West Bengal by dispossessing the present owners in the name of development.

A continuing saga of the battle over possession of land, albeit with a different set of dramatis personae, continues in West Bengal. The essence and spirit of the struggle remains the same. While the opposition parties cry foul, UCRC-equivalent committees and organizations like the Bhumi Uchhed Pratirodh (Resistance to Land Acquisition) Committee and Krishi Jami Raksha (Save Farmland) committee formed to resist eviction, and the government tries to get a grip over the situation through carrot-and-stick measures.

And last but not the least, these struggles affect the vote bank. It was land that propelled the Left Front to power. It is the same land issue that dismantled the coalition from its hegemonic position after thirty-four years. The CPI(M)-led Left Front with 50.71

per cent vote share had bagged as many as thirty-five of the forty-two seats in the state in the 2004 parliamentary election and swept the assembly election two years later in 2006, capturing 235 of the 294 seats in the assembly poll. The main opposition party was decimated in the parliamentary poll in 2004, managing to obtain only one seat. It barely managed to win thirty seats in the state assembly in 2006. Its vote share had also gone down to 21.04 per cent in 2004 compared to 26.04 in the 1999 parliamentary election (Election Commission of India). However, because of the post-land acquisition fiasco, in the 2008 *panchayat* (village-level) election, the CPI(M)'s electoral graph started going down when the party tasted defeat in East Midnapore, which had seen fierce agitation against farmland acquisition and subsequent police violence in Nandigram in March 2007. The opposition not only stormed to power in the East Midnapore village board, but also captured the same in another red bastion South 24-Paraganas district and put up an impressive showing in some other districts like North 24-Paraganas, Nadia, and Hooghly. That its movement against the farmland acquisition for industry had paid off was reflected in the opposition's victory in the village-level poll at Singur. Its winning spree continued even in the subsequent assembly by-elections in Nandigram, Bishnupur, and other districts with impressive margins. The next jolt to the ruling coalition came in the parliamentary elections of 2009. The Left Front managed to win only fifteen of the forty-two seats, while a united opposition (the major opposition parties joined hands before the election to put up an united resistance), romped home with twenty-six seats. Land issue proved too costly for the Left. Buoyed by this success, the opposition stepped up its campaign, which essentially centred on land, with an eye to the Assembly election in April–May 2011. Defeat of the ruling Left Front was a foregone conclusion. Despite their optimism and brave-front, the ruling coalition, which had captured 235 of the 294 seats in the 2006 Assembly elections, barely managed 62 out of 294 with all the prominent party leaders, including the incumbent chief minister, being resoundingly defeated. Curtains finally fell on their uninterrupted reign of thirty-four years. Land proved to be the crux. While, on one hand, the land issue proved to be the potent factor behind the unmaking of the Left, on the other, it catapulted the opposition to power as they decimated the Left Front by winning 226 seats.

The squatters' movement brought to the fore the land issue in post-independence politics. Perhaps herein lies the significance and importance of the squatters' movement. The squatters' movement emphasized human rights not only to reside on land but also to human and familial security by human ownership of land. Perhaps this is where the tension lies when we speak of human and refugee rights to use and live on land versus the right to *own land*.

AUTHOR'S NOTE

The author is grateful to Dr. Indivar Kamtekar and Professor Subhoranjan Dasgupta for helping her gather much of the source materials used in this chapter and for comments and suggestions.

NOTES

1. *Lakh* is a unit in the Indian numbering system that is equal to 100,000.
2. In India's parliamentary system, a prime minister is the head of the government and the head of the council of ministers. The premier is the pre-election equivalent of chief minister, who is the elected head of government of a state. Prior to the first assembly election in 1952, the office of the chief minister was known as that of the premier.
3. The *Jumma namaz* is a congretional prayer of the Muslims, held at the mosque every Friday, considered the holiest day of the week.
4. A *cottah* is approximately 720 square feet.
5. Competent authority means a judicial officer not below the rank of a district judge appointed by the state government in consultation with the High Court.
6. Owner denotes someone who is essentially a person entitled to use or occupation of such land or to receive rent in respect of or derive other pecuniary benefits from such land and includes government and any local authority.

7. In Tollygunge Municipality eleven colonies could not be regularized. Though ninety-two were regularized by 1959, in most of the cases out of the total number of plots only a few could be given *arpanpatras*.
8. The fourteen coalition parties were Bangla Congress, CPI, Forward Bloc, PSP, Lok Sevak Sangh, Gorkha League, Bolshevik Party, CPI(M), SSP, Revolutionary Socialist Party, SCU, Workers' Party, Forward Bloc (M), and RCPI.
9. President's rule is the term used in India when a state government is dissolved or suspended and is placed under direct federal rule. President's rule is enabled by article 356 of the Constitution of India, which gives the central government the authority to dismiss any state government if there has been failure of the constitutional machinery in the state. President's rule also applies when there is no clear majority to any party or coalition in the state assembly. It is called President's rule as the President of India governs the state instead of an elected chief minister, but administratively the state governor is delegated executive authority on behalf of the central (federal) government. The governor normally appoints advisor(s), who are retired civil servants, to help in administration. Generally the ruling party at the centre controls policies (D.D. Basu 82).

7

STIRRING THE CULTURAL FIRE

Mohawk Filmmaker Shelley Niro's It Starts With a Whisper *and* Suite: INDIAN

AGNES KRAMER-HAMSTRA

Across the [Haudenosaunee] Confederacy, Iroquois women traditionally kept the central fire burning....Today, it is Iroquois artists who tend and sometimes stir our cultural fires, acting as tradition-keepers, story-tellers, innovators and social commentators.
—RYAN RICE, *qtd. in Loft, "Radical Indigeneity"*

On Fire

SHELLEY NIRO'S *It Starts With a Whisper* and *Suite: INDIAN* are grounded in the reality of the Haudenosaunee fire that has literally been kept burning in Ontario since 1784 when the Six Nations came to live along the Grand River in a nation-to-nation relationship with the British. Despite a 200-year-old history of continuing attempts to limit this relationship, Niro's films both record and imagine a cultural space full of movement that translates founding values in contemporary and multilayered ways. Fire aptly describes the movement in Niro's work, in the dynamic she creates through and between the sketches in *Suite: INDIAN* and in the crackling movement that the Matriarchal Aunts bring to their relationship with Shanna in the short feature film *It Starts With a Whisper*. Niro's vision is like a fierce flame as she parodies both Native and non-Native stereotypes and icons, and it manifests itself as playful energy that seeks to gather her own people into disarming laughter.[1]

In this chapter's exploration of how Niro counters the geographic, political, and cultural attempts to displace the Haudenosaunee, besides referring to *It Starts With a Whisper* and *Suite: INDIAN*, I will include brief references to some of her photography and other work. I will describe the movement in Niro's films that constantly interrupts frozen images of First Nations communities as "lyric gestures." Canadian poet and philosopher Jan Zwicky writes, "certainly every lyric gesture is…a song of longing. Longing for what? Wholeness, I think. Integrity. A homecoming, which must feel like remembering—*nostos*, a return—even if we have never been home before.…[a longing for] that communion with the world" ("Lyric" 93, 98). As it disrupts the way fixed images presume to contain and to manage Iroquois culture, the "lyric gestures" that Niro makes in her films are testimony that Haudenosaunee culture is alive and drawing on that fire that has been burning all these years. "Wholeness" and "integrity" are manifested in the lyric gestures Niro makes through her reverence for everyday, contemporary life among Haudenosaunee people. They are expressed through her portrayal of Six Nations women, who reanimate artistic and spiritual traditions in a contemporary context and who remind characters within her film-stories (as well as her audiences) of the ancestors and present guardians who constitute a community around them. Meanwhile, her use of humour and parody create new forms of community among laughing audiences. The movement of these many lyric gestures defies the empty spectacle and the image-making that seeks to "capture" and therefore displace the life of any First Nations culture. And although in these films Niro counters these impositions by describing "a homecoming, which must feel like remembering," her references to tradition are not nostalgic but are lively conversations that take place in the mediums of contemporary culture.

Niro catches the movement and sound of fire in the opening scenes of her two films, *It Starts With a Whisper* (1993) and *Suite: INDIAN* (2005).[2] As Niro's films and these fires show something of the dynamic dialogue that is Iroquois culture, they counter the many public media images that distort Haudenosaunee[3] life by fixing it in a mythic past or a hopeless present. The production of these stereotypes reflects what Sander Gilman identifies as the "catastrophic potential" that has increased "at a pace roughly in step with technological advances in our ability to harm one another" (12). While Gilman speaks of how important the "formal recognition and study of stereotyping" are, the nuanced imaginings that characterize Niro's filmwork and photography go beyond study to directly address and break apart the fixed character of stereotypes in the public sphere. The movement and sound of fire in Niro's films signifies freedom of movement in the face of a legacy that continues its attempt to back the Iroquois Confederacy into an ever-narrower place geographically *and* politically. Even as the land promised to the Haudenosaunee has been steadily whittled away, Niro "tends and stirs the cultural fires."

However, geographical and political displacement cannot be separated from how Six Nations peoples are displaced in the public mind; thus, this chapter focuses on the way contemporary media produces fixed images that obscure First Nations' histories, and cultural traditions and values. Niro's films challenge these images, replacing them with stories that weave, for example, the founding story of the Six Nations through the lives and relationships of fictional characters in contemporary settings. She also offers portraits that show how Six Nations' traditions are part of the dynamic work of present day Six Nations artists and artisans.

Finally, Niro's work takes up some traditional or historical values and either reshapes them or highlights them again.[4]

In his Massey Lecture, "You're Not the Indian I Had in Mind," Thomas King speaks of the history of this attempted management and containment using the example of American photographer Edward Sheriff Curtis. Starting about 1900, Curtis spent thirty years "photographing the Indians of North America...producing some forty thousand negatives, of which more than twenty-two hundred were published" (King, *Truth About Stories* 32). According to King, Curtis's work reflects the American Romanticism of his time, portraying through his images of the Indian the notion that, "while Europeans in the New World were poised on the brink of a new adventure, the Indian was poised on the brink of extinction"; yet, despite, or *because* they perceive "their Indian as dying," they suffuse this notion with a "sense of nobility" (*Truth About Stories* 32–33). "Determined to capture that idea, that image, before it vanished," Curtis travelled from one tribe to another with a box of props: "wigs, blankets, painted backdrops, clothing—in case he ran into Indians who did not look" like his "imaginative construct" (King, *Truth About Stories*, 32, 34). Curtis's portraits were literally still lifes, as their frozen composition hid and/or abstracted First Nations from the layered context of their everyday lives. Blind to the particulars of their *continuing* life as he travelled among them, Curtis himself was "captured" by the popular notion of the "noble, dying Indian." He was unable to see that even as he was "fixing" them with his camera, their lives, though devastated, survived and continued to unfold in specific places.[5]

Before I move into synopses of *It Starts With a Whisper* and *Suite: INDIAN*, I want to introduce the concept of "flipping the gaze" by performing a quick close reading of one of Niro's short experimental films, *Overweight With Crooked Teeth*. In this film, Niro reminds the audience of the constructed frame produced by the camera and that the one who peers through it is framing their subject in a particular way. Images are not neutral. The camera's eye is not objective. *Overweight*, then, provides an important context for Niro's *Suite: INDIAN* and *It Starts With a Whisper* through the main character. Just as he pointedly engages with the camera, bringing it into dialogue and thus refusing to be identified as the object of its gaze, so the characters in Niro's two films are active subjects with agency within the everyday contexts of the films.

"Flipping the Gaze" in *Overweight With Crooked Teeth*[6]

In *Overweight with Crooked Teeth* (1997),[7] written by Michael Doxtater, her brother, Niro reminds the audience of the way the camera and its operator construct its image. In *Overweight*'s opening scene, a man in a three-piece suit (played by Niro's brother) walking along a country road slowly comes into view. Despite the brevity of this film, his approach takes time. When he comes nearer, it becomes obvious that he is headed directly towards both the camera and the person who is framing him through its lens.

Niro focuses on his response to the camera as he refuses to pretend the camera's gaze is neutral or that its operator is invisible. Purposefully striding right up to its "eye" (and its "I"), he "flips" its gaze, asking: "What were you expecting, anyway? Were you expecting Sitting Bull? Chief Joseph of the Nez Perce saying…'the earth and I are one'?" He questions perceptions and images that fix First Nations people within a mythic past. These questions confront the expectations born of a steady diet of reductive images, and it becomes clear that the "you" he addresses is the non-Native viewer. Indeed, by watching his approach and his direct gaze, we ourselves as audience also become conspicuous. Niro will not allow us to remain invisible. Through this man who is "overweight with crooked teeth," she "flips the gaze," countering the eye that selects a single image of "the" Indigenous person, the eye that decides to lift this image from the many, the eye that decides to repeat this one image. Suddenly, a monologue is shaken up with the question: What *"were* [we] *expecting"* anyway?!

From Smoldering Embers to Fireworks in *It Starts With a Whisper*

Despite differences in their subjects and structures, both *It Starts With a Whisper* and *Suite: INDIAN* begin with disconsolate characters grieving losses that threaten to disorient them both personally and culturally. In *It Starts,* a fire is smothered as the main character, seventeen-year-old Shanna recalls the names of the First Nations lost through European invasion, settlement, and colonization: "Tutelo, Nanticoke, Tobacco, Neutral." Walking along the Grand River in traditional clothing, she mourns their loss and does not know which path to follow, or even how to go forward in the wake of such a legacy. In the next scene Shanna is portrayed as an isolated figure walking home from work in an urban setting when suddenly her three Matriarchal Aunts magically appear in technicolour against the bleak cityscape of concrete. Dressed in campy clothes, including rhinestone eyeglasses and lurid colours, these fantastical but very real ancestors have arrived to take Shanna to a honeymoon suite in Niagara Falls for a weekend, which one of the aunts has won in a bingo game. They drive along to Niagara Falls, playing practical jokes on Shanna, who is at first reluctant to join in the fun. Their garb ("Niro garb!" as the filmmaker humorously put it in an interview with Larry Abbott) and their freedom to be silly encourage Shanna to "think for herself." As their banter and singing surround her, they challenge Shanna's assumption that she is alone in facing the legacy of displacement begun by Columbus. Once in the honeymoon suite (complete with a heart-shaped bed), Shanna and the Matriarchal Aunts croon their country and western song of First Nations independence, sashaying through the suite.

> *You said I was lazy, crazy. Took me away from my kind.*
> *Made me speak in gibberish instead of my language.*
> *But you can't control my mind....I'm surviving, I'm thriving.*
> *I'm doing fine without you.*

The aunts and Shanna end their celebration with fireworks at the Falls, and here, at quarter to twelve, December 31, 1992, on the quincentenary of Columbus's stumble into the Carib Islands, Niro fulfills her desire to get in "the last word" (Ryan 247).

In 1991, First Nations artists began to think of how to respond to upcoming quincentenary celebrations, to this beginning that resulted in a long legacy of imposed, mistaken and, degraded identities.[8] Niro dreamt of a response[9] that would "make a full circle instead of being at the end of the line and being dumped on all the time. If we can continue the circle around…then from a spiritual point of view, it'll be a fresh start. We can start over again" (qtd. in Ryan 248–49). And so in the aptly entitled *It Starts With a Whisper*, Niro responds with the whispers that accumulate to become a chorus that strengthens Shanna, signalling that "fresh start" that was Niro's goal.

The whisper—to be strong as a young First Nations woman—comes to Shanna in various forms. It is whimsical, challenging notions of "authentic" solemn ancestors, as it comes through her three aunts. The very real political figure of Cree Elijah Harper (Red Sucker Lake First Nation) also appears to Shanna in a dream/vision. His lone stance represents another kind of whisper, one that has tremendous political and historical resonances. In 1990, his was the only dissenting vote, one that stopped the Meech Lake Accord, a proposed amendment to the Canadian constitution that did not acknowledge the place of Indigenous peoples within the Confederation.[10] On this trip Shanna is reminded that those who have walked this path ahead of her also faced continuous threats of displacement and disorientation. Niro also symbolically represents the whispers through an image sequence that shows many tributaries flowing into what becomes the Niagara River, flowing over the escarpment in the tremendous falls.

In the final scene Shanna and the three aunts hold a ceremony beside the Falls. It ends in fireworks that become stylized images of a turtle and a celestial tree, repeating the beadwork design that was on Shanna's leather leggings when she began her journey. Niro's return to this design is not nostalgic but reminds her characters and her audience of the Haudenosaunee worldview; this design "represents the creation of the world" (Niro, *A Time of Visions*). Niro translates this worldview from the ancient medium of beadwork to contemporary fireworks as Shanna and the three Matriarchal Aunts celebrate "the continuation of life" (Niro, *A Time of Visions*).[11] This final lyric gesture presents a layered "communion with the world," challenging the still life representations of First Nations culture. Niro stirs the smoldering cultural fire into fireworks.[12]

Suite: INDIAN: **The Movement of Creativity and Consolation, of Fire and Dance**

A shadow cast by interior fire on the hide wall of a lodge introduces *Suite: INDIAN*'s opening scene, which recalls the consolation that shaped the founding of the Six Nations. The Peacemaker comforts Hiawatha after finding him in self-imposed exile, mourning the death of his two daughters. As he wipes away Hiawatha's tears and touches Hiawatha's wampum (beads) to his forehead, a voice-over explains that "Haudenosaunee life began in the need for creativity." Niro begins *Suite: INDIAN* by making a vital connection between consolation and the creativity that open up options for peacemaking in the face of pain, hatred, and bitterness. In this opening scene Niro recalls the Peacemaker's "offer to pull from the older man the grief which had frozen his thinking and plunged him into despair," and through carefully listening to and addressing Hiawatha's grief, eventually the Peacemaker "brings Hiawatha...to a place of hope" (Mohawk xviii).[13]

According to Taiaiake Alfred, founding Director of the University of Victoria's School of Indigenous Governance, the "heart" of the condolence ceremony has to do with "requickening...bringing something back to life" and includes "gestures" that "pacify those people [who]...are in pain" (Alfred, *Peace* 18). Alfred understands this condolence is of primary importance for establishing good governance because when people are in pain "they can't see properly; they can't hear; and they don't speak the truth. Something serious has happened to them, and the challenge for the strong-minded, the peace-makers, is to....give them something that will make them capable of seeing, hearing, and speaking their way back to peace" (*Peace* 18). Consolation and creativity are closely linked both personally and in the public square. According to Alfred, if Hiawatha, through the condolence that the Peacemaker brings, "can set aside [the] hatred and revenge" that fill him after those two killings that "become a blood feud," a way is opened for peace, not only within Hiawatha but also between enemies (*Peace* 129). And so Niro's opening to *Suite: INDIAN* powerfully recalls a vitally important part of the larger and founding story of the Six Nations: how Hiawatha and the Peacemaker work to help five[14] warring First Nations slowly form a strong alliance, which becomes the "oldest continuously running democratic government in the world" (Coleman, "Imposing" 11–12).[15] The constant action of peacemaking that grounds this particular democracy provides a dynamic legacy. It testifies to the inner strength that was forged in the resolve of the five nations to work together towards unity: the desire to solve problems through diplomacy, good words, good-mindedness (Monture). In this opening and through this connection between consolation and good governance, Niro makes a lyric gesture towards this founding story.

Suite: INDIAN is made up of ten unrelated stories and segements of eight to ten minutes each. Together they suggest the movement of music and reveal Niro's pun on *suite*—sweet. These sketches embody the movement of Six Nations culture: the dynamic of tradition in everyday life circa 2005. Niro responds, through the movement between and within each of these stories and segments, to the rigid stereotypes that she herself signals by her use of "Indian" in the title. *Suite: INDIAN* highlights many kinds of creativity and consolation and ends with the final four movements, contemporary experimental dance pieces by award-winning Mohawk choreographer Santee Smith. The first two of these dances emphasize consolation and are set in the longhouse. "Living with Fire" suggests a woman labouring to give birth, while "From the Ashes" switches between shots of dancers arriving for practice in their everyday dress, shots of the Grand River, and shots of a male and a female dancer again in the longhouse. *Suite: INDIAN* ends with "Dance of the Canoe Pants" and "The Red Army is the Strongest," and in these Niro breaks into hilarity. In an exaggerated parody, Niro juxtaposes wildly different elements. A group of Six Nations dancers in "war paint" and clownish costume move to the oom-pah-pah rhythm of marching band music as well as to the Russian Army Chorus as they are filmed by turns in a hall and along the banks of the Grand River.

In one of the first segments of *Suite: INDIAN*, Niro's camera respectfully documents the movements of their faces and hands as six Haudenosaunee artisans design and create cornbread, a wampum belt, exquisite beadwork, a cornhusk doll, a stone carving, and moccasins. Each person is identified by name as they bend over their work, and eventually each one responds to the person filming them when they show their completed project. Niro's pointed focus in *Overweight* echoes through this segment; there is a dialogue between the one who films them and the artisans, as well as between the artisans and their work. The honour given the process of their labour is apparent not only in the way the camera slowly pans across their hands, faces, and work but also in the underlying soundscape of a solo cello. Niro's portrayal of their work demonstrates great respect for the creative processes as well as for the objects and highlights their enduring cultural and symbolic value.

The beaded headdress and the moccasins reappear in the following movement of *Suite: INDIAN*, "Mars Thunderchild Gets a Calling." At the beginning of this segment, while Mars

Thunderchild sleeps, the camera moves around her room revealing a context in which this traditional dress and a photo of Sitting Bull seem like memorabilia, irrelevant relics. However, despite the pop culture setting of this preppy college-age woman's bedroom, Niro troubles the disconnection between Mars's way of life and these traditional objects and historical figures that have become relics. Niro creates a fusion so that when Sitting Bull appears to Mars Thunderchild in a dream, she acknowledges him, variously calling him "S.B." or "Mr. Bull." When he comes calling, first over the telephone, then by knocking at her door, he challenges the narrow parameters of the consumer culture and materialism that Mars appears to be living within, calling her to a deeper purpose that begins with a reverence and wonder for the created world. The respect he challenges her to is *both* a return to a foundational value of Haudenosaunee culture and something that Mars will need to translate in a way that is contemporary to her world. The movement between past, present, and future in this and other sketches includes the dialogue between cultures and the fusions that are especially evident in Niro's use of Native music, classical cello pieces, and country and western songs in *Suite: INDIAN*.

"Home," one of the middle movements in *Suite: INDIAN*, is set in the city of Brantford's Victoria Park and complicates Niro's portrayal of the continuum of Iroquois culture. This movement follows a homeless Haudenosaunee young woman for a day and highlights the tension of "the painful paradox of living in a town named after a Mohawk (Joseph Brant) where contemporary Haudenosaunee 'feel that they are the intruders and quietly exist, never really claiming the identity that made it possible for others to share the space'" (Niro qtd. in Higginson 179). The Chicago Blackhawks hockey shirt that the main character wears also signals the history of appropriations. This hockey team uses the name of the Black Hawks, who were driven from the area now known as Illinois when, in three short years (1845–1848), the American state doubled its territory through expropriating land from First Nations

(Powell 12). The main character and her friends sleep in the shadow of a monumental statue of Joseph Brant. At the end of the day, in the dark, this young woman walks back into the park carrying a flame to her companions there, recalling the central role of the fire-keeper at the cultural heart or hearth of the Haudenosaunee. In this segment Niro asks, "Do we care for one another?" repeating the same question that sparked the beginning of the Iroquois Confederacy.

> I see the foundation as being made up of individuals weakened by sickness and disease. Survivors...had to know their limits and realize that if they were to thrive in the face of adversity they had to join forces and help each other in that fight. That is where the strength of community lies—coming together, giving thanks, contributing—that is the seed that holds people together. Otherwise people starve [as they]...just focus on things. (Niro, Guest Lecture)

Although the camera includes the light of a full moon that seems to breathe peace over the homeless Six Nations young people, Niro maintains an uneasy and necessary tension in the closing scene of "Home." Even as they continue to experience displacement, they have a home under this moon, and the fire that the young woman brings to the group recalls this seed that "holds people together," signalling the continuous life of both the earth and the Haudenosaunee.

A Ubiquitous Image: The Masked Mohawk Warrior Context

Almost 100 years after Edward Curtis's fixed construction of "the Indian [he] had in mind," the stereotype continues, this time changing from a romanticized image to one couched in hopelessness. In *It Starts With A Whisper*, Shanna speaks of the overwhelmingly negative images of First Nations people that are repeatedly broadcast by the news media: "so self-destructive.

Suicide. Alcohol. Drugs." After the 1990 summer events at Oka, Quebec, these and other media images are part of what Niro was responding to when she began to write *It Starts*. It was at Oka that the Mohawk of Kanehsatake stood their ground over a small area called the Pines, which the town council of Oka planned to make into a nine-hole addition to a local golf club. This planned expropriation reflected the history of how the lands of this area had been coercively exchanged between the English and the French for centuries, in violation of treaty agreements. The Mohawk of Kanehsatake united to resist the town council's action to take over this traditional burial grounds and the place where they have gathered medicines for generations.

One of the ways the non-Native media contained and managed all that was happening at Oka was through one particular image: a masked Mohawk warrior. Used repeatedly, this image became a reductive symbol of the struggle over this land for non-Native viewers. This image was not "worth a thousand words," as the saying goes; rather, it was a monologue that silenced all other voices. This image erased how the federal and provincial governments had ignored distinct differences between European and First Nations' worldviews for over 100 years. The image of the masked Mohawk warrior erased the lengths to which the government would go to hold onto its own view of land and ownership. This image hid the fact that even as negotiations were being held, the federal government was increasing its armed presence at Oka to 2,600 Canadian soldiers.

Especially in the context of the way Niro's work plays on portrayals of the tradition of the "noble warrior" image and her respectful portrayals of Six Nations women and their role in Haudenosaunee culture, it is important to note that this ubiquitous image of the masked Mohawk warrior obscured the leadership that Kanehsatake women gave in the struggle. Standing their ground as tanks and tear gas and other weapons of intimidation surrounded them, these women led the Mohawk presence on the front lines. They stood firm because the rifles aimed at them made them "more mad than afraid" (*Kanehsatake*).[16]

The Warrior Unmasked: From Spectacle to the Everyday

Although he is speaking from a disparate political context (the way media worked in South Africa to deepen displacement during the apartheid regime) South African writer Njabulo Ndebele's description of how a "spectacle" is created and how it works resonates with the repetition of the image of the masked warrior in news coverage of Oka. The repetition of this image created a "vast sense of presence without offering intimate knowledge" (49–50). This "vast sense of presence" that spectacle produces, he writes, is "demonstrative, preferring exteriority to interiority," and it effectively erases historical context, setting up a tyranny of the moment. Such images—along with another of spectacle's many tools, the sound byte of the thirty-second "news"—makes respectful dialogue impossible. The public character of this exteriority negates the layered particularities, such as the examples listed above from the context of the Mohawk's struggle at Oka. The spectacle displaces, in the public mind, the everyday life of the people as it continues on this piece of land: that richly layered context that Ndebele calls the "ordinary" and which Niro's filmwork creates as the "everyday."

Niro's portrayal of the everyday is multilayered. It includes, for example, her choice to cast her sisters in the role of the Matriarchal Aunts in *It Starts With a Whisper* as well as in the photographic series *Mohawks in Beehives*. Of this choice she says: "I began using my family in my work [because] these familiar images are the common images I live with [and] the more images you see of somebody that looks like you the more you accept yourself" (*Time of Visions*). These subjects are women by whom her Haudenosaunee audiences have felt welcomed because "they can see their own aunts or their sisters in these images" (Niro, *Time of Visions*).

In choosing the women in her family as subjects and characters, Niro recalls many things. For one, in the Matriarchal Aunts she is recalling the role of clan mothers in the ancient governance practice of the Iroquois Confederacy, a practice that is ongoing. As noted earlier, it was the clan mothers, not warriors, who decided it was time to stand their ground as their land was threatened; their decision began their challenge both at Oka, Quebec in 1990 and in Caledonia, Ontario in February 2006.

In these and other portrayals Niro also imagines a Mohawk nationhood guarded by women who make their protective stance flexible rather than fixed. For example, Niro features her mother under a hairdryer in her sister's kitchen in a photograph whose title plays on anthropological language: "The Iroquois is a Highly Developed Matriarchal Society." This title, she notes, "sounds so serious, and I sometimes think some people start believing these things they hear and…that they have to be so stiff. It *is* a matriarchal society, but you can loosen it up a bit too. And it comes from your mum" (qtd. in Ryan 66). When Niro was beginning her work, it was not only the images of "heroes and warriors" that were abstract from the culture she knew, but First Nations women also were being portrayed as "humourless depictions of nubile princess, nurturing earth mother, sultry vixen, and servile squaw," images that "have long been fixed in the popular imagination" (Ryan 62). Niro's camera counteracts these portrayals by depicting particular women who, while they assume leadership positions in a traditionally matriarchal society, re-envision what that leadership means. Niro's approach is a sometimes playful counternarrative to the posture of leadership that is motivated by fear, greed, or defensiveness. This counter-narrative parallels the approach of Ellen Gabriel, one of the clan mothers at the front lines during the 1990 summer at the Pines, who explains that in the Mohawk language "warrior" signifies "one who bears the burden of peace" (*Keepers of the Fire*). One posture suggests a leadership in the throes of a constant power struggle where one seeks to lord it over another, while the other seems based on a perspective propelled by a desire for peace based on justice, a peace within which a people have the opportunity to flourish. By creating various "Matriarchs" who "bear the burden of peace" in ordinary, everyday ways, Niro counters the hollowness of spectacular images with a nuanced portrayal of commitment.

The ordinary or everyday that is inherent in Niro's work is a force to be reckoned with. In another response to Oka that provides "a personal and collective antidote to the numerous images of Mohawk warriors and of women and children under siege," Niro created the photograph "Portrait of the Artist Sitting with a Killer Surrounded by French Curves" (Ryan 72).[17] In the hand-tinted black-and-white photograph, she is lounging with her sisters on hot pink cushions; the cigarette in her hand is the "killer," and its smoke curves up around Niro's head as all four sisters directly face the camera, two of them wearing sunglasses. This photograph makes a powerful gesture as it "flips the gaze" on the posturing of the Canadian military and all levels of government at Oka. The "stance" of the women in this portrait recodes the "killer," as it plays on James Joyce's famous title, makes the "artist" central, and surrounds her with the "French curves." Niro adapts the black and white of the photograph by using hot pink and red to carefully highlight the cigarette smoke, the women's lips, their shoes, and the cushions. The "killer" and its resulting smoke are subtle compared to the "French curves," which contrast "idealized notions of (white) femininity with familial images of Native reality" (Ryan 77). These women are also leaders, but this portrait suggests their interpretation of leadership is formed by knowledge that is collective. Leadership is indeed shared in the context of being sisters or "mums" who are matriarchs in a society based on clans. (However, these clans are not necessarily organized in a familial way.) The pillows in "Portrait of the Artist Sitting With a Killer Surrounded by French Curves" suggest the lounging women are here to stay and are fierce (hot pink) in their identification with the relationships of their clan. Through them, Niro confronts the viewer with a strong force that cannot be ignored.

Lyric Gestures: Disarming Humour and Parody

Using a kind of humour that eschews cynicism and that ranges from slapstick to subtle and biting wit, Niro creates an intimacy that draws people in. Of her own audience, clan and community, Niro says: "to take the time to make people laugh comes from the core feeling of love and community" (*Honey Moccasin*). In the context of the familiarity and trust that grounds one's own community, one can also afford to call another "overweight with crooked teeth." The Matriarchal Aunts in *It Starts With a Whisper* act as guardian angels; they carry Shanna along with their practical jokes, outrageous outfits, and tacky Niagara Falls honeymoon tourism.

This humour has "teeth" for her non-Native audience, as Niro juxtaposes this backdrop of Niagara Falls with the Columbus quincentenary. When she is dealing with the issue of the ongoing devastation of Native communities, Niro realizes that her work has the potential to "turn a lot of people off, and so," she says, "you have to bring them a little bit closer to make them want to listen. I think that is where humour comes in. It pulls them in a little bit and gets them to wait for the punchline" (*Time of Vision*). Using the honeymoon capital as her setting highlights that there was never a "honeymoon"; the tackiness of the setting recalls the betrayals of trust. The touristy consumerism that characterizes much of the area around Niagara Falls recalls the trap that many treaties evolved into as they were re-interpreted in subsequent years in ways that put commerce before respect and justice. Niro's humour disarms before its bite is felt.

While *It Starts* refers to the way Elijah Harper called attention to the force of political denial that was inherent in the Meech Lake Accord, Niro highlights the way certain images are another form of denial and injustice; she does this through laughter and playfulness. For example, she uses parody to disarm the power of stereotypes about both Native and non-Native communities, imitating them through exaggeration and/or by putting them in new contexts. The final two movements of Niro's *Suite: INDIAN* are full of such exaggerated over-the-top imitations.

In "Dance of the Canoe Pants" and "The Red Army is the Strongest" the dancers are each wearing "canoe pants" reminiscent of Disney costumes. Made of fabric, the bow and stern of each canoe puffs out behind and in front of the dancer. The dancers are sitting in their canoes, which are the size of shorts, and the effect of these stuffed fabric canoes is hilarious as they get in the way of their "war dance," complete with fake hatchets raised. In "The Red Army is the Strongest,"[18] the same dancers in their canoe pants mock-march to the music of the former USSR's Red Army Chorus in a wild juxtaposition that adds another layer to this send-up of the warrior stereotype. This chorus's music was used to lift the spirits of the flagging armies on the Russian front. Niro evokes laughter even as in this scene she calls her own "red army" to be strong on what are still "front lines."

In "Modern Parody and Bakhtin," Linda Hutcheon contests the idea that parody is simply ridicule and demonstrates that it involves imitation in many registers: "Even in mocking, parody reinforces; in formal terms, it inscribes the mocked conventions onto itself....and is the custodian of artistic legacy, defining not only where art is, but where it has come from" (Hutcheon 100). In these dances Niro's parody layers "creative imitation" with a context that mixes "filial rejection with respect," illustrated for example, by her representation of the warrior in *Suite*'s final dances (Hutcheon 91).

Parody also gives Niro a vehicle to explore the dynamic of past/present/future. She takes conventional representations of Haudenosaunee culture, like the canoe, as well as objects often portrayed as relics and sets them in new contexts, "revising, replaying and inverting" them to see and hear if and how they will resonate (Hutcheon 92). For example, the moccasins and beadwork headdress exquisitely crafted in the early movement of *Suite: INDIAN* appear in an entirely different context in Mars Thunderchild's bedroom. Within this story of how Sitting Bull comes calling, they are recoded not in terms of "nostalgic imitation of past models" but in terms of how narrow Thunderchild's vision has become (Hutcheon 90). Sitting Bull's call to Mars Thunderchild is not *back* to some mythic past but forward into a context larger than materialism. In this sense, in the context of Sitting Bull's call, the parodic form of imitation (i.e., the moccasins and head dress) here is not made "at the expense of the parodied text" but is a recoding: from a nostalgic stance to the challenge of reinterpreting foundational Haudenosaunee values in the context of contemporary culture (Hutcheon 88). Niro also "replays" the almost stereotypical figure that Sitting Bull has become, as one of the most widely known historical figures (along with, for instance, Geronimo) in pop culture. Sitting Bull, a Lakota, becomes Niro's choice over less widely known Haudenosaunee leaders such as Levi General (Deskaheh), who went to the League of Nations in 1923 to appeal for Six Nations recognition as an independent nation (Coleman, "Imposing" 10–11). In choosing a pop culture figure of Native authenticity/leadership/resistance, Niro animates this framed trophy into a living, vital figure when he comes calling through the dream sequence.

Towards Wonder and Spirituality

This chapter identifies spirituality with the lyric gesture that Zwicky describes as "a song of longing…for wholeness…integrity…a homecoming" ("Lyric" 93, 98). In *Wasáse: Indigenous Pathways of Action and Freedom*, Alfred calls First Nations to nothing short of a spiritual revolution in response to the West's rampant consumerism with its appeals to human greed. His call is not only to Native communities; the devastation and displacement that this consumption wreaks on humans and the environment is a signal that spiritual renewal is needed in both Native and non-Native communities.

The "song of longing" that permeates Niro's work suggests that "wholeness, integrity and homecoming" have to do with a return to respect for relationships, both with the rest of creation and with the relationships inherent in the shape of Haudenosaunee governance through clans. Niro manifests this respect in many ways in her work. Indeed, it begins with wonder. *It Starts With a Whisper* and *Suite: INDIAN* go beyond recalling the tradition of the Six Nations, its founding story, history, and the ethos that Niro links with Haudenosaunee creativity. Haudenosaunee creativity points to a spirituality that calls one to imagine and to be part of a much larger world. This largeness has to do not only with one's place in creation but with one's place in community, a place that includes being part of the generations. Often, in these two films, an older generation appears to walk alongside a younger one. Elijah Harper appears to Shanna in *It Starts*; Sitting Bull appears to Mars Thunderchild in *Suite*. Indeed, Niro is behind these sketches, implicitly calling to a younger generation and giving them a sense of being part of a living tradition.

In this way, Niro's work recalls Swan Lake Alberta Cree, Ray Aldred's description of the worldview implicit in First Nations' oral traditions. This description, as it critiques the Enlightenment notion of a human originator who assumes that truth is individually gained, carries important wisdom for communities shaped by other spiritual traditions.

> *Another proper ethic among storytellers is that they do not "know" a story but they "understand" something. The difference between these two words being...that knowing something meant that one had originated the idea. Thus, the person who said "I know" was displaying arrogance because they assumed that wisdom had begun with them. On the other hand the person who said, "I understand" was acknowledging that wisdom was something that flowed from the Creator and they were merely entering into a "river of understanding" as it*

> *were. So then, a storyteller may exercise creativity but the story is in control, not the storyteller. (Aldred)*

Being part of something bigger than oneself has to do with identity that does not focus on the individual but that is understood by the Aboriginal people to include those who have come before and those who will come after. This is illustrated by "praying for one's grandchildren, even before there are any grandchildren...This expanded view of identity is an alternative to the modern autonomous individual" (Aldred). Aldred's articulation of Indigenous spirituality flies in the face of and provides a radical alternative to Western notions of the atomistic individual as well as a view of human rights that erases the context of communally held values. Since freedom in the West is equated with being autonomous, what is assumed in this interpretation of spirituality provides a powerful counter-narrative: communion as an intrinsic part of being human, and freedom as a freedom to be responsible within one's relationships.

This perspective is implicit in Niro's work. In the opening sequence of *Suite: INDIAN*, Niro recalls Hiawatha's recruitment to the way of the Good Mind through the consolation that the Peacemaker brings him. Niro's retelling of the condolence given by the Peacemaker, the vital role of the Matriarchal Aunts in *It Starts*, the connections that the young Six Nations homeless woman maintains despite being radically displaced—these all implicitly signal the perspective that each person is part of a larger community of meaning and purpose. Niro's image of the tributaries that are gathered into and become the powerful river that plunges spectacularly over Niagara Falls suggests that this larger communion is a thing of wonder and great power. In turn, this wonder counters the stereotypes that displace as they flatten and gloss over the deep value that community holds in the Haudenosaunee worldview.

While each of the tributaries in *It Starts* can be read to signify the generations who continue Haudenosaunee history in a specific place, these tributaries also speak of the wonder of creation and the Creator. Aldred writes that those "telling the story...do not just speak for themselves. They are speaking as representative of *something bigger than themselves*" (5, emphasis added). This foundational sense, of being a part of "something bigger than themselves" that includes a much larger mystery—that of being a part of the life that shapes and sustains the earth—is implicit in Aldred's discussion of oral tradition and explicit in Niro's "Mars Thunderchild" movement in *Suite: INDIAN*.

Although in *Overweight with Crooked Teeth*, the man in the three-piece suit is *not* Sitting Bull, not the expected, not the "Indian you had in mind," Sitting Bull *does* appear in "Mars"—first in the photograph framed on her bedroom wall. There it sits, or he sits, Niro seems to suggest, along with Mars's trophies, in this thoroughly modern context. This is the Western modern secular tradition that Jacqui Alexander says divorces "the sacred" from tradition (296). She elaborates that this "secularism renders the Sacred as tradition, but it is also that tradition...is always made to reside elsewhere and denied entry into the modern" (296). Besides recalling the discussion earlier that traced how media images "fix" First Nations' cultures and traditions, what Alexander is saying here is that the Western mindset also fixes the sacred into a still life, rendering its influence stillborn. Ancestors for Mars Thunderchild seem to have the status of relics and carry no weight in terms of an ethos or value. However, Sitting Bull steps out of this frame. He brings substance as he calls Mars in another of the dreams/visions that Niro weaves seamlessly through her films. When Sitting Bull appears, he ignores Mars's attempts to connect with her tradition through her half-hearted attention to her weekly Mohawk language immersion class, for example. Rather, by suggesting that she "is just fooling around with [her] Indian identity," he challenges the values of the material culture that have begun to permeate her life, a challenge similar to the one issued by Alfred.

Sitting Bull calls Mars Thunderchild to a deeper purpose. He calls her through wonder, offering her a new perspective of the world as a gift. In her dream he stands at her door with a glittering "world" in his hands, and he offers her this world when she marvels at its beauty. She barely dares to hold it and tucks it under her pillow. The next morning, however, when she slowly wakes and recalls the dream, she carefully approaches her pillow and finds "the world" is still there. Her response in the scene is one of thanksgiving for the perspective that had come to her so profoundly in her dream/vision: that all of the life that makes up creation, which includes her own life, is presented to her as a gift. This wonder leads Mars into a sense of responsibility: to wrestle with what it means to live in respect for this world and all of the relationships that make up its life. In this movement of *Suite: INDIAN*, Niro suggests that humans cannot account for, manage, or contain the goodness and the wonder of creation.

Niro works with this sense of a larger world in another way as well. The "world" that Sitting Bull presents to Mars is in the form of a mirror ball, inserted in the middle of what looks like a war club or a mace, blending a tacky disco object with traditional-looking Native gear. This glittering world is from unauthentic pop disco culture, much like the heart-shaped bed in the Niagara Falls honeymoon suite in *It Starts With a Whisper*. Niro insists that wonder and respect can be regenerated even in relation to these campy, degraded items from consumer culture. Traditional values are consistently reached through these kitschy objects.

▶ *It Starts With a Whisper* begins with the smothering of a fire and it ends with fireworks that signify a (very modern) continuation of Haudenosaunee life, recalling George McMaster's words that "symbolically, fire's energy represents regeneration....In Iroquoian speeches, fire metaphors—such as: 'Quicken the fire' or 'partake of the warmth of the fire'—are basic to government and peace" (14).

In Niro's depiction, Shanna experiences this regeneration as she becomes aware, through the "lyric gestures" of her aunts, of Elijah Harper, and of the wonder of the falls, that she is not alone. All of these moments counter the displacement Shanna has experienced with the powerful message that she belongs to a vital community. This community includes not only those who came before her, but also the clownish matriarchs and the elders who are presently working with the welfare of the future seventh generation in mind.

In *Suite: INDIAN* the fire that is implied in the opening becomes the cultural fire that Niro helps to stir through *Suite*'s movements, until she imagines it crackling into the exuberant laughter that the final two stylized dances evoke. Countering the displacement that freezes First Nations into a fixed past, Niro's wide-angle lens presents the rich context of the continuing history and culture of Haudenosaunee people. She plays with the expectation of a mythic aura around "authentic" First Nations values ("What did you expect? The earth and I are one?"), insisting that the foundational value of respect can be communicated through the medium of pop culture. Niro displaces the gaze that tries to freeze-frame the dynamic of Haudenosaunee life by showing the layered movements that make up the everyday life of her characters in dialogue with Haudenosaunee tradition and consumer and pop culture. As Audra Simpson says:

> Because [her] work is historical, political, and playful [it] serves as precious windows on our worlds, worlds that are finally envisioned by us, and windows that have finally been made by us. At the same time, her works serve as vehicles for Iroquois to contemplate each other, to laugh, to find resonance in these images, and in doing so, to remove us from the domain of history and give us a past and a present that is all of our own. (5)

Niro's eye counters displacement's reductive gaze, catching all the life that moves through and beyond the narrow parameters that displacement attempts to set around Haudenosaunee life. The play of her camera work and her narratives bring consolation through the space that her imagination opens up as she invites her characters and her First Nations audience to ever greater freedom of movement.

NOTES

1. In *The Trickster Shift: Humour and Irony in Contemporary Native Art*, Allan Ryan notes: "Niro is not alone in viewing humour as a means of survival. Aboriginal peoples have employed humour's preservative power for a long time" (72).
2. *It Starts With a Whisper* was co-directed with Anna Gronau.
3. Literally, People of the Longhouse, the Haudenosaunee/ Rotinohshonni are also known as the Six Nations (Alfred, *Peace* 125). Taiaiake Alfred identifies how displacement is also manifested through reduction of language: "Today we recognize the significance and symbolic value of terminology and the use of our own recovered languages is important not only for the purposes of communication but as a symbol of our survival....As Native people... relearning the languages stripped from us in the past, we are coming to realize the gross insult of most common 'Indian' names....The struggle to break the bonds placed on our minds and spirits by derogatory or ignorant labels is ongoing" (*Peace* 23).
4. Catherine Higginson explores, for example, Niro's reinterpretation of sovereignty by comparing Niro's 1991 photographic series "Mohawks in Beehives" to Mohawk Pauline Johnson's poem "Ode." Higginson writes, "The strength that Johnson attributed to the Queen, Niro gives to her sisters—shifting the Loyalist focus to a familial one and nudging the sovereigntist fraternal analogy with a prioritizing of the *sister*hood instead" (170).
5. Sander Gilman notes that texts such as Curtis's photographs "provide a very good basis for analyzing the historical forces at work in the shaping of stereotypes" ("Preface," *Difference* 11). Indeed, King argues that Curtis's work underscored the milieu or spirits at work in the literary "American Romantic Period" with its "emphasis on feeling, its interest in nature, its fascination with exoticism, mysticism and eroticism, and its preoccupation with the glorification of the past" (33).
6. "Flipping the gaze" is Armand Ruffo's expression and it builds on Franz Fanon's exploration of the gaze that works to only ever colonize another (Indigenous Studies Lecture, Fall 2007, McMaster University). For a

discussion of stereotype, voyeurism, and surveillance that especially engages the work of Franz Fanon and Edward Said, see Homi Bhabha's "The Other Question: Stereotype, Discrimination and the Discourse of Colonialism" in *The Location of Culture*.

7. This film's title is characteristic of Niro's ongoing humorous engagement with the glossed exteriority of the "ideal" human figure that is the stock in trade of many mass media images.

8. The peoples of the Carib Islands were mistaken for people of India, hence the name "Indian," which painted the immense variety of First Nations cultures in the Americas with the same brushstroke. Those cultures judged to be nomadic were popularly seen as uncivilized beside European settlers. In his work on the subject, J. Edward Chamberlin offers a clear-eyed critique of the very categories of "the settler" and "the nomad": "Think about it. Aborigines who know the names of every plant and the location of all the water holes, as perpetual nomads...we call Them wanderers? Europeans in a place ten thousand miles from home, as settlers?...It's hard to imagine a more cockeyed set of categories" (*If This is Your Land* 30).

9. Niro initially dreamt that "we take a plane to Spain....And then we'll climb up the rock of Gibraltar and have our little flag and plant it on the top of the mountain and claim Spain in the name of Elijah Harper...or whoever else is the 'King of Indians' at the time. Do that and [get] Indian organizations to give us something to bury in a time capsule....[I]t will be really symbolic... [because] we really don't want Spain...or anything else. We really don't want anybody else's continent" (Ryan 248–49).

10. In her book, *Canada's First Nations: A History of Founding Peoples from the Earliest Times* (3rd ed., 2002), Olive Dickason includes a discussion of Elijah Harper's role in the Meech Lake Accord. For coverage of the Meech Lake constitutional talks as they happened, see CBC, http://archives.cbc.ca/society/native_issues/clips/6496/.

11. Another layer in Niro's desire to put in a "last word" is realized in the venue of the film's New Year's premiere: the Six Nation's Iroquois Lodge—a senior citizen's home. The subject of the film—a young woman coming to realize she walks in solidarity with her ancestors—and the place of the first viewing aptly embody Nero's hope to "continue the circle around or take it back" (Ryan 249).

12. *It Starts With a Whisper* also signalled another beginning as "one of the first films broadcast on the newly created Women's Television Network cable channel, which went on the air in Canada in early 1995" (Ryan 252 n.76).

13. This encounter "provides the model for the condolence practices in the installation of leaders and provides some of the process by which peace treaties were to be conducted in this part of the world for a long time" (Mohawk xviii). In *Peace, Power and Righteousness*, Taiaiake Alfred shows how this founding relationship remains vital to Haudenosaunee governance and how the practice of the condolence ceremony is a gift that the Confederacy is able to offer other cultures whose political models do not take reconciliation into account.
14. The Tuscaroras joined the original The Five Nations—Onondaga, Mohawks, Oneidas, Cayugas, and Senecas—to make up the Six Nations of the Iroquois Confederacy.
15. In recalling the Peacemaker's role as he attends Hiawatha in his grief and despair, bringing him "eventually to a place of hope," the Peacemaker "defined righteousness as the result of the best thinking of collective minds operating from principles which assume that a sane world requires that we provide a safe environment for our children seven generations into the future" (Wallace xx).
16. The world's attention on Oka and the support sent by First Nations from all over North America, as well as the formation of a peace camp, were also minimized by the image of the masked Mohawk warrior.
17. A part of the series *Mohawks in Beehives*.
18. The five dance sequences that make up the last movements of *Suite: INDIAN* were choreographed by Santee Smith.

8

CREATIVITY AS A FORM OF RESILIENCE IN FORCED MIGRATION

MAROUSSIA HAJDUKOWSKI-AHMED

> *The oppressed are victims of social injustice; their significance, however, does not reside in the fact of their victimisation, but in the possibility that their agency will transform their lived relations.*
> —PETER HITCHCOCK, Dialogics of the Oppressed

THE IMPACT of globalization on self and identity is a crucial contemporary issue, and the processes involved in the negotiation of self and identity in the context of globalization are intensely dialogical. This is even more the case with refugees whose experience of forced displacement obliges them to confront new contexts and new voices and locates them in a constant "in-between" subject position. Despite increasing awareness of the complexities of subjectivity and of the roles that culture and gender play in shaping refugees' subject positions, a medicalized trauma discourse that identifies refugees as victims, prevails in popular understandings of refugee experience. This chapter uses three qualitative research projects involving refugee women who have experienced forced migration to bring the medical trauma discourse of refugee as victim into dialogical interface with a psychosocial approach, one whose participatory counselling and therapy emphasizes the agency and resilience of refugees identified as survivors.

Bringing together experiential knowledge gained in these research projects, recent developments in research on the dialogical self, and theories of resilience,[1] this chapter will focus on women refugees' creativity as expressions of resilience. Creativity as a form of resistance among women refugees, I will show, is shaped by refugees' past experience, gender, and culture. In the course of my analysis, it will also become apparent that creativity is a form of resilience that is conducive to refugees' well-being. Creativity also contributes to the enrichment of art and culture and to participatory democracy in the host society. To indicate that theory and experience are mutually dependent, this chapter will take the shape of a contrapuntal interface between my experiences in participatory action research (PAR), the voices of refugee women who participated in various PAR projects, and theoretical considerations. As the PAR methodology tends to blur the dividing lines between researchers and participants, making them into co-learners, when a collective first person plural (we-us-our) is used in this chapter, it intentionally reflects this common agency.

Research Projects with Refugee Women: Experiential and Theoretical Context

> *It is in exactly such marginal groups [survivors] that we find people of highly developed consciousness, who have been able to exploit their situation to develop new thinking and artistic creativity...That position on the "edge" also provides for insight that can transcend boundaries.*
> —INGER AGGER, *The Blue Room: Trauma and Testimony Among Refugee Women*

My interest in the resilience of refugee women originates in experience I acquired in three qualitative research projects with refugee women. These projects were informed by a dialogical approach to identity and its corollary, namely an ethics and a politics of recognition. The first research project, entitled "Healing from Torture" (2000), on which I was the principal investigator, involved seven refugee women survivors of torture from Iran, Cambodia, Bosnia, Siberia, Argentina, and Chile. Living in Hamilton, Ontario, at the time of the research, they participated in the project on a regular basis from 1994 to 1997. The respondents came from different religious backgrounds, including Muslim, Jewish, Buddhist, and Bahai. They were tortured because of religious affiliations, social and political activism, and union activism (Hajdukowski-Ahmed et al., "Healing" 20). Our qualitative approach included focus groups and in-depth interviews in safe spaces during times chosen by the participants. Refugee participants shared knowledge on issues they faced, such as loss of trust in people, isolation, Post-Traumatic Stress Disorder (PTSD) symptoms, and self-splitting.[2] They identified spirituality, hope, and community (re)building as factors that shaped their resilience. Trust-building was an essential component of the research process because of the nature of the trauma, which "in some measure occurred with the intent purpose of destroying trust in human relationships and personal integration" (Hajdukowski-Ahmed et al., "Healing" 20). Discussion of the torture itself was not perceived as desirable or helpful to the participants, who preferred to focus on aspects of their own healing from torture. Communication between the women and between the researchers and the women also occurred indirectly through creative activities. Hence, there was sharing without confession, and the women enjoyed being productive. The articulation of a structured goal and end-product to these sessions gave the participants a sense of achievement (Hajdukowski-Ahmed et al., "Healing" 48). The group decided to conduct concrete activities, each with specific but overlapping goals: mask making aimed to reconnect participants with themselves; refugee women chose knitting as a way to bring together individuals from different generations and both genders;[3] bread making and herb planting endeavoured to help the women reconnect with elemental forces; and participating in the Canadian celebration of the Thanksgiving holiday sought to connect them with their new community.

The second project, "Saying 'I,'" was conducted in spring 2003 over a period of several weeks at the Workers Arts and Heritage Centre (WAHC), a community development organization based in Hamilton, Ontario. In collaboration with a wide range of partners, WAHC explores issues of race, class, gender, and homelessness through creative expressions to preserve the history and enrich and disseminate the culture of working class people in Canada. Financially supported by Status of Women Canada and the Ontario Arts Council, WAHC organized workshops with refugee women under the guidance of a professional lead artist—herself a former refugee from Afghanistan. These workshops had several goals: for the women to share artistically their experience and their culture, to explore their talent, and to find new strength. Nine refugee women participants came from various countries, and, because of circumstances leading to their forced displacement, several of them had journeyed through other countries prior to landing in Canada; all together they came from or had travelled through Afghanistan, Turkey, Sudan, Egypt, Somalia, Kenya, Uganda, Colombia, USA, Iraq, and Pakistan. They expressed their pain and resilience in drawings, poems, and a collectively painted mural, which is now part of WAHC's art collection. Participants organized discussion sessions, during which they first shared the circumstances of their flight and their subsequent settlement in Canada. After each session, they were asked to write about their experience, emotions, and ideas in a journal provided for them. During the third and fourth sessions, they translated their experience and emotions into drawings. In the fifth session the women discussed, explored, and chose visual symbols they felt could convey to a broader audience what they perceived to be their common past and present experience. They composed the symbols in one drawing that was enlarged into a six-by-three-foot canvas and spent the remaining sessions painting it under the guidance of the lead artist. This painting (see Figure 8.3) was the final activity that captured both the solidarity, the shared symbols, and the hope and optimism generated by the weeks of collaboration (Petersen). Their final action was to participate in the March 21, 2003 international conference, "Saying 'I': Refugee Women Reclaim their Identity," where they displayed their individual drawings and their collective painting and read to the community the narratives they had composed and selected.

The third and last project discussed in this chapter took place between 2002 and 2004 and involved eleven refugee women from Sudan who had survived the war there.[4] They came from north and south Sudan and belonged to different cultures (Dinka and Nuer), religions (Christian and Muslim), and linguistic areas. They took part in focus groups and in-depth interviews. A grounded theory method was used in the analysis of their narratives. Following this method, common themes were identified, coded, and used in determining factors that affected participants' mental health and their resilience.

Together, the three studies elicited a number of theoretical and methodological questions, which shape this chapter. How does a dialogical perspective on refugee identity allow researchers and practitioners to gain a fuller understanding of refugees' vulnerability and resilience in the field of refugee studies and intervention more generally? What is resilience and what factors contribute to it? How does creativity contribute to the resilience of refugees, particularly to that of refugee women? What are the benefits of a qualitative approach to resilience for research and therapy with refugees? What have both refugees and researchers learned from these projects?

The assertion that "an official culture...determines the meaning of physical [and, one could add, mental] pains and pleasures" (Hirshkop 282) resonates with particular acuity in the field of refugee studies and intervention, particularly when researchers or therapists discuss issues such as trauma, suffering, and resilience. In looking at the socio-ideological construction of identity and mental health of refugees from a gender perspective, I will foreground what academic and dominant discourses about refugees often omit when characterizing their identity—namely the fact that refugees are *not* the helpless victims that are often represented by media and humanitarian organizations. Rather, they are resilient survivors. Examining the factors that shape their identity will help us understand the process of resilience building.

My discussion will be informed primarily by the works of Mikhail Bakhtin and Boris Cyrulnik and by Michael Ungar's recent works on identity and resilience in Canada. Since refugees are normal people who have faced abnormal situations, it is appropriate to use Bakhtin's dialogical approach, which gives full importance and significance to the socio-historical context that surrounds refugee-ness, refugees' identity as a construct, and to aspects such as body and language, agency and responsibility, while taking into account their processual interaction. In 1929, Bakhtin himself experienced refugeeness; he was sentenced to six years of internal exile in Kazakhstan during the Stalin era (Emerson 75) and suffered from a crippling bone disease (osteomelytis) that kept him homebound and physically exiled. Against these odds, he never stopped writing and created an oeuvre that has greatly influenced diverse fields, including contemporary literary criticism, cultural theory, and applied psychology. Bakhtin was "completely alien to the victim mentality" and demonstrated a remarkable resilience until his death in 1975 (Emerson 4). He concentrated his energies on his intellectual endeavours and creativity with the help of his wife Elena Alexandrovna and his friends and followers, who all significantly contributed to his resilience.

Dialogism and Resilience

> *Dialogism is neither dialogue in the sense of "consensual conversation" nor Hegelian dialectics as it does not imply a resolution or "Aufhebung." It is a non-teleological, open-ended process of interlocution in which worldviews are confronted and are relationally transformed by the interlocutors. Dialogism refers to an interaction between competing meanings or worldviews and can occur within a single consciousness.*
>
> —M.M. BAKHTIN, *The Dialogic Imagination*

The concept of resilience originates from the field of engineering and comes from the Latin *resalire*, "to jump up again." It is the property of material (i.e., rubber or metal) to absorb energy and to bounce back once that energy is dissipated. This term was adopted in the field of medicine—used in the sense that one bounces back from a physical trauma. More recently, the term has shifted to the field of mental health, particularly the area of trauma studies related to children's and adolescents' mental health—we are familiar with the expression "children bounce back" (Boyden qtd. in Ungar, *Handbook* 6). Resilience refers to an individual's ability to overcome trauma (a catastrophic event or situation) and to continue his or her normal development. The term has now permeated the semantic field of refugee studies, particularly in the area of refugee mental health. In a context of risk and adversity, resilience is affected by individual and group strengths as well as environmental factors. Michael Ungar, who heads the International Resilience Project (IRP) at Dalhousie University, proposes a hybrid definition that conveys the tension between a Darwinian approach, which emphasizes the survival of the fittest (Tisseron 21) and a constructionist approach: "Resilience is both an individual's capacity to navigate health resources and a condition of the individual's family, community, and culture to provide those resources in culturally meaningful ways" (Ungar, *Handbook* 225). This definition makes a crucial shift in our understanding of resilience from the individualistic concept often assumed by Western-trained researchers and service providers to a more relational, multifactorial, and contextual understanding. Resilience therefore results from a dialogical interface between the intrinsic capacity to withstand adversity and environmental factors (Lighezzolo and De Tychey 139). Thus, agency and responsibility are more evenly distributed between the individual and the social actors and factors involved.

Ungar also perceives a dialogical relationship between the risk and protective factors that manifests itself in a jagged push-pull movement in the process of resilience building (*Handbook* 341). Resilience is about (re)constructing a healthy self-definition through various forms of negotiation. Ungar's concept of resilience derives from a concept of self that is similar to that developed by Bakhtin and later adopted by Hubert Hermans, for whom the self is an open-ended, multivoiced construct that is relational, social, historical, and cultural (Ungar, *Handbook*; Bakhtin, *Dialogic*; Hermans and Kempen). Similarly, factors that are conducive to resilience are transactional processes that are multi-dimensional and contextually dependent (Ungar, *Handbook* xxv). Resilience can be expressed through verbal and non-verbal—including corporeal—language, even through silence. For Bakhtin, Hermans, and Ungar, body and mind are dialogically intertwined,[5] and our bodies live in relation with the world, with others, and with verbal language that can also harm or heal (Bakhtin, *Formal* 12; Butler 5). In my earlier essay, "A Dialogical Approach to the Identity of Refugee Women," and in concurrence with Cathy Caruth (163) and Inger Agger (123), I explain that "the body of a refugee (especially of women) possesses its own memory and 'speaks' its own language of somatization, particularly when the woman has experienced a trauma that is unspeakable, such as sexual violence" (Hajdukowski-Ahmed, "Dialogical" 45). A refugee who participated in an earlier research project encapsulated this unspeakable voice in a powerful statement: "Nobody knows, but my body knows" (Hajdukowski-Ahmed et al., "Healing" 25). Engaged in a relationship with the conscious mind that has "forgotten," the body's memory can resurface and reactualize a physical reaction to a past traumatic experience (Agger 123), and it can also stimulate the healing forces of reconnection and creativity. Refugees are often like Sisyphus who experienced the "syndrome of repetition"[6] (Moussa 24) through incidences of somatization and flashbacks, which dialogically struggle in a "push-pull" manner with their present until the past is successfully integrated in their psyche. The identity of a refugee is thus not that of a victim who then becomes a survivor, but of a victim continually engaged in a dialogical interaction with the survivor.

In adversity, as in resilience, the language of the refugee's body is an integral part of trauma research. Researchers, psychosocial therapists, as well as participants consider that the body's language is involved in creativity. It is the hand that traces, paints, knits, sculpts; it is the face that one paints, adorns, or moulds; it is the whole body that dances. It is also through her body language and other forms of non-verbal communication that the survivor expresses her pain as well as her reconnection with herself, her past, her community, and with the material world. The language of the body (or of creativity) can even contradict the spoken word. Within a dialogical approach, such contradictions are acknowledged without being considered abnormal or pathological or deceitful; they are simply part of the process of identity expression and (re)construction. What appears as conflicts between voices or worldviews within the same discourse are not defects of logic, but forces at work in a normal life (DeSantis 1). Viewed as an open-ended process of interlocution between competing meanings and worldviews, Bakhtin's concept of dialogism is particularly suited to the task of understanding those whose lives have been radically affected and transformed by a plurality of experience, such as trauma, upheaval, and resettlement, expressed in a plurality of langauge.

Non-Verbal Forms of Communication and Trauma

Refugees who have experienced trauma such as sexual violence, murder, kidnapping, or torture directly or—as in the case of family members—indirectly have experienced a speechless terror that remains actualized at a raw stage and cannot be organized in memory and conveyed in verbal language. It becomes "organized on a somato-sensory or *iconic level*: as somatic sensations, behavioural re-enactments, nightmares, and flashbacks" (Caruth 172, emphasis added). I contend that it is precisely this non-verbal *iconic* nature of the mnemonic trace of such experience that makes trauma easier to express through non-verbal forms of creativity.

> *Non-verbal forms of communication (NVFC) comprise an exchange of information through non-linguistic signs…They encompass the entire range of cultural expressions exclusive of language (Poyatos 1–3), such as clothing, gestures, postures, body art, music, fashion, crafts, display of objects, etc.*
>
> *NVFC have at once a representative and a performative function in the linguistic, discursive, and therapeutic spheres. NVFC dialogically contribute to the reconstruction of self and memory.* (Hajdukowski-Ahmed, "Non-Verbal" 222)[7]

NVFC therefore provide an important (re)connection with all facets of life. They are particularly relevant when expressing trauma. As I have explained elsewhere, "NVFC constitute a more accessible and less stressful form of communication when refugees have a limited knowledge of official language(s), or when verbal forms of expression are not an option. Survivors may also come from cultures which emphasize and validate the use of NVFC (e.g., dance, mime, street theatre, carnivals, religious practices)" (Hajdukowski-Ahmed, "Non-Verbal" 216). Individuals can also self-censor verbal expression and control what they say and with whom they communicate; while non-verbal expression and creativity can facilitate access to deeper knowledge more quickly and safely.

The Complexity of Identity Construction in Forced Migration

Creativity that strengthens resilience is intimately connected with identity (re)construction and makes identity into a foundation on which a self and a life can be (re)built. It is for this reason that such significance is accorded to identity by researchers and practitioners who work with refugees (Hajdukowski-Ahmed et al., *Not Born* 14–19). In our increasingly globalized world, people experience intense mobility and border crossing—chosen and forced—resulting in encounters between differences, voices, and countervoices. In this context, life requires constant adjustments, as "fundamental differences in an intensely interconnected world society not only require dialogical relationships between people to create a liveable world, but also a self that has developed the capacity to deal with its own differences, contrasts, tensions and uncertainties" (Hermans and Dimaggio, "Self, Identity, and Globalization" 35). This assertion is particularly relevant in the situation of forcibly displaced people who encounter many different voices or discourses in their exilic journey and who are increasingly marginalized and denied any form of belonging, whether it is called home or citizenship. The numbers of refugees and situations that engender forced displacements have expanded considerably as political or economic conflicts are no longer the sole causes for refugeeness.[8] Through their journey, refugees are constantly confronted with new knowledge, new forms of communication, and new ways of being in the world. On its exilic journey, their "I" or self encounters multiple voices that challenge previous worldviews and represent potential new possibilities. Refugees are in a perpetual state of becoming, always occupying in-between spaces, thresholds, and bridges.

It is within this shifting context that a dialogical encounter or struggle that contains the seeds of transformation takes place. Janet Dench, executive director of the Canadian Council for Refugees, has called it the space of "productive tension." Every new location or new situation challenges the self, which is constantly renegotiated and opened up to new possibilities. When a Sri Lankan refugee widow who intends to remarry decides to become a welder to afford a dowry, she confronts at the same time a masculinist worldview on women's employability; Western feminism opposed to the practice of dowry giving; and, in certain instances, her religious mores that forbid widows to remarry (Hyndman and de Alwis 91). Those changes do not occur "without doubts and struggles," which are also reflected in the tension between the humanitarian discourse that constructs women as "victims" and the development discourse that constructs them as "empowered" survivors (Rajasingham-Senanayake 154–55). When researchers are translating or intervening in refugees' discourse from a dialogical perspective, it is important to ensure that differences between self and Other remain distinct and embodied, that all voices are heard, and that power relationships are taken into account. Such an approach is also imbued with "an ethics of recognition of the Other and an ethics of answerability because each subject is viewed as unique, invested with historical agency and responsibility, and, as such, each mutually transforms and is transformed" (Hajdukowski-Ahmed et al., *Not Born* 31). The gaze and the words of the Other also shape one's identity and affect one's self-perception, particularly in an asymmetrical power relationship, such as when individuals have experienced a traumatic event that leads to their being shamed by their community. As Boris Cyrulnik, the French authority on resilience—himself a Holocaust survivor—remarked: "If you feel disgust, pity, or horror for what has happened to me, it is your view that will transform my ordeal into trauma" ("A Person" 165). Women who were raped, trafficked, or enslaved are particularly vulnerable to the consequences of such stigmatization. But even in the most disempowering circumstances, refugees can retain some agency through resisting discourses, creative initiatives, strategic essentialism, or even silence.

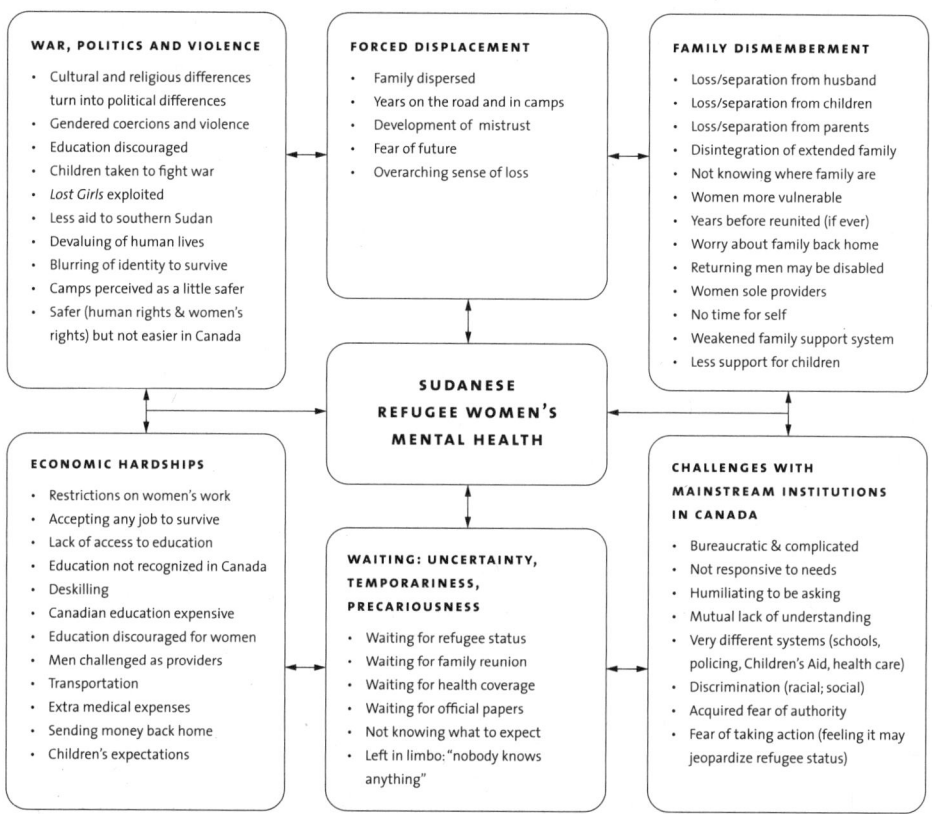

FIGURE 8.1: *Circumstances Affecting the Resilience and Mental Health of Refugee Women from Sudan to Host Country (Canada),* Refugee Women from Sudan and Their Mental Health, v.

Factors that Hinder Resilience and Factors that Enhance It

In the participatory project undertaken with refugee women from Sudan, participants identified factors that were perceived as impediments to their resilience and well-being, as well as factors that contributed to them (see Figures 8.1 and 8.2). While those factors appear separately in the diagrams, they relate dialogically in the process of identity construction.

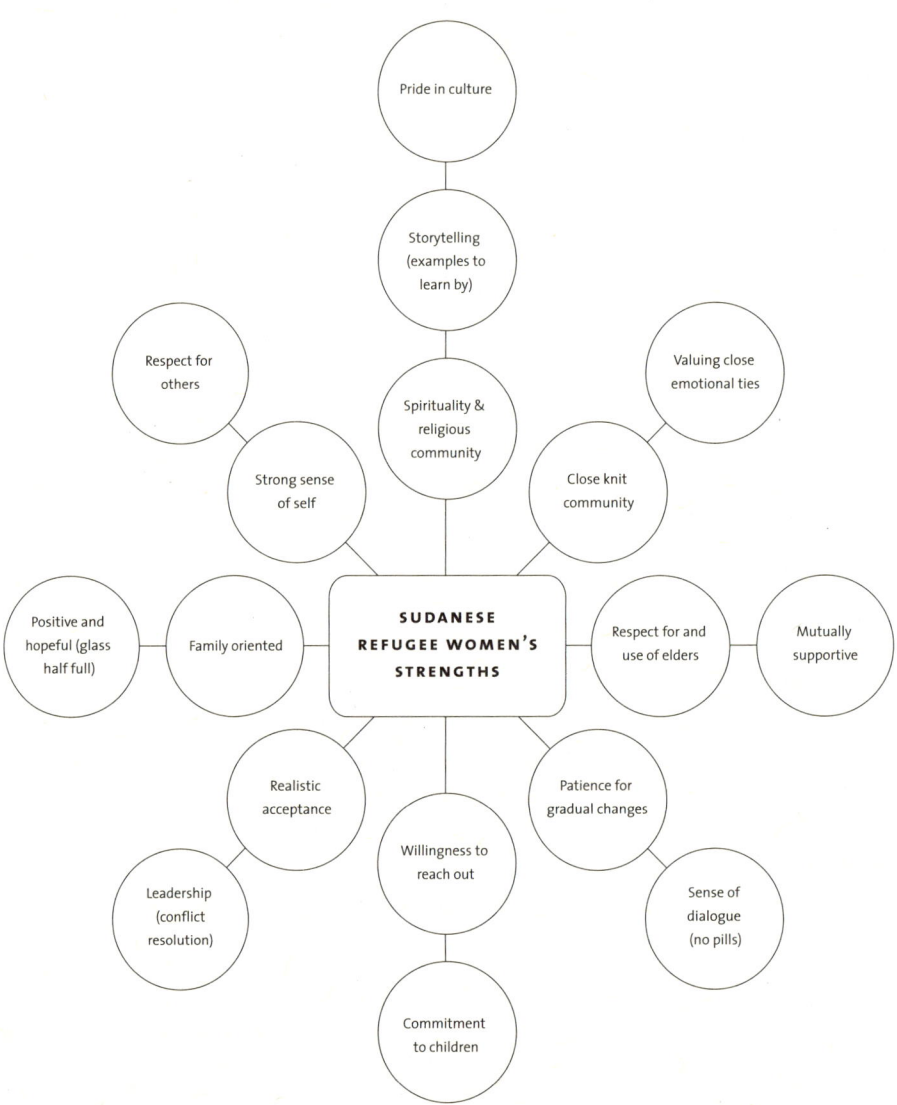

FIGURE 8.2: *Strengths of Sudanese Refugee Women that Contribute to Positive Mental Health*, Refugee Women from Sudan and Their Mental Health, *vi.*

A cursory reading of Figure 8.1 informs us of external factors that have a disempowering effect on the refugee women's identity and agency and that threaten to turn them into helpless victims. War, political violence, forced displacement, family dismemberment, waiting time, bureaucracy, economic hardships are external factors that render refugees vulnerable, as well as create dependency on services, which can lead to a loss of agency and self(worth). The diagram demonstrates that the powerlessness of refugees is largely structurally and externally constructed (i.e., by policy makers and mainstream organizations).

As shown in Figure 8.2, most of the factors that construct resilience are of a relational nature and emphasize the importance of dialogue, experience-sharing, community, and mutual support. For example, mutual support took the form of a small association and credit union founded by the Sudanese community for the purpose of celebrating their cultures, organizing humanitarian assistance for families left behind in Sudan, and lending money to families from a common fund to answer various immediate needs (i.e., airfare for an emergency visit to Sudan). The "sense of dialogue (no pills)" expression refers to a quotation—"We want to talk, they give us pills"—by Sudanese refugee women who complained about doctors who shorten the time of visits, quickly dismiss the refugees' need to share their concerns, and prefer instead to prescribe medication ("pills") that in effect silence them. Participants also pointed to family togetherness as a major contributor to their resilience, as one deleterious effect of refugeeness is the dispersal and dismemberment of families. Thus, keeping their family together was identified as a major objective in which religion—in its spiritual and societal function—plays an important unifying role, whether for Christian Sudanese of the south or Muslim Sudanese of the north. Common prayer times, religious rituals and celebrations, communal meals, and community life held in places of worship all provide a sense of structure and comfort. Other factors that construct resilience revolved around the notion of hope, such as "giving a chance," "patience for gradual changes," "positive and hopeful," "realistic acceptance," and "commitment to children." It is noteworthy that patience and hope have a common Latin root which means to "bear" (Johnston and Scholler-Jaquish 102). As Cyrulnik, reported, community support and cultural grounding are conducive to resilience (*Autobiographie* 15). So is the availability of shared cultural narratives that can lead to collective healing (*Autobiographie* 17). Thus, surviving individuals whose community has been destroyed by genocide or whose victimhood is shamed by their community have more difficulty rebuilding their self. As we shall see later, both the expressions of connection and hope figured prominently in the visual and verbal creativity of refugee women.

Creativity and Resilience Building

By creativity, I mean any activity that involves the use of an artistic form, language, or technique to express and communicate an emotion or an idea. Put simply, creativity is the act of making something new by using one's imagination within a form of expression (verbal, pictural, musical, etc.). In rejecting all dichotomies, Bakhtin does not distinguish between high and low art, between theory and practice, between body and verbal language, or between aesthetics and ethics. Ethics is what contributes to the unity of the work of art and life within the concept of the act or, in Bakhtin's terms, *postupok*. That is, an act is a step towards a horizon rather than a specific teleology. This step, taken by us as historical agents, is what Bakhtin called our "being as event," for which we are answerable (Bakhtin, *Toward* 12). Technology (or aesthetics) separated from that answerable deed is viewed as an empty and dangerous theoreticism.[9] Bakhtinian creativity is thus not only a set of aesthetic principles and rules enacted upon a created object. It is the historical manifestation of our agency, of the uniqueness of our answerable being in the world, and of our legacy to culture and history. Bakhtin's understanding of the meaning and place of creativity helps those who work with refugees, including researchers, practitioners, and policy makers, recognize the historical and cultural agency of refugees, which in turn enhances refugees' sense of self-worth and strengthens their resilience. However, this creativity is not about cultural essentialism; it cannot be reified into some folk art to be displayed at official multicultural events because individuals and cultures are part of multiple and constantly evolving contexts and mediums.

For people who have faced trauma, there is a reluctance to express themselves verbally in the first person, and the recourse to creativity becomes a sort of narrative in the third person, mediated by the chosen mode of expression. Creative work helps, therefore, to situate one's experience outside of oneself and to locate it in time. Looking at the created object establishes an objective distance that allows the individual to visualize herself and to comment on the object and the experiences it represents. This objective distance can also allow the individual to discard the experience symbolically. For refugees, creativity is an adaptive strategy conducive to resilience. It is also an oppositional discourse that entertains a dialogical relationship with the political, socio-cultural, and medical silencing that they may experience in traumatic or exilic situations, both as refugees and as women.[10] Our participatory projects exemplified the notion of "creative culture" described by Cyrulnik, as refugee participants were full protagonists in the projects they had themselves initiated. Similarly, in the project's report, the participants' narratives of their experience—in their own voices—were central, and their agency in the participatory research process was therefore fully acknowledged.

Creative initiatives can represent individual responses, but in the "Healing from Torture" project, they took relational forms of group knitting, mask making, community gardening, and collective mural painting, and these initiatives were carried out within the refugees' communities. Through these activities, refugee women expressed their deep desire to reclaim control over their agency and to (re)connect with their communities, with past and present generations, with earth, with their culture, with time and history, and with themselves. A participant in the "Healing from Torture" project who experienced trauma when her father, a former union leader in Chile, had been imprisoned and tortured under General Pinochet's dictatorship, wrote a section of the report on the group's activities. About the herb planting session, she remarked:

> *Working with one's hands provides a sense of control and direct contact with reality. The feeling of nurturing a living and growing thing can recreate a sense of connection to other living things and to the emotions. As an activity, planting is a concrete and yet creative way to channel energy: it is creating one's own reality. This reality becomes visual with the growth of the plants—utopia could be a beautiful garden. (Hajdukowski-Ahmed et al., "Healing" 49)*

Participants also understood the choice of this activity metaphorically: they were in a process of "transplanting" themselves in a new soil. About bread baking, the same participant commented:

> *The preparing of food is also a very homosocial and community creating activity. The activity of baking bread together showed a reverence for life and the sense of care of a united group....The celebration of Thanksgiving became a way to learn about the traditions of the host society and a means to integrate and "normalize" the rhythm of their family and social life, and adjust to the social rhythm of Canadian seasons. (Hajdukowski-Ahmed et al., "Healing" 50)*

Sharing bread also conveys the sacred connotation of the Christian communion. Annette Gagnon, who conducted the knitting workshop, found that knitting "fostered a sense of pride in the creative effort, intergenerational blending and fun" (Hajdukowski-Ahmed et al., "Healing" 50). Those creative activities were also designed to help a young girl from a refugee family who had become very withdrawn and whose behaviour had left her teacher and family deeply worried. Gagnon and the participants noted positive changes in the young girl, which made the whole experience most worthwhile. A definite process of resilience building and healing had occurred. The girl joyfully participated in all activities and became "a beautiful knitted piece [her]self" (Hajdukowski-Ahmed et al., "Healing" 50). Mask making was the closing activity for the "Healing from Torture" project, and it "served as a powerful closing ritual and a symbol of creating their own healthier, perhaps integrated 'face' to the world" (Hajdukowski-Ahmed et al., "Healing" 52), wrote Myrna Pond, the coordinator of the project. She further remarked that "the process of healing amounts to finding who they really are, finding themselves, unlearning the wrongs done to them by torture, discarding the masks they had to make and wear in order to survive" (Hajdukowski-Ahmed et al., "Healing" 54). Participants told the coordinator that being members of a support group, including their families in activities, organizing activities that reconnected them with their body and their human and natural environment, had consolidated their resilience and affected their health in a very positive way (Hajdukowski-Ahmed et al., "Healing" 57). Through their experience, they established their agency, strengthened their self-esteem, explored their talent, learned new skills, started a fresh support group, furthered their integration in their host society, and left a testimony for future generations and for the host society.

In the "Saying 'I'" project, nine refugee women collectively created a painting entitled, "Pedalling Towards a Future of Peace." At the "Saying 'I'" conference, the women described the painting as a pictorial narrative. As the reproduction of the painting in Figure 8.3 conveys, the painting exudes a high level of energy, which contradicts the stereotype of the refugee woman as passive. In an allegorical mode reminiscent of social realism, a woman with an impressive stature looks upward while engaged in intense physical labour, perhaps constructing the solid new home near her. One

FIGURE 8.3: WAHC Refugee Project, collective painting, "Pedalling Towards a Future of Peace," Hamilton, Ontario, 2003.

can easily understand why survivors-participants chose construction as a metaphor to represent their life and hope. In contrast, the empty refugee camp tent conveys deprivation and the erasure of identity, agency, and humanness. Gradually, and from left to right, darkness gives way to light and bright colours; stones figuring the absence of humanness are replaced with the presence of female bodies engaged in vigorous activity; and precariousness becomes stability. The adolescent girl pedalling on her bicycle represents a being in process, a growing seed, a link between past and present and between generations. She is hope and future in motion. The enslaving chain has been broken, freeing refugee women under the protective wings of peace. Looking at the painting, a participant expressed the collective wish of her group in these words: "Let us make ourselves the bridge of peace between Canada and different regions around the world" (Petersen).

How did participants build and express their resilience during the course of these projects? Their collective experience had a transformative effect and opened new possibilities. For the refugee women who had been voiceless and spoken for at all stages of their journey and who had been acted upon (especially if they were tortured), their participation in the research project as well as their public performance at the international conference "Saying 'I'" affirmed their presence and agency in the public sphere. In the process, they reclaimed their voices, sense of purpose, control over their life, and place in society. While reading their own narratives, they could objectively look back on their journey as in a mirror, taking the exotopic position of inside-outsider, and reflect on their transformation. They created the flow of a narrative from their fragmented hectic journey, and looking back helped them to look forward as they could feel pride in seeing how much they had already accomplished and how many hurdles they had overcome. This further stimulated their confidence and energy so that they could pursue their constructive journey. When writing her life journey, one of the participants derived comfort and hope in realizing that she had overcome political persecution, an earthquake, a break-up that left her with two young children, and that she had completed ESL classes to improve her English, and had even fallen in love with her teacher whom she eventually married (Petersen). The linear continuity of a narrative helps the survivors to reconstruct their sense of self (Klugman 174), especially after their identity has been shattered through various dehumanizing instances of silencing. In the course of this WAHC-sponsored project, the participants forged friendships in a safe space that consolidated their resilience through solidarity and mutual support. The sessions also provided many hours of respite from their daily routine and worries, and this refreshed their energies. Because the women came from different cultural backgrounds, they gained knowledge and understanding of each other's cultures and engaged with diversity outside of their own ethno-cultural community. This transcultural exchange created solidarity as it brought to light what refugee women had in common and allowed identification across cultures, without erasing the mutual recognition of their distinctive cultural differences, in accordance with Charles Taylor's "politics of recognition."

Refugee women could apply their new insights, knowledge, and skills to further their education or facilitate access to employment. They also learned how to enhance technically their creativity and use it to express their resilience visually and verbally. Their experience provided a new venue for expressing their emotions and concerns and for resolving them creatively. As in the "Healing from Torture" project, creativity enabled a better understanding of the impact of trauma and had a cathartic effect on them (Lohman 12). Like in a grief narrative, the narrators gained insight in their own process, educated others, and created a testimony (Klugman 169). Knowing that they were not alone and isolated, that they had friends, mentors, and advocates, and that their experience and creativity would be disseminated in mainstream society enhanced their sense of self-worth and usefulness and strengthened their hope—thus their resilience—in working toward a better future for themselves and their families. As a participant stated: "I felt I am not alone. I felt more strong when I heard their stories....We can help each other to solve our problems" (Petersen). Collective creativity had a therapeutic effect, attested to by another participant: "I think all of this is good for relaxation and a kind of therapy. We can become more strong than before" (Petersen). The voices of participants themselves give powerful testimony to the process of resiliency building. The following eloquent and self-affirming comments from another refugee woman exemplify the process of resilience building:

> *The first time [story sharing] was such a great experience. Very emotional full of stories and tears...It was a rich session where I learned*

from other women different aspects of their lives and issues they have to deal with....I am happy to share my history without any regret and able to talk loud knowing that I am not going to be judged by anyone...I feel honoured to be in this kind of project because my experience can probably help other women and open the doors for understanding and become conscious about specific topics. A lot of people out there are not even aware that there is a whole other world around the corner...

It was something that moved my ground and brought me a lot of moments from the past that I want to forget, but it let me realize this is a good way to release and heal my pain. So I need to work with these feelings and turn them to find the answers I am looking for. It fills my soul with hope, strength and I will continue fighting for a better future....I am in ecstasy, I am in heaven, I am in earth, I am in dream, I am in unreal world, I am in pain, I am in hell, I am in death.... I want to live, I want to love, I want to breathe, I want to grow, I want to do, I want to be....It is time, it is real, it is here, it is right, it is necessary, it is urgent, it is now, it is for us, it is.... (Petersen)

For the refugee women, creativity was experienced as a form of communication, a refuge, a stage in the healing process, and a legacy. Creativity allowed the participants to explore their talent and skills, which shaped or reinforced their agency and self-esteem in the process. It facilitated their socialization and bonding, particularly in group activities. It created a safe space in which they shared their knowledge, emotions, and culture. Their painting now adorns the entrance wall of the Workers Art and Heritage building as well as the cover of a book, *Not Born a Refugee Woman: Contesting Identities, Rethinking Practices* (Hajdukowski-Ahmed et al.) In the qualitative resilience-building projects, we researchers and participants realized that creativity was an effective tool in analysing the dynamic, non-linear process of transformation of refugee women who had experienced trauma. Being forced into displacement is already in itself a traumatic experience. The research process was also a product in its own right as it empowered all participants to acquire an increased measure of self-awareness and well-being. Taking up their own agency, refugees transform and enrich knowledge, policies, and practices related to their situation (Ungar and Teram 152, 158), and in the process bridge various disciplines in the humanities, social sciences, and medical sciences (Hajdukowski-Ahmed, "Bakhtin"; Ungar and Teram 149–59).

Participatory Creativity, Psychosocial Research and Therapy: A Path to Resilience

Participatory creativity affirms the value and usefulness of psychosocial research and therapy, particularly with women who have been constructed as voiceless. Psychosocial research and therapy is distinct from medicalized trauma research and therapy. An official discourse grounds trauma research firmly

> *in the discipline of psychiatry and medicine....It is a discourse that is comfortable with publication and statistics...What it often does not tell is the refugees' own stories and how they conceptualise their experiences, how they feel they were affected and, possibly more importantly, what they think might be the best ways to address the consequences of the suffering. (Loughry 167)*

Western therapists who principally rely on verbal language and tend to consider nonverbal forms of communication as only supplementary—especially when they do not understand them—potentially will not recognize information crucial for therapeutic purposes.

During the healing process, the common, secular approach may overlook or dismiss narratives of refugees that convey their religious beliefs and view their practices as insignificant or harmful superstitions (Agger 115; Hajdukowski-Ahmed et al., *Not Born* 52). Furthermore, a medicalized approach, such as the one exemplified by the standard use of the Harvard Trauma Scale, tends to essentialize, pathologize, and individualize the experience of refugees, and in the process, obfuscates external causes and public responsibility. As Ungar remarks, "medicalized accounts of human responses to misfortune detract from the political, economic and social nature of the adversity in the world today" (Ungar, *Handbook* 14). As a result, those who fail to bounce back are at risk of being blamed or abandoned, which is not to deny the existence of pathologies in certain cases (Lighezzolo and De Tychey 139–40).

Psychosocial research and therapy take into consideration the multiple external factors that impact the well-being and resilience of refugees. The psychosocial approach is non-hierarchical and involves the participants as active collaborators in the therapeutic process (Hermans and Hermans-Jansen, *Self-Narratives* 129). To recognize that so-called mental illness or deviance is also a cultural construct predicated on contextual norms reshapes our thinking and intervention. This awareness results in a shifting of policies and intervention from a controlling/policing/repression paradigm to one of expression/prevention. Such shifting, which also occurs at the epistemological, ethical, and political level, fosters the practice of democracy through co-participation and power-sharing between researchers and participants (Denton et al., *Women's* 44). In psychosocial research and therapy, socially marginalized—and often vilified—groups who have been exiled from mainstream discourse and intervention find themselves empowered to reclaim subjecthood and agency.[11] Because of the present post–9/11 border closing and fence building,

> *the words "refugee" and even more that of "asylum seeker" are increasingly becoming a term [sic] of abuse...As such, they are words loaded with negativity that is both empowering for their usual speakers...and disempowering for those they purport to describe (dehumanised and objectified as refugees and as asylum-seekers). (Rotas 59, emphasis original)*

This new context increases the vulnerability of refugees and asylum seekers, thus making their voicing even more crucial in research and therapy. The conceptualization of refugees as social agents recognizes both their strengths and weaknesses, and, further, does not isolate them into the slot of helpless victims or destructive delinquents, as is often the case, for example, with trafficked women who are treated as prostitutes. Participatory psychosocial research and therapy constitute a compelling path to resilience and creativity. Participants are engaged in their self-definition and their healing process, and all parts of their self are validated. This approach considers that distress can also contain a seed of opportunity (Ungar, *Handbook* 10; Johnston and Scholler-Jaquish). Its objective is to empower participants/refugees so that they "re-establish the relationship to reality in a process where the person regains his or her history and the capacity to relate to other people, and where the person again has a vision of a meaningful future" (Agger and Jensen 105). Theory and methodology entertain a dialogical association with policies and politics.

> *"To make the ugly beautiful" is one of the most important themes for victims of violence, whether it is violence in the family, incest, rape, or organized political violence.*
> —INGER AGGER, *The Blue Room: Trauma and Testimony Among Refugee Women*

▶ Creativity is an alchemy that can transform pain into art, testimony, and hope. It has transformed refugee women into agents in control of their life. They have reconnected with their self and transformed it, finding meaning and purpose in what could have been perceived as only pain and chaos. I may seem to be overstating the positive impact of creativity in the projects conducted with refugee women, but years of experience have made me aware of the long-term effects of such collaboration—effects that cannot be captured by an exit questionnaire.

In the longer term of a life span, such creative projects that strengthen resilience can become seeds that grow into unforeseen flourishing occupations, community leadership, artistic or educational accomplishments. Creativity, whether verbal or non-verbal, should dialogically find its place in qualitative research and psychosocial therapy. Creativity is conducive to resilience in refugee women who have participated in creative projects and whose own words attest to their increased well-being. It could also help us rethink the purpose of research whose validity should not be measured only in terms of scientific data, but also in terms of its ability to construct a better world.

Is it art or is it therapy? In my opinion, it is irrelevant to discuss or question the artistic value of creativity in this context, or to reduce it to a therapeutic exercise, because one could argue that any art is also a form of therapy, as it was the case for such prominent artists as Van Gogh (his disturbing self-portraits), Frida Kahlo (her dramatic portrayals of severe physical and psychological wounds suffered after her accident in 1925), or Picasso (his haunting *Guernica*). Creativity is multidimensional and multifunctional as it manifests itself, to different degrees, in art, communication, therapy, and testimony, and as it works contextually and in the continuum of time. The projects have also affected the researchers, who were humbled by their experience, which has been a learning process for them as well. They learned to question their own perception of refugee women as helpless victims, as well as any residual Othering and fence-building dichotomy. In this process, the distinction between the learners and the mentors became unclear as the researchers' own resilience was strengthened by the refugee women's life examples, inventiveness, and talents.

I cannot express better the meaning of resilience in creativity than Madeleine Gagnon, a French Canadian award-winning poet and novelist; she writes: "Among those physically or psychologically wounded by war, we have found an unfathomable aptitude for happiness, which can be translated only into art: music, dance, painting and poetry" (Gagnon 160). And she then offers the following example:

> *It is of a young woman in Bosnia whose parents were killed and her lover missing, dead or imprisoned, but who, in her immense solitude, went to work every morning, even though work did not exist anymore, since the building where she had worked had been destroyed. But she went everyday nonetheless, walking eight kilometres and, despite the danger, walked back the same distance to return home. What she told us was astonishing: every day, she would put on her best clothes and fix her hair and makeup. Why? For whom? For nothing and for no one. "To stay alive," she plainly answered. This verse from an anonymous poet I had read a long time ago later came to mind, "The ultimate proof of love is to adorn oneself for a lover who is blind." (Gagnon 161)*

In a simple yet powerful and poignant manner, this young woman embodied the profound meaning of resilience; she has re-created herself and transformed herself into a work of art. In her own creative way, she has affirmed the force of life against the forces of death and destruction. Refugee creativity is a testimony. It leaves a trace and contributes to our common heritage for all to enjoy and appreciate, to understand and reflect upon in our efforts towards eradicating trauma and forced displacement, for which, ultimately, we should all feel responsible.

NOTES

1. For recent research on theories of dialogical self, refer to Sunil Bhatia and Anjali Ram, "Locating the Dialogical Self in the Age of Transnational Migrations, Border Crossings and Diasporas," *Culture and Psychology* 7.3 (2001): 297–309; Hubert Hermans, and Giancarlo Dimaggio, "Self, Identity, and Globalization in Times of Uncertainty: a Dialogical Analysis," *American*

Psychological Association. 11.1 (2007): 31–61; and *The Dialogical Self in Psychotherapy*, New York: Brunner-Routledge, 2004.

For recent work on theories of resilience, see, for example, Michael Ungar, *Handbook for Working with Children and Youth: Pathways to Resilience Across Cultures and Contexts,* Thousand Oaks, CA: SAGE 2005; Margaret Waller, "Resilience in Ecosystemic Context: Evolution of the Concept," *American Journal of Orthopsychiatry* 71.3 (2001): 290–97; and Boris Cyrulnik, "A Person Should Never be Reduced to his or her Trauma," Interview with Anne Rapin, *Focusing on the Humanities—Interview with a Neuropsychiatrist*, web, accessed 17 October 2008, as well as Boris Cyrulnik, *Autobiographie d'un épouvantail*, Paris: Odile Jacob, 2008.

2. A split self is the result of repression or inhibition of part of a self that is not consciously accepted, of an "undesirable" part of the self (for example, a woman repressing being raped). It creates a breach between the real self and the lived experience, a sense of ill well-being, and it can lead to mental disorders.

3. The project was woman-centred, but the women chose to include men in the knitting activity. In so doing, they deconstructed the traditional "woman-craft" of knitting while giving it a symbolic meaning as they knit the threads of family ties.

4. We are referring to the Second Sudanese Civil War, which started in 1983, and which followed by ten years the First Sudanese Civil War (1955–1972), and took place mostly in southern Sudan. Nearly two million civilians were killed and four million were forcibly displaced. A peace agreement was signed in 2005, but did not resolve all issues or alleviate the effects of the war on the Sudanese population. Officially, the war is described as opposing southern, non-Arab populations and northern, Arab-dominated government, but it is as much about the control of resources (oilfields and water), in which multi-national companies and foreign governments are also involved ("History of Sudan," *Wikipedia.org*.)

5. "Bakhtin rejected dichotomies that separate the material, the organic and the mental and even created the Russian neologism *telo-znak* or 'body/sign'" (Bakhtin and Medvedev 12).

6. According to Greek mythology, Sisyphus was condemned to roll a great boulder to the top of a hill as a punishment for a crime committed against the gods. But every time he would reach the summit, the boulder would roll back down again. The recurrence of the same ordeal is often compared to the myth of Sisyphus.

7. Participatory Action Research (PAR) methodology proved to be particularly productive in eliciting, identifying, and interpreting NVFC. See Hajdukowski-Ahmed, "A Dialogical Approach to the Identify of Refugee Women," especially page 51, for a discussion of PAR with immigrants and refugees.
8. The number of people forcibly uprooted by conflict and persecution worldwide reached 42 million at the end of 2008. According to the UNHCR's 2009 *Annual Report*, "The total includes 16 million refugees and asylum seekers and 26 million internally displaced people uprooted within their own countries" (Press Release 2009). The generic terms "uprooted" or "forcibly displaced" now include that of "refugee," which reflects the change in the causes for forced displacement, originally related to conflict and now covering a wide spectrum, including natural disasters. For example, "The rise in the number of victims of natural disasters over the past decade and ever-greater levels of displacement caused by development projects have added millions to the number of forcibly displaced people in the world. According to the International Federation of the Red Cross and Red Crescent Societies, the total number of people affected by natural disasters has tripled over the past decade to 2 billion people, with the accumulated impact of natural disasters resulting in an average of 211 million people directly affected each year. This is approximately five times the number of people thought to have been affected by conflict over the past decade" (United Nations High Commissioner for Refugees, *Statistical Yearbook*, 27). Even "natural disasters" can be traced to human actions (i.e., a flood caused by a poorly constructed dam), thus blurring the distinction between categories.
9. For Bakhtin, technological, theoretical, or artistic creativity cannot be dependent only on their intrinsic timeless laws. They cannot be separated from life and from the answerability of the creator as historical agent: "All that which is technological, when divorced from the one-occurrent unity of life and surrendered to the will of law immanent to its development, is frightening; it may from time to time erupt in this once occurrent unity as an irresponsibly destructive and terrifying force" (Bakhtin, *Toward* 7). Art is at once timeless in its form but the artist as a historical and unique being and agent is answerable for his artistic deed, which enriches the common historico-cultural heritage.
10. Emphasizing the role of social context in resilience building, Cyrulnik sees in the contemporary Western forms of culture an impediment to the process of resilience: "In order for culture to provide resilient support, it has to generate protagonists rather than spectators. It's why I set the 'creative culture' against

the 'passive culture' that dominates our consumer and entertainment societies" (Cyrulnik, "A Person").

11. Such decentering of knowledge taught us, for example, that from a psychosocial perspective, adolescents' deviance or substance addiction are not moral defects but coping strategies when they face adversity (Ungar and Teram 153). And independence perceived as a norm and sought as a desirable outcome in Western therapy is regarded as "abnormal" in many non-Western cultures.

WORKS CITED

Adams, Howard. *Prison of Grass: Canada from a Native Point of View*. 1975. Rev. ed. Saskatoon, SK: Fifth House Publishers, 1989. Print.
"AFSPA (Armed Forces [Special Powers] Act, 1958)." *South Asia Terrorism Portal*. Institute for Conflict Management. 2001. Web. 21 December 2011.
Agamben, Giorgio. "We Refugees." *Symposium* (Summer 1995): 114–19. Print.
Agger, Inger. *The Blue Room: Trauma and Testimony Among Refugee Women: A Psycho-Social Exploration*. London: Zed Books, 1992. Print.
Agger, Inger, and Soren Buus Jensen. *Trauma and Healing Under State Terrorism*. London: Zed Books, 1995. Print.
Ahmed, Rafiul, and Prasenjit Biswas. *Political Economy of Underdevelopment of North-East India*. New Delhi: Akansha Publishing House, 2004. Print.
Ahmed, Sara. "Home and Away: Narratives of Migration and Estrangement." *International Journal of Cultural Studies* 2 (1999): 329–47. *EBSCOhost*. Web. 2 April 2008.
Aldred, Ray. "The Resurrection of Story." *Veritas Forum*. York University, Toronto. 10 Nov. 2005. Lecture.
Alexander, M. Jacqui. *Pedagogies of Crossing: Meditations on Feminism, Sexual Politics, Memory, and the Sacred*. Durham, NC: Duke University Press, 2005. Print.
Alfred, Taiaiake. *Peace, Power, Righteousness: An Indigenous Manifesto*. 2nd ed. Don Mills, ON: Oxford University Press, 2009. Print.
———. *Wasáse: Indigenous Pathways of Action and Freedom*. Peterborough, ON: Broadview Press, 2004. Print.

Ali, Mahmud S. *The Fearful State: Power, People and Internal War in South Asia.* London: Zed Books, 1993. Print.

Amnesty International. "India: Briefing on The Armed Forces (Special Powers) Act, 1958." 9 May 2005: 1–34. *Amnesty.org*. Web. 8 Aug. 2008.

———. "India: Briefing. The Armed Forces Special Powers Act (AFSPA) Review Committee takes One Step Forward and Two Backwards." 23 Nov. 2006: 1–8. *Amnesty.org*. Web. 8 Aug. 2008.

Amrita Bazar Partika (English daily newspaper). Calcutta: Basumati Corporation, 8 Nov. 1949. Print.

Anand, Oinam. "Where Have the Students Gone?" *Epao.net*. E-Pao, 17 March 2008. Web. 2 June 2008.

Anderson, Benedict. *Imagined Communities: Reflections on the Origin and Spread of Nationalism.* London: Verso, 1983. Print.

Angus, Ian. *A Border Within: National Identity, Cultural Plurality, and Wilderness.* Montreal & Kingston: McGill-Queen's University Press, 1997. Print.

———. *(Dis)Figurations: Discourse/Critique/Ethics.* New York: Verso, 2000. Print.

Anonymous Group of Live-In Caregivers. "Operetang Maynila, abridged version." Video. Written by Petronila Cleto. Performed at 2008 *John Douglas Taylor Conference, "Displacements: Borders, Mobility and Statelessness."* McMaster University, Hamilton, Ontario. 9 March 2007. *"Displacements" Conference Archives.* www.literaryculture.ca.

Appiah, Kwame Anthony. *Cosmopolitanism: Ethics in a World of Strangers.* New York: Norton, 2006. Print.

Armstrong, Jeanette. "Literature of the Land: An Ethos for These Times." *Association for Commonwealth Literature and Language Studies Fourteenth Triennial Conference.* University of British Columbia, Vancouver. 18 Aug. 2007. Lecture.

Armstrong, Jeanette, and Douglas Cardinal. *The Native Creative Process.* Penticton, BC: Theytus Books, 1991. Print.

"Army Demolishes Village Housing Over 200 Palestinians, West of the Barrier." *B'Tselem*, The Israeli Information Center for Human Rights in the Occupied Territories. 25 Nov. 2007. Web. 17 Sept. 2008.

Babiak, Todd. "Consent, not dissent, the order of the day." *Edmonton Journal* 7 Feb. 2008: C1. Print.

Babiuk, Colin. *Oil Sands and the Earth: Framing the Environmental Message in the Print News Media.* Charleston, SC: VDM Verlag, 2008. Print.

Bacon, D. "For an Immigration Policy Based on Human Rights." *Immigration.* Ed. S. Jonas and S.D. Thomas. Wilmington, DE: Scholarly Resources, 1999. 157–73. Print.

Badil Resource Centre. *Displaced by the Wall: Forced Displacement as a Result of the West Bank Wall and Its Associated Regime*. Bethlehem and Geneva: Badil Resource Center for Palestinian Residency and Refugee Rights, 2006. Print.

Bagchi, Jasodhara, and Subhoranjan Dasgupta. *The Trauma and the Triumph: Gender and Partition in Eastern India*. Kolkata: Stree, 2003. Print.

Bahuguna, Nitin Jugran. "Formidable Force." *The Statesman* 4 July 2006: n. pag. *Unodc.org*. Web. 18 May 2008.

Bakhtin, Mikhail, and Pavel Medvedev. *The Formal Method in Literary Scholarship*. Trans. Albert J. Werhle. Cambridge, MA: Harvard University Press, 1985. Print.

Bakhtin, M.M. *The Dialogic Imagination: Four Essays by M.M. Bakhtin*. 1981. Ed. Michael Holquist. Trans. Caryl Emerson and Michael Holquist. Austin: University of Texas Press, 1992. Print.

———. *Art and Answerability: Early Philosophical Essays by M.M. Bakhtin*. Ed. Michael Holquist and Vadim Liapunov. Trans. and notes Vadim Liapunov. Supp. trans. Kenneth Brodstrom. Austin: University of Texas Press, 1990. Print.

———. *Toward a Philosophy of the Act*. Trans. Vadim Liapunov. Austin: University of Texas Press, 1993. Print.

Balibar, Étienne. "What we owe to the *sans-papiers*." *Social Insecurity*. Alphabet City Series no. 7. Toronto: Anansi, 2000. 42–44. Print.

———. *We, the People of Europe?* Princeton, NJ: Princeton University Press, 2004. Print.

Bammer, Angelika. Introduction. *Displacements: Cultural Identities in Question*. Ed. Angelika Bammer. Bloomington and Indianapolis: Indiana University Press, 1994. xi–xx. Print.

Banerjee, Paula. "Second Civil Society Dialogue on Peace: A Report." Kolkata: Mahanirban Calcutta Research Group, 2002. N. pag. *Mcrg.ac.in*. Web. 4 July 2008.

Baruah, Sanjib. *Postfrontier Blues: Toward a New Policy Framework for Northeast India*. Washington, DC: East-West Center, 2007. *Eastwestcenter.org*. Web. 20 March 2008.

Barutciski, Michael. "Tensions Between the Refugee Concept and the IDP Debate." *Forced Migration Review* 3 (Dec. 1998): 11–14. Print.

Basu, D.D. *Introduction to the Constitution of India*. New Delhi: Wadhwa and Company Law Publishers, 2002. Print.

Basu, Dakshinaranjan, ed. *Chhere Asha Gram*. Calcutta: Jijnasa, 1975. Print.

Ben, Aluf. "Olmert to Haaretz: Two-state solution, or Israel is done for." *Haaretz*. 29 Nov. 2007. Web. 18 Sept. 2008.

Benhabib, Seyla. *The Rights of Others: Aliens, Residents, and Citizens*. Cambridge: Cambridge University Press, 2004. Print.

———. *Situating the Self: Gender, Community, and Postmodernism in Contemporary Ethics*. New York: Routledge, 1992. Print.

Bertell, Rosalie. "The Standard is Zero." *Alberta Views* 10.9 (Nov. 2007): 18–19. Print.

Bhabha, Homi. *The Location of Culture*. New York: Routledge, 1994. Print.

Bhabha, Jacqueline. "Belonging in Europe: Citizenship and Post-National Rights." *International Social Science Journal* 51.1 (1999): 11–23. Print.

Bhagat, Ram. "Conceptual Issues in Measurement of Internal Migration in India." Paper Presented at the XXV IUSSP International Conference, Tours, France, 18–23 July 2005: 1–18. *Princeton.edu*. Web. 8 Aug. 2008.

Bhagat, Rasheeda. "Anguish of an Alienated People." *Business Line*. 4 Aug. 2004: n. pag. *thehindubusinessline.in*. Web. 16 April 2008.

Bhaloo, Shaheen, Ana Carias, M. Hajdukowski-Ahmed, Lynda Hayward, Jenny Ploeg, Karen Trollope-Kumar, and Madina Wasuge. *Refugee Women from Sudan and their Mental Health*. Hamilton, ON: McMaster University Community Care Research Centre Report, 2005. Print.

Bhatia, Sunil, and A. Ram. "Locating the Dialogical Self in the Age of Transnational Migrations, Border Crossings and Diasporas." *Culture and Psychology* 7.3 (2001): 297–309. Print.

Bil'in (Village Council) v. Green Park International Inc. 2009. QCCS 4151 affirmed 2010 QCCA 4151. Filed in the Superior Court of Montreal, Quebec. Docket number 500-17-044030-081. 7 July 2008. Print.

Bishara, Azmi. *From the Jewish State to Sharon: A Study in the Contradictions of the Israeli Democracy*. Ramallah: MUWATIN-The Palestinian Institute for the Study of Democracy, 2005. (In Arabic). Print.

Biswas, D. "Col. Jagmohan Singh And Ors. vs. The State Of Manipur And Ors. on 23 June, 2005—Judgment." *Indiankanoon.org*. Web. 15 Aug. 2008.

Blaser, Mario, Harvey A. Feit, and Glenn McRae, eds. *In the Way of Development: Indigenous Peoples, Life Projects, and Globalization*. London: Zed Books; Ottawa: International Development Research Centre, 2004. Print.

Boddy, Trevor. "The Canadian Museum." *The Architecture of Douglas Cardinal*. Edmonton, AB: NeWest Press, 1989. Print.

Bosniak, Linda. *The Citizen and the Alien*. Princeton, NJ: Princeton University Press, 2006. Print.

———. "Citizenship Denationalized." *Indiana Journal of Global Legal Studies* 7.2 (2000): 447–510. Print.

Bott, Robert. "Canada's Oil Sands." 2nd ed. Ed. David M. Carson and Tami Hutchinson. *Canadian Centre for Energy Information*. Sept. 2007. Web. 29 May 2008.

Bourdieu, Pierre. *Esquisse d'une théorie de la pratique*. Genève: Droz, 1972. Print.

Brooymans, Hanneke. "Oilsands' Newest Project: A Greener Image." *Edmonton Journal* 14 Oct. 2007: A1. Print.

———. "Syncrude Duck Deaths Kept Quiet." *Edmonton Journal* 1 April 2009. A1. Print.

Brueggemann, Walter. *Deep Memory, Exuberant Hope: Contested Truth in a Post-Christian World*. Minneapolis, MN: Fortress Press, 2000. Print.

Burton, Antoinette. "Who Needs the Nation? Interrogating 'British' History." *Journal of Historical Sociology* 10.3 (1997): 227–48. Print.

Butler, Judith. *Excitable Speech: A Politics of the Performative*. New York: Routledge, 1997. Print.

Cardinal, Harold. *The Unjust Society*. 1969. Rev. ed. Vancouver: Douglas and McIntyre; Seattle: University of Washington Press, 1999. Print.

Caruth, Cathy. *Trauma: Explorations in Memory*. Baltimore, MD: Johns Hopkins University Press, 1995. Print.

Chakrabarti, Prafulla. *The Marginal Men: The Refugees and Left Political Syndrome in West Bengal*. Calcutta: Naya Udyog, 1999. Print.

Chakraborty, Saroj. *With Dr. B.C. Roy and other Chief Ministers: A Record up to 1962*. Calcutta: Benson's, 1974. Print.

Chambers, Iain. *Migrancy, Culture, Identity*. London: Routledge, 1994. Print.

Chamberlin, J. Edward. *If This is Your Land, Where Are Your Stories?: Finding Common Ground*. Toronto: Vintage Canada, 2004. Print.

Chapman, K.J., et al. "The Oil Sands Survey: Albertans' Values Regarding Oil Sands Development." Edmonton, AB: Cambridge Strategies Inc., 2008. Print.

Chatterjee, Partha. *The Nation and Its Fragments: Colonial and Postcolonial Histories*. Princeton, NJ: Princeton University Press, 1993. Print.

Chatterji, Kedarnath, ed. *The Modern Review* (Calcutta) 88 (July–December 1950). Print.

Chaube, Shibani Kinkar, Sunil Munsi, and Amalendu Guha. "Regional Development and the National Question in North-East India." *Social Scientist* 4.1 (1975): 40–66. *JSTOR*. Web. 4 Feb. 2008.

Chaudhuri, Sukumari. Interview by Subhoranjan Dasgupta. *The Trauma and the Triumph: Gender and Partition in Eastern India*. Ed. Jasodhara Bagchi and Subhorajan Dasgupta. Kolkata: Stree, 2000. Print.

Chimni, B.S. "The Birth of a 'Discipline': From Refugee to Forced Migration Studies." *Journal of Refugee Studies* 22.1 (2009): 11–29. Print.

Choudhury, Deba Prosad. "The North-East Frontier of India." *Modern Asian Studies* 4.4 (1970): 359–65. *JSTOR*. Web. 4 Feb. 2008.

Chow, Rey. *Writing Diaspora: Tactics of Intervention in Contemporary Cultural Studies*. Bloomington: Indiana University Press, 1993. Print.

Chowdhury, Neerja. "Can you Hear the Women?" *The New Indian Express*. 23 Aug. 2004: n. pag. Web. 11 March 2008.

Code, Lorraine. *Ecological Thinking: The Politics of Epistemic Location*. Toronto: Oxford University Press, 2006. Print.

Cole, Ellen, Oliva M. Espin, and Esther D. Rothblum, eds. *Refugee Women and Their Mental Health: Shattered Societies, Shattered Lives*. Binghamton, NY: Haworth Press, 1992. Print.

Coleman, Daniel. "Imposing subCitizenship: Canadian White Civility and the Two Row Wampum of the Six Nations." *Narratives of Citizenship: Indigenous and Diasporic Peoples Unsettle the Nation-State*. Ed. Aloys Fleischmann, Nancy Van Styvendale, and Cody McCarroll. Edmonton: University of Alberta Press, 2011. 177–211. Print.

Constituent Assembly of India (Legislative) Debates, Part I. "Questions and Answers, Starred Questions and Answers, Oral Answers, 30 August 1948." New Delhi, 1949. Print.

———. "Questions and Answer, Starred Questions and Answers, Oral Answers, 19 February 1949." New Delhi, 1950. Print.

———. "Questions and Answer, Starred Questions and Answers, Oral Answers, 24 February 1949." New Delhi, 1950. Print.

Coutin, Susan Bibler, Bill Maurer, and Barbara Yngvesson. "In the Mirror: The Legitimation Work of Globalization." *Law & Social Inquiry* 27.4 (2002): 801–43. Print.

Coutin, Susan Bibler. "Denationalization, Inclusion and Exclusion: Negotiating the Boundaries of Belonging." *Indiana Journal of Global Legal Studies* 7.2 (2000): 585–93. Print.

Cruikshank, Julie. "Colonial Echoes in 'Postcolonial' Worlds: Boundaries and Managers." *Do Glaciers Listen?* Vancouver: UBC Press, 2005. Print.

Curthoy, Ann. "An Uneasy Conversation: The Multicultural and the Indigenous." *Race, Colour and Identity in Australia and New Zealand*. Ed. John Docker and Gerhard Fischer. Sydney: University of New South Wales Press, 2000. 21–36. Print.

Cyrulnik, Boris. "A Person Should Never be Reduced to his or her Trauma." Interview with Anne Rapin. *Focusing on the Humanities—Interview with a Neuropsychiatrist*. 2001. République Française: Ministère des Affaires Étrangères. Web. 17 Oct. 2008.

———. *Autobiographie d'un epouvantail*. Paris: Odile Jacob, 2008. Print.

———. *Les Nourritures affectives*. 1993. Paris: Odile Jacob, 2000. Print.

———. *Parler d'amour au bord du gouffre*. Paris: Odile Jacob, 2007. Print.

The Daily Jugantor. (Bengali daily newspaper). 10 May 1955. Print.

The Daily Jugantor. (Bengali daily newspaper). 16 Jan. 1960. Print.

Dasgupta, Jyotirindra. "Community, Authenticity, and Autonomy: Insurgence and Institutional Development in India's North-East Community." *The Journal of Asian Studies* 56.2 (May 1997): 345–70. JSTOR. Web. 4 Feb. 2008.

De Genova, Nicholas. "Migrant 'Illegality' and Deportability in Everyday Life." *Annual Review of Anthropology* 31 (2002): 419–47. Print.

———. *Working the Boundaries: Race, Space and "Illegality" in Mexican Chicago*. Durham, NC: Duke University Press, 2005. Print.

Dench, Janet. "Opening Plenary: Canadian Settlement and Integration: A Manifesto for Unsettlement and Dis-Integration." CARMS *Inaugural Conference on Refugees and the Insecure Nation*. York University, Toronto. 17 June 2008. Lecture.

Denton, Margaret, Maroussia Hajdukowski-Ahmed, Mary O'Connor, and Isik Urla Zeytignolu. *Women's Voices in Health Promotion*. Toronto: Canadian Scholars' Press, 1999. Print.

DeParle, Jason. "A Good Provider Is One Who Leaves." *The New York Times Magazine* 22 April 2007. Print.

DeSantis, Alan. D. "Caught Between Two Worlds: Bakhtin's Dialogism in the Exile Experience." *International Journal of Refugee Studies* 14 (2001): 1–19. Print.

Dickason, Olive Patricia. *Canada's First Nations: A History of Founding Peoples From Earliest Times*. 3rd ed. Toronto: Oxford University Press, 2002.

Dolendru, Thonjum. Personal Interview by Pavithra Narayanan. Imphal, Manipur, 2005.

Doxtator, Deborah. "Godi'Nigoha': The Women's Mind and Seeing Through to the Land." *Godi'Nigoha: The Women's Mind*. Brantford, ON: Woodland Cultural Centre, 1997. 29–41. Print.

Dugard, John. "Report of the Special Rapporteur on the Situation of Human Rights in the Palestinian Territories Occupied since 1967." Human Rights Council, Fourth Session. A/HRC/4/17. 29 Jan. 2007. Print.

Dumoulin, Philippe. Personal Communication with Catherine Graham. 4 March 2009.

During, Simon. Introduction. *The Cultural Studies Reader*. Ed. Simon During. London: Routledge, 1993. 1–25. Print.

Election Commission of India. "Past Elections," *Election Commission of India*, 2010. Web. 21 Aug. 2011.

Emerson, Caryl. *The First Hundred Years of Mikhail Bakhtin*. Princeton, NJ: Princeton University Press, 1997. Print.

Farsakh, Leila. "Independence; Cantons or Bantustans: Whither the Palestinian State?" *Middle East Journal* 59.2 (Spring 2005): 230–45. Print.

Finch, David. *Pumped: Everyone's Guide to the Oilpatch*. Calgary, AB: Fifth House, 2007. Print.

"Flamenco." *Encyclopaedia Britannica Online*. Encyclopedia Briticannica. 2011. Web. 18 Aug. 2011.

Fleischmann, Aloys, Nancy Van Styvendale, and Cody McCarroll, eds. *Narratives of Citizenship: Indigenous and Diasporic Peoples Unsettle the Nation-State*. Edmonton: University of Alberta Press, 2011.

Franda, Marcus, *Political Development and Political Decay in Bengal*. Calcutta: Firma K.L. Mukhopadhyay, 1971. Print.

Frank, Arthur W. "For a Sociology of the Body: an Analytical Review." *The Body: Social Process and Cultural Theory*. Ed. Mike Featherstone, Mike Hepworth, and Bryan S. Turner. London: SAGE, 1991. 36–102. Print.

Fraser, Nancy. *Justice Interruptus: Critical Reflections on the "Post-Socialist" Condition*. New York: Routledge, 1997. Print.

Gagnon, Madeleine. "Writing on Women and War." *Not Born a Refugee Woman: Contesting Identities, Rethinking Practices*. Ed. M. Hajdukowski-Ahmed, N. Khanlou, and H. Moussa. New York: Berghahn Books, 2008. 150–63. Print.

Gangte, Gin. "N-E Students Flock to Delhi." *The Times of India*. 15 Oct. 2001: n. pag. Web. 19 March 2008.

Ganguly, Indubaran. *Colony Smriti*. Calcutta: Self-published, 1997. Print.

Gilgun, Jane F., and Laura S. Abrams. "Gendered Adaptations and the Perpetration of Violence." *Handbook for Working with Children and Youth: Pathways to Resilience Across Cultures and Contexts*. Ed. M. Ungar. Thousand Oaks, CA: SAGE, 2005. 57–70. Print.

Gilman, Sander. Preface and Introduction. *Difference and Pathology: Stereotypes of Sexuality, Race and Madness*. Ithaca, NY: Cornell University Press, 1985. 11–35.

Gilroy, Paul. *The Black Atlantic: Modernity and Double Consciousness*. Cambridge, MA: Harvard University Press, 1993. Print.

Goodnow Katherine, and Jack Lohman. *Museums, the Media and Refugees*. New York: Berghahn Books, 2008. Print.

Goswami, Roshmi. "Women in Armed Conflict Situations in India—Report." North East Network (NEN), 2005: 1–120. *Iwraw-ap.org*. Web. 4 May 2008.

Goswami, Uddipana. "Internal Displacement, Migration, and Policy in Northeastern India." Working Paper No 8. Washington, DC: East-West Center, 2007: 1–67. *Eastwestcenter.org*. Web. 20 March 2008.

Government of India. "The Armed Forces (Special Powers) Act, 1958 Act 28 of 1958, 11th September, 1958." South Asia Terrorism Portal, 2001: n. pag. *Satp.org*. 4 July 2008.

Government of West Bengal. *Five Years of Independence, August 1947–August 1952*. Calcutta: Government of West Bengal, 1953. Print.

Grant, George. *Philosophy in the Mass Age*. 1959. Ed. William Christian. Toronto: University of Toronto Press, 1995. Print.

———. *Technology and Justice*. Toronto: Anansi, 1986. Print.

Grant, Jennifer, Simon Dyer, and Dan Woynillowicz. "Fact or Fiction: Oil Sands Reclamation." *Pembina.org*. May 2008. 29 May 2008.

Grewal, Inderpal, and Caren Kaplan. *An Introduction to Women's Studies: Gender in a Transnational World*. Boston: McGraw-Hill, 2006. Print.

Grossberg, Lawrence. "Cultural Studies vs. Political Economy: Is Anybody Else Bored with This Debate?" *Critical Studies in Mass Communication*. 12.1 (Mar 1995): 72–81.

Guha, Amalendu. "Nationalism: Pan-Indian and Regional in a Historical Perspective Nationalism." *Social Scientist* 12.2 (Feb. 1984): 42–65. JSTOR. Web. 10 March 2008.

Hajdukowski-Ahmed, Maroussia. "A Dialogical Approach to the Identity of Refugee Women." *Not Born a Refugee Woman: Contesting Identities, Rethinking Practices*. Ed. M. Hajdukowski-Ahmed, N. Khanlou, and H. Moussa. New York: Berghahn Books, 2008. 28–55. Print.

———. "Bakhtin Without Borders: Participatory Action Research in Social Sciences." *Bakhtin/ "Bakhtin."* Ed. P. Hitchcock. Spec. issue of *North Atlantic Review* 95.3-4 (1998): 643–69. Print.

———. "The Non-Verbal Forms of Communication of Refugee Women Survivors of Torture." *Exile*. Ed. Magda Stroinska, and Vicki Cecchetto. Geneva: P. Lang, 2003. 213–29. Print.

Hajdukowski-Ahmed, Maroussia, Myrna Pond, Isik Urla Zeytinoglu, and Lori Chambers. "We are Making a Difference: The Women's Worksite Action Group: A Participatory Action Research Project." *Women's Voices in Health Promotion*. Ed. M. Denton, M. Hajdukowski-Ahmed, Mary O'Connor, and Isik Urla Zeytinoglu. Toronto: Canadian Scholars' Press, 1999. 122–38. Print.

Hajdukowski-Ahmed, Maroussia, Myrna Pond, Minoo Farragheh, and Shaista Justin. "Healing from Torture: Women Survivors of Torture Living in Hamilton: A Participatory Action Health Promotion Project." McMaster Research Centre for the Promotion of Women's Health (MRCPOWH), Report No. 10, 2000. Print.

Hall, Stuart. "Cultural Identity and Diaspora." *Colonial Discourse and Post-Colonial Theory: A Reader*. Ed. Patrick Williams, and Laura Chrisman. New York: Columbia University Press, 1994. 392–403. Print.

Hanus, Michel. *La résilience, à quel prix?* Paris: Maloine, 2001. Print.

Hass, Amira. "Did the Transfer of the Closed Areas Begin?" *Haaretz*. 24 Feb. 2004. Web. 18 Sept. 2008.

Hatch, Christopher, and Matt Price. "Canada's Toxic Tar Sands: The Most Destructive Project on Earth." *Environmental Defence.ca*. Environmental Defence, Feb. 2008. Web. 2 March 2008.

Hebdige, Dick. "From Culture to Hegemony." 1979. *The Cultural Studies Reader*. Ed. Simon During. London: Routledge, 1993. 357–67. Print.

Henderson, James (Sákéj) Youngblood. "The Context of the State of Nature." *Reclaiming Indigenous Voice and Vision*. Ed. Marie Battiste. Vancouver: UBC Press, 2000. 11–38. Print.

———. "*Sui Generis* and Treaty Citizenship." *Citizenship Studies* 6.4 (2002): 415–40. Print.

Henton, Darcy. "If Syncrude Convicted, Oilsands 'Doomed': Defense." *Edmonton Journal* 29 April 2010. A1. Print.

Hermans, Hubert J.M., and E. Hermans-Jansen. *Self-narratives: The Construction of Meaning in Psychotherapy*. New York: Guilford Press, 1995. Print.

Hermans, Hubert, and Giancarlo Dimaggio. "Self, Identity, and Globalization in Times of Uncertainty: a Dialogical Analysis." *American Psychological Association*. 11.1 (March 2007): 31–61. Print.

———, eds. *The Dialogical Self in Psychotherapy*. New York: Brunner-Routledge, 2004. Print.

Hermans, Hubert J.M., and Harry J.G. Kempen. *The Dialogical Self: Meaning as Movement*. San Diego, CA: Academic Press, 1993. Print.

Hermans, Hubert, and W. Lyddon, eds. *The Dialogical Approach to Counselling*. Spec. issue of *Counselling Quarterly* 19.1 (2006): 1–120. Print.

Higginson, Catherine. "Shelley Niro, Haudenosaunee Nationalism, and the Continued Contestation of the Brant Monument." *Essays in Canadian Writing* 80 (2003): 141–86. Print.

Hirschkop, Ken, *Mikhail Bakhtin: An Aesthetic for Democracy*. Oxford: Oxford University Press, 1999. Print.

Hitchcock, Peter. *Dialogics of the Oppressed*. Minneapolis: University of Minnesota Press, 1992. Print.

Hodge, Jarrah. "'Unskilled Labour': Canada's Live-in Caregiver Program." *National Anti-Racism Council of Canada*. Action Web, n.d. Web. 31 Aug. 2009.

Holston, James, and Arjun Appadurai. "Cities and Citizenship." *Cities and Citizenship*. Ed. J. Holston. Durham, NC: Duke University Press, 1999. 1–18. Print.

The Holy Bible: New Revised Standard Version. Grand Rapids, MI: Zondervan Bible Publishers, 1990. Print.

Horowitz, M., N.J. Wilner, and W. Alvarez. "Impact of Events Scale: A Measure of Subjective Stress." *Psychosomatic Medicine* 41 (1979): 209–18. Print.

House of the People. *Part I. Questions and Answers, Starred Questions and Answers, Oral Answers to Questions, 4 March 1952*. New Delhi: Government of India, 1953. Print.

Human Rights and Natural Disasters: Operational Guidelines and Field Manual on Human Rights Protection in Situations of Natural Disaster. United Nations High Commissioner for Refugees Brookings-Bern Project on Internal Displacement, March 2008. Web. 22 June 2009.

Humberman, Irwin. *The Place We Call Home: A History of Fort McMurray as Its People Remember, 1778–1980*. Edmonton, AB: Historical Book Society of Fort McMurray, 2001. Print.

Hunter, William M., et al. "Our Fair Share, Report of the Alberta Royalty Review Panel." *Alberta Royalty Review*. Alberta Royalty Review Panel, 18 Sept. 2007. Web. 12 Nov. 2007.

Hussain, Wasbir. "Contemporary North-East India: Problems and Prospects." *Trends in Social Sciences and Humanities in North-East India (1947–97)*. Ed. J.P. Singh. New Delhi: Regency Publications, 1998. 128–36. Print.

Hutcheon, Linda. "Modern Parody and Bakhtin." *Rethinking Bakhtin*. Evanston, IL: Northwestern University Press, 1989. 87–103. Print.

Hyndman Jennifer, and Malathi de Alwis. "Reconstituting the Subject: Feminist Politics of Humanitarian Assistance." *Not Born a Refugee Woman: Contesting Identities, Rethinking Practices*. Ed. M. Hajdukowski-Ahmed, N. Khanlou, and H. Moussa. New York: Berghahn Books, 2008. 84–101. Print.

"India Human Rights Report 2007—Manipur." Asian Centre for Human Rights. N. pag. *Achrweb.org*. Web. 8 Aug. 2008.

Inoue, Kyoko. "Integration of the North-East: the State Formation Process." *Sub-Regional Relations in the Eastern South Asia: With Special Focus on India's North-Eastern Region*. Eds. Mayumi Murayama, Kyoko Inoue, and Sanjoy Hazarika. Chiba, Japan: The Institute of Developing Economies (IDE) Publication, 2005: 16–31. *Ide.go.jp*. Web. 14 April 2008.

Internal Displacement Monitoring Centre. "Democratic Republic of the Congo (DRC): Massive Displacement and Deteriorating Humanitarian Conditions." Country Update. 12 Aug. 2009. Print.

International Court of Justice (ICJ). *Legal Consequences of the Construction of a Wall in the Occupied Palestinian Territory*, Advisory Opinion, I.C.J. Reports 2004, 136. Print.

Isin, Engin. *Being Political*. Minneapolis: University of Minnesota Press, 2002. Print.

"Israel's Security Fence." *Ministry of Defense*. 30 April 2007. Web. 18 Sept. 2009. (In Hebrew).

It Starts With a Whisper. Dir. Shelley Niro and Anna Gronau. Toronto: Canadian Filmmakers Distribution Centre, 1993. Film.

Johnston, Nancy, and Alwilda Scholler-Jaquish, eds. *Meaning in Suffering*. Madison: University of Wisconsin Press, 2008. Print. Interpretive Studies in Healthcare and the Human Sciences 6.

"Kadima's Political Platform." *Kadima Reconstructionist Jewish Community*. N.d. Web. 8 Dec. 2009.

Kälin, Walter. *Guiding Principles on Internal Displacement—Annotations*. Washington, DC: The American Society of International Law and the Brookings Project on Internal Displacement, 2000. *Asil.org*. Web. 18 March 2009.

Kalinowski, T. "Boards Attack Removal of Kids: Students Used to Lure Parents." *Toronto Star* 1 May 2006. Print.

Kanehsatake: 270 Years of Resistance. Dir. Alanis Obomsawin. Toronto: National Film Board of Canada, 1993. Film.

Karnad, Raghu. "The Sucessionist Movement." *Outlook India* 14 May 2007: n. pag. Web. 5 April 2008.

Katinas, Tom. "An Apology from Syncrude—And a Promise to do Better." *Syncrude*. 2 May 2008. Web. 12 June 2008.

Keepers of the Fire. Dir. Christine Welsh. Toronto: National Film Board of Canada, 1994. Film.

Kertzer, Jonathan. "Bio-Critical Essay." *The Rudy Wiebe Papers, First Accession: An Inventory of the Archive at the University of Calgary Libraries*. Calgary: University of Calgary Press, 1986. Print.

Keung, Nicholas. "Women Face Dilemma: Abuse or Deportation?" *Toronto Star* 3 Aug. 2004. Print.

King, Thomas. "Borders." *One Good Story, That One*. Toronto: Harper Perennial, 1993. Print.

———. *The Truth About Stories: A Native Narrative*. Toronto: Anansi, 2003. Print.

Klaszus, Jeremy. "Athabasca Blues." *Alberta Views* 10.9 (Nov. 2007): 30–35. Print.

Klugman, Craig "Narrative Phenomenology: Exploring Stories of Grief and Dying." *Meaning in Suffering*. Ed. Nancy Johnston, and A. Scholler-Jaquish. Madison:

University of Wisconsin Press, 2008. 144–86. Print. Interpretive Studies in Healthcare and the Human Sciences 6.

Kogawa, Joy. *Woman in the Woods*. New York: Mosaic Press, 1985. Print.

Kroetsch, Robert. *Alberta*. 2nd ed. Edmonton, AB: NeWest Press, 1993. Print.

Kumar, Vinay. "Manmohan reaches out to Manipuris." *The Hindu* 21 Nov. 2004: n. pag. Web. 18 April 2008.

Lefebvre, Henri. "Preface to the Study of the Habitat of the 'Pavillon.'" *Key Writings*. Ed. Stuart Elden, Elizabeth Lebas, and Eleonore Kofman. New York: Continuum, 2003. Print.

Les Murs Tombent, Les Mots Restent. Théâtre du Public and Theater for Everybody. Centre culturel Marcel Hicter de la Marlagne, Wépion, Belgique. 29 Sept. 2006. Performance.

Levant, Ezra. "Shed no tears for Ft. McMurray's ducks." *National Post* 5 May 2008. Web. 8 June 2008.

"License to Kill—Manipur, AFSPA." Independent People's Inquiry Commission. 2000. Print.

Lighezzolo, Joelle, and Claude De Tychey. *La resilience. Se [re]construire apres le traumatisme*. Paris: In Press Editions, 2004. Print.

Lillebuen, Steve. "Native Groups Sue Gov't Over Oilsands." *Edmonton Journal* 5 June 2008: A3. Print.

Loft, Steven, and Marcia Crosby. "Radical Indigeneity: Claiming Cultural Space." *FUSE Magazine* 30.4 (Sept. 2007): 41–46. Print.

Lohman Jack. "How Do We Sing Our Song in a Strange Land? Belonging: Voices of London's Refugees in the Museum of London." *Museums, the Media and Refugees*. Ed. K. Goodnow. New York: Berghahn Books, 2008. 9–12. Print.

Longjam, Ibotombi. "Nupi Lan—the Women's War in Manipur, 1939: An Overview." *The Manipur Page*. N.d., n. pag. Web. 4 June 2008.

Loughry, Maryann. "The Representation of Refugee Women in our Research and Practice." *Not Born a Refugee Woman: Contesting Identities, Rethinking Practices*. Ed. M. Hajdukowski-Ahmed, N. Khanlou, and H. Moussa. New York: Berghahn Books, 2008. 166–73. Print.

Lovelace, Bob. "Steps Toward Freedom in an Uncertain World." Guest Speaker of Amnesty International. McMaster University, Hamilton, Ontario. 10 Dec. 2008. Lecture.

Lowry, Michelle, and Peter Nyers. "'No One Is Illegal': The Fight for Refugee and Migrant Rights in Canada." *Refuge* 21.3 (2003): 66–74. Print.

MacAllister, Karine. "Applicability of the Crime of Apartheid to Israel." *Al-Majdal* (Summer 2008): 11–21. Print.

Mahaffy, Cheryl. "The Hidden Face of Prosperity." *Alberta Views* 10.9 (Nov. 2007): 36–41. Print.

Mamdani, Mahmood. *From Citizen to Refugee: Ugandan Asians Come to Britain.* London: Frances Pinter, 1973. Print.

Manufactured Landscapes. Dir. Jennifer Baichwal. Zeitgeist Films Ltd., 1996. Film.

Mara'ba v. The Government of Israel, Tak-A1 2007(3). Petitioners' Briefs HCJ 10716/06. 2007: 3434. Print.

Marsden, William. *Stupid to the Last Drop: How Alberta is Bringing Environmental Armageddon to Canada (and doesn't seem to care).* Toronto: Knopf Canada, 2007. Print.

Masalha, Nur. *Expulsion of the Palestinians: The Concept of "Transfer" in Zionist Political Thought 1882–1948.* Washington, DC: Institute of Palestine Studies, 1992. Print.

———. *A Land Without a People: Israel, Transfer and the Palestinians 1949–96.* London: Faber and Faber, 1997. Print.

McCubbin, Laurie D., and M.I. Hamilton. "Culture and Ethnic Identity in Family Resilience Dynamic Processes in Trauma and Transformation of Indigenous People." *Handbook for Working with Children and Youth: Pathways to Resilience Across Cultures and Contexts*. Ed. M. Ungar. Thousand Oaks, CA: SAGE, 2005. 27–44; 39–58. Print.

McMaster, George. "Rebuilding the Spirit." *Unbury my Heart: An Exhibition of the Art of Shelley Niro: February 25–April 8, 2001*. Hamilton, ON: McMaster Museum of Art, 2001. 10–17. Print.

McNevin, Anne. "Political Belonging in a Neoliberal Era: The Struggle of the *Sans-Papiers*." *Citizenship Studies* 10.2 (2006): 135–51. Print.

———. Untitled Lecture. Acts of Citizenship plenary panel. *2008 John Douglas Taylor Conference,"Displacements: Borders, Mobility and Statelessness."* McMaster University, Hamilton, Ontario. 7 March 2008. *"Displacements" Conference Archives*. www.literaryculture.ca. Web.

Menjívar, Cecilia. *Fragmented Ties: Salvadoran Immigrant Networks in America.* Berkeley: University of California Press, 2000. Print.

Mentschel, Binalakshmi Nepram. "Armed Conflict, Small Arms Proliferation and Women's Responses to Armed Violence in India's North-East." Working Paper No. 33. Heidelberg: Heidelberg Papers in South Asia and Comparative Politics, 2007: 1–27. *Archiv.ub.uni-heidelberg.de*. Web. 2 July 2008.

———. "A Narrative on the Origin of the Meira Paibis." *E-Pao*. 9 Jan. 2005: n. pag. Web. 2 July 2008.

Mercer, David. "Aboriginal Self-determination and Indigenous Land Title in Post-Mabo Australia." *Political Geography* 16.3 (1997): 189–212. Print.

———. "*Terra Nullius*, Aboriginal Sovereignty, and Land Rights in Australia: the Debate Continues." *Political Geography* 12.4 (1993): 299–318. Print.

"The Merciless Killing of Thangiam Manorama." *Worldpress*. 23 July 2004: n. pag. Web. 11 April 2008.

Milloy, John S. *A National Crime: The Canadian Government and the Residential School System, 1879–1986*. Winnipeg: University of Manitoba Press, 1999. Print.

Ministry of Information and Broadcasting. *Jawaharlal Nehru's Speeches: Volume One. September 1946–May 1949*. New Delhi: Ministry of Information and Broadcasting, 1967. Print.

Ministry of Rehabilitation. *Annual Report on Evacuation, Relief and Rehabilitation of Refugees (September 1947 to August 1948)*. New Delhi, 1949. Print.

Ministry of Rehabilitation. *Annual Report: 1960–61*. New Delhi, 1961. Print.

———. *Estimates Committee (1959–60) Ninety-Sixth Report*. New Delhi, 1960. Print.

Ministry of Supply and Rehabilitation. "Report of the Working Group on the Residual Problem of Rehabilitation in West Bengal." New Delhi, 1976. Print.

Mitra, Asok. *Census of India, 1951*. Vol. VI, Part III. Calcutta City, 1953. Print.

Mohapatra, Manas. "Learning Lessons from India: The Recent History of Antiterrorist Legislation on the Subcontinent." *The Journal of Criminal Law and Criminology* 95.1 (Autumn 2004): 315–44. JSTOR. Web. 18 May 2008.

Mohawk, John C. Prologue. *The White Roots of Peace*. By Paul A.W. Wallace. 1946. Saranac Lake, NY: Chauncy Press, 1986. xv–xxiii. Print.

Monitoring Israeli Colonizing Activities in the Palestinian West Bank and Gaza. "Alarming Demolition Orders in Nazlet 'Isa Village." *Applied Research Institute Jerusalem*. 21 Jan. 2003. Web. 18 Sept. 2008.

Monture, Rick. English 331—Early American Literature and Culture. Redeemer University College, Hamilton, Ontario. 16 Jan. 2008. Guest Lecture.

Morris, Benny. *Righteous Victims: A History of the Zionist-Arab Conflict 1881–2001*. New York: Vintage Books, 2001. Print.

Moussa, Helene. *Traumatismes et ruptures. Colloque international. Conseil des Eglises du Moyen Orient 26–27 Octobre 2002*. The Middle East Council of Churches, Beirut, Lebanon, 2003. Print.

The National Center on Women, Violence and Trauma (USA). "Free Trauma Models." 24 Aug. 2005. Web. 18 Oct. 2008.

Ndebele, Njabulo S. "The Rediscovery of the Ordinary." *South African Literature and Culture*. Manchester: Manchester University Press, 1994. 41–59. Print.

Neimeyer, Robert A., and M. Buchanan-Arvay. "Performing the Self: Therapeutic Enactment and the Narrative Integration of Traumatic Loss." *The Dialogical*

Self in Psychotherapy. Ed. H.J.M. Hermans, and C. Dimaggio. New York: Brunner-Routledge, 2004. 173–89. Print.

Nikiforuk, Andrew. *Tar Sands: Dirty Oil and the Future of a Continent*. Vancouver: Greystone Books, 2008. Print.

"Nilin Village Non-Violent Struggle Against the Wall." *YouTube*. N.d. Web. 30 May 2009.

Niro, Shelley. "Artist Statement." *Unbury my heart: an exhibition of the art of Shelley Niro: February 25–April 8, 2001*. Hamilton, ON: McMaster Museum of Art, 2001. Print.

———. *Honey Moccasin* installation review. *National Museum of the American Indian*. n.d. Web. 25 Nov. 2007.

———. Independent Film and Video Class. McMaster University, Hamilton, Ontario. 23 Oct. 2008. Guest Lecture.

———. Interview with Larry Abbott. *A Time of Visions: Interviews by Larry Abbott*. Web. N.d. 13 April 2007.

No One Is Illegal. "About No One Is Illegal-Toronto." *No One Is Illegal*. N.d. Web. 1 Sept. 2009.

Nyers, Peter. "Abject Cosmopolitanism: The Politics of Protection in the Anti-Deportation Movement." *Third World Quarterly* 24.5 (2003): 1069–93. Print.

———. "Introduction: What's Left of Citizenship?" *Citizenship Studies* 8.3 (2004): 203–15. Print.

———. *Rethinking Refugees: Beyond States of Emergency*. New York: Routledge, 2006. Print.

O'Brien, Susie, and Imre Szeman. *Popular Culture: A User's Guide*. Scarborough, ON: Thomson Nelson, 2004. Print.

OCHA. "The Barrier Gate and Permit Regime Four Years On: Humanitarian Impact in Northern West Bank." *United Nations Office for the Coordination of Humanitarian Affairs*. Nov. 2007. Web. 17 Sept. 2008.

———. "The Humanitarian Impact of the Barrier: Four Years After the Advisory Opinion of the International Court of Justice on the Barrier." *United Nations Office for the Coordination of Humanitarian Affairs*. Update No. 8. July 2008. Web. 17 Sept. 2008.

O'Connor, Flannery. "The Displaced Person." *Flannery O'Connor: Collected Works*. New York: Library of America, 1988. 285–327. Print.

Oinam, Bhagat. "Manipur." *Sub-Regional Relations in the Eastern South Asia: With Special Focus on India's North-Eastern Region*. Eds. Mayumi Murayama, Kyoko Inoue, and Sanjoy Hazarika. Chiba, Japan: The Institute of Developing Economies (IDE) Publication, 2005: 65–110. *Ide.go.jp*. Web. 14 April 2008.

Ong, Aihwa. *Buddha is Hiding: Refugees, Citizenship, the New America*. Berkeley: University of California Press, 2003. Print.

———. *Neoliberalism as Exception*. Durham, NC: Duke University Press, 2006. Print.

Overweight With Crooked Teeth. Dir. Shelley Niro. 1997. Film.

"PACBI Call for Academic and Cultural Boycott of Israel." *Palestinian Campaign for Academic and Cultural Boycott of Israel*. 21 Dec. 2008. Web. 28 May 2009.

"Palestinian Call for Boycott, Divestment and Sanctions Against Israel until it Complies with International Law and Universal Principles of Human Rights." BDS *Movement: Boycotts Divestment and Sanctions for Palestine*. Global BDS Movements, 9 July 2005. Web. 28 May 2009.

———. "State of Independence." *Imphal Free Press* 15 Aug. 2011. Web. 27 Aug. 2011.

Pappe, Ilan. *The Ethnic Cleansing of Palestine*. London: One World, 2006. Print.

Parratt, Saroj N. Arambam, and John Parratt. "The Second 'Women's War' and the Emergence of Democratic Government in Manipur." *Modern Asian Studies* 35.4 (Oct. 2001): 905–19. JSTOR. Web. 11 March 2008.

Perera, Suvendrini. "A Pacific Zone? (In)Security, Sovereignty, and Stories of the Pacific Borderscape." *Borderscapes: Hidden Geographies and Politics at Territory's Edge*. Ed. Prem Kumar Rajaram and Carl Grundy-Warr. Minneapolis: University of Minnesota Press, 2007. 201–27 Print.

Petersen, Inessa. *Saying "I": Refugee Women Re-claim their Identity. A Community Arts Project*. Hamilton, ON: Workers Arts and Heritage Centre, Immigrant Culture and Arts Association, and the Settlement and Integration Services Organization, 2003. Print.

Peutz, Nathalie. "Embarking on an Anthropology of Removal." *Current Anthropology* 47.2 (2006): 217–41. Print.

Phanjoubam, Pradip. "Population Displacement in Manipur in the last 100 years." *A Status Report on Displacement in Assam and Manipur*. Eds. Monirul Hussain and Pradip Phanjoubam. Kolkata: Mahanirban Calcutta Research Group (CRG), 2007: 22–41. *Mcrg.ac.in*. Web. 20 March 2008.

"Political Action Plan." *Kadima*. 25 Jan. 2009. Web. 29 May 2009.

Powell, Timothy B. Introduction. *Ruthless Democracy: A Multicultural Interpretation of the American Renaissance*. Princeton, NJ: Princeton University Press, 2000. 5–29. Print.

Poyatos, Fernando, ed. *Cross-Cultural Perspectives in Non-verbal Communication*. Toronto: C.J. Hogrefe, 1987. Print.

Prasad, Kiran. "Women's Movement and Media in India: Reshaping Notions of Power." *Women in Action* 3 (2004): n. pag. *Isiswomen.org*. 8 Aug. 2008.

Pratt, Larry. *The Tar Sands: Syncrude and the Politics of Oil*. Edmonton, AB: Hurtig Publishers, 1976. Print.

"Press Release: Victory for Worker Solidarity." *Congress of South African Trade Unions*. 6 Feb. 2009. Web. 29 May 2009.

Radhakrishnan, R. *Diasporic Mediations: Between Home and Location*. Minneapolis: University of Minnesota Press, 1996. Print.

Rajaram, Prem Kumar, and Carl Grundy-Warr. Introduction. *Borderscapes: Hidden Geographies and Politics at Territory's Edge*. Ed. Prem Kumar Rajaram and Carl Grundy-Warr. Minneapolis: University of Minnesota Press, 2007. ix–xl. Print.

———, eds. *Borderscapes: Hidden Geographies and Politics at Territory's Edge*. Minneapolis: University of Minnesota Press, 2007. Print.

Rajasingham-Senanayake, Darini. "Between Victim and Agent: Women's Ambivalent Empowerment in Displacement." *Refugees and the Transformation of Societies: Agency, Policies, Ethics and Politics*. Ed. Philomena Essed, Georg Frerks, and Joke Schrijvers. *Studies in Forced Migration*. Oxford: Berghahn Books, 2004. 151–67. Print.

Razack, Sherene H. *Dark Threats and White Knights: The Somalia Affair, Peacekeeping, and the New Imperialism*. Toronto: University of Toronto Press, 2004. Print.

Rejwan, Nissim. *Israel's Place in the Middle East: A Pluralist Perspective*. Gainesville: University Press of Florida, 1999. Print.

"Report of the Committee, headed by Justice (Retd.) B.P. Jeevan Reddy, to Review the Armed Forces (Special Powers) Act 1958." *The Hindu* 2005: n. pag. Web. 4 March 2008.

"Review of Armed Forces Act Will be Considered: Manmohan." *The Hindu* 2 Nov. 2004: n. pag. Web. 12 Feb. 2008.

Ricoeur, Paul. "The Poetics of Language and Myth." Interview with Richard Kearney. *Debates in Continental Philosophy: Conversations with Contemporary Thinkers*. New York: Fordham Press, 2004. 99–125. Print.

Robinson, Courtland. "Risks and Rights: The Causes, Consequences, and Challenges of Development-Induced Displacement." Washington, DC: The Brookings Institution—Sais project on internal displacement, May 2003: 1–102. *Adb.org*. Web. 11 May 2008.

Rodinson, Maxime. *Israel: A Colonial-Settler State?* New York: Pathfinder Press, 1973. Print.

Rotas Alex. "Is Refugee Art Possible?" *Third Text* 18.1 (2004): 51–60. Web. 18 July 2008.

Routray, Bibhu Prasad. "Manmohan Singh's North-East India Sojourn: A Healing Overture?" *Society for the Study of Peace and Conflict* 11 Dec. 2004: n. pag. *Sspconline.org*. Web. 1 March 2008.

Rowe, Stan. "'Homo Ecologicus'—A Wiser Name." *Earth Alive: Essays on Ecology*. Edmonton, AB: NeWest Press, 2006. Print.

Roy, Sanjay K. "Conflicting Nations in North-East India." *Economic and Political Weekly* 40.21 (21–27 May 2005): 2176–82. JSTOR. Web. 4 June 2008.

Rushdie, Salman. *Imaginary Homelands*. New York: Penguin Books, 1991. Print.

Ryan, Allen. "The Re/Creation of Identity." *The Trickster Shift: Humour and Irony in Contemporary Native Art*. Vancouver: UBC Press, 1999. 13–91. Print.

Sachdeva, Gulshan. "India's North-East: Rejuvenating a Conflict-riven Economy." *Faultlines: Writings on Conflict & Resolution* 6 (2001): n. pag. *Satp.org*. Web. 8 May 2008.

Sahni, Ajai, and J. George. "Security & Development in India's North-East: An Alternative Perspective." *Faultlines: Writings on Conflict and Resolution* 4 (2000): n. pag. *Satp.org*. Web. 8 May 2008.

Said, Edward W. *The Question of Palestine*. London: Routledge and Kegan Paul, 1980. Print.

Salameh Theatre Troupe. Introductory Notes to the performance *Finding our Song*. 2008 John Douglas Taylor Conference, "Displacements: Borders, Mobility and Statelessness." McMaster University, Hamilton, Ontario. March 2008. *"Displacements" Conference Archives*. The Canada Research Chair Symposium for Diversity in Literary Cultures. Web. p. 7 of 8.

Sassen, Saskia. *Guests and Aliens*. New York: The New Press, 1999. Print.

———. *Losing Control? Sovereignty in an Age of Globalization*. New York: Columbia University Press, 1996. Print.

———. "The Need to Distinguish Denationalized and Postnational." *Indiana Journal of Global Legal Studies* 7.2 (2000): 575–84. Print.

———. "The Repositioning of Citizenship and Alienage: Emergent Subjects and Spaces for Politics." *Globalizations* 2.1 (2005): 79–94. Print.

———. *Territory, Authority, Rights: From Medieval to Global Assemblages*. Princeton, NJ: Princeton University Press, 2006. Print.

———. "When National Territory is Home to the Global: Old Borders to Novel Borderings." *New Political Economy* 10.4 (2005): 523–41. Print.

Sen, K.K. "Industrial development in Assam." *The Assam Tribune* 25 July 2008: n. pag. Web. 8 Aug. 2008.

Shafir, Gershon. "Zionism and Colonialism: A Comparative Approach." *The Israel/Palestine Question*. Ed. Ilan Pappe. New York: Routledge, 1999. 81–96. Print.

Sharma, Nandita. "Global Apartheid and Nation-Statehood: Instituting Border Regimes." *Nationalism and Global Solidarities: Alternative Projections to Neoliberal Globalization*. Ed. J. Goodman and P. James. London: Routledge, 2007. 92–109. Print.

———. "Immigrant and Migrant Workers in Canada: Labour Movements, Racism and the Expansion of Globalization." *Canadian Woman Studies* 21.4 (2002): 18–26. Print.

Shiell, Leslie, and Colin Busby. "Greater Saving Required: How Alberta can Achieve Fiscal Sustainability from its Resource Revenues." *C.D. Howe Institute Commentary*. No. 263, May 2008. Web. 29 May 2008.

Shimray, U.A. "Feeling "Diaspora: An Essay." *Kangla Online*. N.d. Web. 4 July 2008.

———. "Youth on the Move: North-East Experience." *Kangla Online*. N.d. Web. 4 July 2008.

Shohat, Ella. "Notes on the Post-Colonial." *Social Text* 31.32 (1992): 99–113. JSTOR. Web. 5 Jan. 2007.

Shukin, Nicole. "Industrial Mobility." *Animal Capital: The Politics of Rendering*. Unpublished Dissertation. 2005. 129–211. Print.

Simpson, Audra. "The Empire Laughs Back: Tradition, Power, and Play in the Work of Shelley Niro and Ryan Rice." *IroquoisART: Visual Expressions of Contemporary Native American Artists*. Altenstadt, Germany: Christian F. Feest, 1998. 48–54. Print.

Singh, B.P. "North-East India: Demography, Culture and Identity Crisis North." *Modern Asian Studies* 21.2 (1987): 257–82. JSTOR. Web. 4 Aug. 2008.

Singh, Gurharpal. "Resizing and Reshaping the State: India from Partition to the Present." *Right-sizing the State—The Politics of Moving Borders*. Eds. Brendan O'Leary, Ian S. Lustick, and Thomas Callaghy. Oxford: Oxford University Press, 2001. 138–68. Print.

Singh, Manmohan. "Independence Day Speech, 2008." 15 Aug. 2008: n. pag. *Pmindia.nic.in*. Web. 16 Aug. 2008.

Singha, Anil, *Jabardakhal Colony*. Calcutta: Self-published, 1979. Print.

Smith, Dorothy E. *Conceptual Practices of Power*. Toronto: University of Toronto Press, 1990. Print.

"Smritikatha," *Ganashakti* (Bengali daily newspaper). Calcutta: Communist Party of India (Marxist), 2000. Print.

Soguk, Nevzat. "Border's Capture: Insurrectional Politics, Border-Crossing Humans, and the New Political." *Borderscapes*. Ed. Prem Kumar Rajaram, and Carl Grundy-Warr. Minneapolis: University of Minnesota Press, 2007. 283–308. Print.

South Asia Human Rights Documentation Centre (SAHRDC). "Armed Forces Special Powers Act: A Study in National Security Tyranny." New Delhi (Nov. 1995): n. pag. *hrdc.net/sahrdc/resources*. Web. 6 July 2008.

South Asia Terrorism Portal, Institute of Conflict Management. *Satp.org*. Web. 8 May 2008.

———. "United National Liberation Front." 2001: n. pag. *Satp.org*. Web. 8 May 2008.

Soysal, Yasemin. *Limits of Citizenship*. Chicago: University of Chicago Press, 1994. Print.

Spivak, Gayatri Chakravorty. *A Critique of Postcolonial Reason: Toward a History of the Vanishing Present*. Cambridge, MA: Harvard University Press, 1999. Print.

Stasiulis, Daiva, and Abigail Bakan. *Negotiating Citizenship*. Toronto: University of Toronto Press, 2005. Print.

Stiell, Bernadette, and Kim England. "Domestic Distinctions: Constructing Difference Among Paid Domestic Workers in Toronto." *Gender, Place and Culture* 4.3 (1997): 339–59. Print.

"Stop The Wall: Latest News." *Stop the Wall Grassroots Palestinian Anti-Apartheid Wall Campaign*. Web. 18 Sept. 2008.

Suite: INDIAN. Dir. Shelley Niro. Brantford, ON: Turtle Night Productions, 2005. Film.

Sultany, Nimer. "The Legacy of Justice Aharon Barak: A Critical Review" *Harvard International Law Journal* 48 (2007): 83–92. Print.

Syncrude Canada Ltd. "2006 Sustainability Report." *Syncrude.com*. Web. 23 Aug. 2007.

Tactaquin, C. "Illegal Immigrants are Treated Unfairly." *Illegal Immigration*. Ed. W. Barbour. San Diego, CA: Greenhaven Press, 1994. 138–44. Print.

Taruni, Keisam. Personal Interview by Pavithra Narayanan. Imphal, Manipur, 2005.

Taylor, Charles. "The Politics of Recognition." *Multiculturalism: Examining the Politics of Recognition*. Ed. Amy Gutmann. Princeton, NJ: Princeton University Press, 1994. Print.

Teveth, Shabtai. *Ben Gurion and the Palestinian Arabs: From Peace to War*. Jerusalem: Schoken, 1985. (In Hebrew) Print.

Thangjam, Homen. "Armed-conflict and Women's Well-being in Manipur." *Manipur Research Forum*. N.d., n. pag. Web. 4 April 2008.

Théâtre du Public and Theater for Everybody. Publicity pamphlet for *Les Murs Tombent, Les Mots Restent*. N.d. Print.

Thingnam, Sanjeev. "Redefining Frontier Through LEP: A Colonial Articulation of Manipur." *Look East Policy and India's North East: Polemics and Perspectives*. Ed. Thingnam Kishan Singh. New Delhi: Published for Centre for Alternative Discourse, Manipur by Concept Pub. Co., 2008: 93–111. Print.

Thokchom, Khelen. "She Stoops to Conquer." *The Telegraph* 25 July 2004: n. pag. Web. 4 Aug. 2008.

Tilley, V., ed. "Occupation, Colonialism, Apartheid? A Re-assessment of Israel's Practices in the Occupied Palestinian Territories Under International

Law." *Human Sciences Research Council of South Africa*. Middle East Project Democracy and Governance Programme, May 2009. Web. 29 May 2009.

Tisseron, Serge. "Ces mots qui polluent la pensée: 'Résilience' ou la lutte pour la vie." *Le Monde Diplomatique* 21 Aug. 2003. Print.

Todorov, Tsvetan. *The Conquest of America: The Question of the Other*. New York: Harper & Row, 1984. Print.

Torpey, John. "Coming and Going: On the State Monopolization of the Legitimate 'Means of Movement.'" *Sociological Theory* 16.3 (1998): 239–59. Print.

Tully, James. *Strange Multiplicity: Constitutionalism in an Age of Diversity*. Cambridge: Cambridge University Press, 1995. Print.

Ungar, Michael. "A Constructionist Discourse on Resilience: Multiple Contexts, Multiple Realities Among at-risk Children and Youth." *Youth & Society* 35.3 (2004): 341–65. Print.

———. *Handbook for Working with Children and Youth: Pathways to Resilience Across Cultures and Contexts*. Thousand Oaks, CA: SAGE, 2005. Print.

Ungar, Michael, and Eli Teram. "Qualitative Resilience Research: Contributions and Risks." *Handbook for Working with Children and Youth: Pathways to Resilience Across Cultures and Contexts*. Thousand Oaks, CA: SAGE, 2005. 149–59. Print.

Ungar, Michael, and Linda Liebenberg. "The International Resilience Project: A Mixed Methods Approach to the Study of Resilience across Cultures." *Handbook for Working with Children and Youth: Pathways to Resilience Across Cultures and Contexts*. Thousand Oaks, CA: SAGE, 2005. 27–44. Print.

United Central Refugee Council. *Shorosh Sammelan O Subarna Jayanti Utsab*. Calcutta: UCRC, 2000. Print.

United Nations Centre for Human Settlements (Habitat). *Survey of Slum and Squatter Settlements*. Dublin: Tycooly International Publishing Limited, 1982. Print.

"UNHCR Annual Report Shows 42 Million People Uprooted Worldwide." Press Release. *United Nations High Commissioner for Refugees*. 16 June 2009. Web. 22 June 2009.

United Nations High Commissioner for Refugees. *Statistical Yearbook, 2006*. Web. 17 Oct. 2008.

Upadhyay, R. "Manipur—In a strange whirlpool of Cross-Current Insurgency." *South Asia Analysis Group*. Paper No. 1210, 3 Jan. 2005: n. pag. Web. 8 May 2008.

Van Voorhis, Rebecca M. "Culturally Relevant Practice: A Framework for Teaching the Psychosocial Dynamics of Oppression." *Journal of Social Work Education* 34.1 (1998): 121–33. Print.

Varadarajan, Siddharth. "Anybody Remember Manipur?" *The Hindu* 29 June 2005: n. pag. Web. 11 July 2008.

———. "Repeal Armed Forces Act—Official Panel." *The Hindu* 8 Oct. 2006: n. pag. Web. 11 July 2008.

Varsanyi, Monica W. "Interrogating 'Urban Citizenship' *vis-à-vis* Undocumented Migration." *Citizenship Studies* 10.2 (2006): 229–49. Print.

Vital, David. *The Origins of Zionism*. Oxford: Oxford University Press, 1975. Print.

Viveknagar Colony Subarnajayanti Samkalan. Calcutta: Viveknagar Colony Subarnajayanti Committee, 2000. Print.

Wallace, Paul A. *The White Roots of Peace*. 1946. Saranac Lake, NY: Chauncy Press, 1986. Print.

Waller, M.A. "Resilience in Ecosystemic Context: Evolution of the Concept." *American Journal of Orthopsychiatry* 71.3 (2001): 290–97. Print.

Walters, William. "Deportation, Expulsion, and the International Police of Aliens." *Citizenship Studies* 6.3 (2002): 265–92. Print.

Welch, M. "The Immigration Crisis." *Immigration*. Ed. Jonas, S., and S.D. Thomas. Wilmington, DE: Scholarly Resources, 1999. 191–206. Print.

West, Amy R. "The Refugee-Media Nexus." Interviewed by Soenke Zehle. *Nongovernmental Politics*. New York: Zone Books, 2007. 407–17. Print.

West Bengal Legislative Assembly. *Proceedings of the West Bengal Legislative Assembly*. Calcutta: Government of West Bengal, 1956. Print.

———. *Proceedings of the West Bengal Legislative Assembly*. Calcutta: Government of West Bengal, 1957. Print.

———. *Proceedings of the West Bengal Legislative Assembly*. Calcutta: Government of West Bengal, 1958. Print.

Whaley, Susan. *Rudy Wiebe and His Works*. Toronto: ECW Press, 1986. Print.

"Where 'Peacekeepers' Have Declared War." New Delhi: National Campaign Against Militarization and Repeal of the Armed Forces (Special Powers) Act, 1997. Print.

Wiebe, Rudy. "Passages By Land." *The Narrative Voice: Short Stories and Reflections by Canadian Authors*. Ed. John Metcalf. Toronto: McGraw-Hill Ryerson, 1972. Print.

———. "The Angel of the Tar Sands." *The Angel of the Tar Sands and Other Stories*. Toronto: McClelland & Stewart, 1982. Print.

Wiebe, Rudy, and Theatre Passe Muraille. *Far as the Eye Can See*. Edmonton, AB: NeWest Press, 1977. Print.

Williams, Raymond. "Culture is Ordinary." 1958. *The Raymond Williams Reader*. Ed. John Higgins. Oxford: Blackwell Publishers, 2001.10–24. Print.

Wright, Cynthia. "Moments of Emergence." *Refuge* 21.3 (2003): 5–16. Print.

Wright, Ronald. *Stolen Continents: The New World Through Indian Eyes*. Toronto: Penguin Books, 1992. Print.
Yaeger, Patricia. "Editor's Column: The Death of Nature and the Apotheosis of Trash; or, Rubbish Ecology." *PMLA* 123.2 (March 2008): 321–39. Print.
Yan, Miu Chung, and Yuk-Lin Wong. "Rethinking Self-Awareness in Cultural Competence: Toward a Dialogic Self in Cross-Cultural Social Work." *Families in Society* 86.2 (2005): 181–88. Print.
Zetter, Roger. "More Labels, Fewer Refugees: Remaking the Refugee Label in an Era of Globalization." *Journal of Refugee Studies* 20.2 (2007): 172–92. Print.
Zhang, Benzi. "The Politics of Re-homing: Asian Diaspora Poetry in Canada." *College Literature* 31.1 (Winter 2004): 103–25. *JSTOR*. Web. 18 July 2008.
Žižek, Slavoj. *In Defense of Lost Causes*. New York: Verso, 2008. Print.
Zureik, Elia T. *The Palestinians in Israel: A Study in Internal Colonialism*. London: Routledge and Kegan Paul, 1978. Print.
Zwicky, Jan. *Lyric Philosophy*. Toronto: University of Toronto Press, 1992. Print.
———. "Lyric, Narrative, Memory." *a ragged pen: essays on poetry and memory*. Ed. Robert Finlay, et al. Kentville, NS: Gaspereau Press, 2006. 93–100. Print.
———. "Talk and Reading for the Environmental Research and Studies Centre." University of Alberta, Edmonton. 4 Oct. 2007. Lecture.
———. *Wisdom and Metaphor*. Kentville, NS: Gaspereau Press, 2003. Print.

CONTRIBUTORS

DANIEL COLEMAN, a professor at McMaster University, teaches and carries out research in Canadian Literature, critical race studies, diaspora, the literary and cultural production of categories of privilege such as whiteness, masculinity, and Britishness, and, most recently, the spiritual and cultural politics of reading. He has published *Masculine Migrations* (1998), *The Scent of Eucalyptus* (2003), and has co-edited seven scholarly volumes. His book, *White Civility: The Literary Project of English Canada* (University of Toronto Press, 2006), won the Raymond Klibansky prize for the best English-language book in the humanities in Canada in 2006–2007. His most recent book, *In Bed With the Word: Reading, Spirituality, and Cultural Politics* was published by the University of Alberta Press in March 2009.

SUBHASRI GHOSH received her doctoral degree in modern history from Jawaharlal Nehru University, New Delhi and is at present a post-doctoral fellow at the Rabindranath Tagore Centre for Human Development Studies at the University of Calcutta. She worked previously as publications coordinator in a Calcutta-based women's rights organization named Swayam.

ERIN GOHEEN GLANVILLE is a PHD candidate in the English and Cultural Studies Department at McMaster University. She is researching and writing on Canadian refugee narratives and church-based refugee activism but has broader interests in postcolonial and diaspora studies. She has chapters in multi-author volumes published by Routledge and by Regent University Press as well as contributions to *The Literary Encyclopedia*. During her doctoral years, Erin has lectured at Redeemer University College, Hamilton, Ontario, given workshops at several teacher-training conferences, and provided short courses on refugee and postcolonial narratives for local high school students: Recently, she relocated from Sydney, Australia to Vancouver, BC with her husband Mark and daughter Mahla.

JON GORDON has taught in English and Film Studies at the University of Alberta and Writing Studies at Maskwachees Cultural College. He is currently teaching writing studies at the University of Alberta. He has published on hog production and mountaineering literature; his article in this collection is part of a larger project examining the relationship between literature and the cultural assumptions that enable bitumen production.

CATHERINE GRAHAM is an associate professor of Theatre and Film Studies at McMaster University, where she also contributes to graduate programs in Cultural Studies and Critical Theory, Gender Studies and Feminist Research and French. She is an associate editor of *Canadian Theatre Review*, has worked in and around activist theatre for thirty years, and has published articles in this field in Canada, the United States, and Belgium. Her research for this article was supported by a grant from the Social Sciences and Humanities Research Council of Canada.

MAROUSSIA HAJDUKOWSKI-AHMED teaches in the departments of French and Women's Studies and the Institute on Globalization and the Human Condition at McMaster University. Her present research focuses on migration and identity issues, and on the socio-cultural determinants of the mental health of immigrant and refugee women. She was a principal investigator (1993–1999) and co-chair (1997–1999) of the McMaster Research Centre for the Promotion of Women's Health. She is a co-author and co-editor of *Not Born a Refugee Woman: Contesting Identities, Rethinking Practices*, and *Women's Voices in Health Promotion*. She is also the co-author of working papers, reports and essays on topics such as women and forced migration, dialogism and post-colonial theory, dialogism in the social sciences, and fiction by francophone women authors. She has been a long-standing member of the Board of Directors of settlement organizations for immigrants and refugees in Hamilton.

WAFAA HASAN is a PHD candidate in the Department of English and Cultural Studies and was also the founding associate director of the Canada Research Chair Symposium on Canadian Literary Culture. Her dissertation conducts a discursive analysis of Israeli-Palestinian feminist dialogues in the 1990s to reflect on the contemporary dialogue-boycott proposed by Palestinian women in the region. She has published in the *CLCWeb: Comparative Literature and Culture* journal and has two forthcoming articles entitled "How Do We Speak? The Marginalization of the Canadian Arab Federation" (with UBC Press) and "Arab Scholars' Take on Globalization" (with Routledge). Hasan lives in Toronto, Ontario.

AGNES KRAMER-HAMSTRA received her doctoral degree in Canadian literature and culture at McMaster University and currently is professor of literature at St. Stephen's University, St. Stephen, New Brunswick. Her research interests include the relationship between stories and home-making away from home in contemporary Canadian and First Nations fictional narratives. Her abiding passions include how stories can be as important as bread, narratives of/in exile, fictional representations of First Nations/Settler relations in Canada, and postcolonial and ecocritical theory. Besides presenting at conferences, she has published "Rumours of a Larger Story: The Intersection of Mystery and Mastery in Eden Robinson's *Monkey Beach*" in *Canadian Journal of Native Studies* (2009).

MAZEN MASRI is currently a PHD candidate at Osgoode Hall Law School. Prior to resuming graduate studies at Osgoode, Mazen served as legal advisor to the Negotiations Affairs Department of the Palestine Liberation Organization (PLO). He holds a bachelor of law degree (LLB) from the Hebrew University and a master of law degree (LLM) from the University of Toronto. He has worked in the legal field in both Israel and the West Bank. His current research interests include constitutional law and international law.

JEAN MC DONALD is a SSHRC post-doctoral fellow based out of the Institute on Globalization and the Human Condition at McMaster University. Her research focuses on processes of migrant illegalization within the realm of service provision in Toronto, with particular attention to issues of gender violence, racism, nationalism, and global capitalism. She has extensive activist and community organizing experience with the migrant justice organization No One Is Illegal and through campaigns for greater access to services and social rights for non-status immigrants living in Toronto. Recent publications include "Migrant Illegality, Nation-Building and the Politics of Regularization in Canada," *Refuge* 26.2 (2011): 65–77, and "Citizenship, Illegality and Sanctuary" (2007) in *Interrogating Race and Racism*, edited by Vijay Agnew.

PAVITHRA NARAYANAN is an Associate Professor of English and faculty affiliate of the Centre for Social and Environmental Justice at Washington State University Vancouver. Economic, political, and social policies, class, caste, and gender disparities, and concepts of globalization are central issues in her research. Narayanan's monograph, *What are you reading? The World Market and Indian Literary Production*, published by Routledge India is forthcoming in 2011. She is also a documentary filmmaker. Her first film, *India and Free Trade: A Closer look at Bhopal*, examines the implications of free trade policies.

Narayanan's current film project, *Facing North-East: Remembering Manipur, Manorama Unforgotten*, focuses on civil liberties.

INDEX

Page numbers in *italics* refer to photographs or maps. Page numbers with an italicized *t* refer to a table or figure.

Aberhart, William, as literary character, 6–7, 19
"Abject Cosmopolitanism" (Nyers), xxv–xxvi
Action Committee for Non-Status Algerians, xxvi
"A Dialogical Approach to the Identity of Refugee Women" (Hajdukowski-Ahmed), 212
AFSPA. See *Armed Forces (Special Powers) Act*
Agamben, Giorgio, xvii
Agger, Inger, 206, 212, 230
Albanna, Rami, 96, 100
Alberta
    "acceptable" trade-offs, 9–12
    coal mining, 3, 6–9
    Wiebe on literature and land, 19
    See also oil sands

Alberta (Kroetsch), 20
Aldred, Ray, 196–98
Alexander, Jacqui, 198
Alfred, Taiaiake, xxiii–xxv, xxix, xl, 184–85, 195, 201*n*3, 203*n*13
Ali, Mahmud, 123, 131, 132
Altamirano, Isabel, xxiv
Anand, Oinam, 142
Anderson, Benedict, 122–23
"The Angel of the Tar Sands" (Wiebe)
    as alternative narrative, 2, 13–14, 18–20
    angel and lyric thinking, 4, 20–22, 28, 30*n*8
    Judaeo-Christian worldview, 22, 24, 28, 30*n*8
    synopsis of, 3
Angus, Ian, 14, 21
Appadurai, Arjun, 37, 46–47
Appiah, Kwame Anthony, 90–91, 97, 113
Arab Abu Farada, West Bank, 70, 72–73
Arab Aramadin, West Bank, 70, 72–73

Arambam Somorendra Singh, 132
architecture and Indigenous peoples, Canada, xxxi–xxxiii
Arendt, Hannah, xxi–xxii
Ariel, West Bank, 66
Armed Forces (Special Powers) Act (India)
  overview of, 124–27, 129–30, 148n6
  protests for repeal of, *116*, 117–18, 121, 127, 138–41, *141*, 144–45, 149n17
  recommendations for repeal of, 133–34, 144–45, 149n15–16
Armstrong, Jeanette, xxxii–xxxiii, 18
art, culture, and displacement
  alternative narratives, 2–3
  Appiah on art as a new way of seeing, 90–91, 97, 113
  art and therapy, 231
  Bakhtin on art and artists, 220–21, 233n5, 234n9
  Cardinal's architecture, xxxi–xxxiii
  creativity as countering displacement, xxix–xxxi, xli
  creativity of refugees, 206–09, 221–24, 230–32
  cultural studies, xii–xiv
  cultural styles of exclusion, 94–96
  Displacements conference performances, xv, xxxiv–xli
  painting by women refugees, 223–24, *224*, 227
  quincentenary of Columbus, 183, 193
  re-presentation of narratives (Spivak), 2, 18, 20
  Wiebe on land and literature, 19
  See also "The Angel of the Tar Sands"; music and song; photography; theatre; Zwicky, Jan, lyric thinking
Arunachal Pradesh, India, 121–22, 124
Asfour, Georgina, 96, 97, 106
Assam, India, 120, 124, 128
Assam Rifles, India, 125, 133, 140–41, 148n10
asylees. *See* refugees and asylees
Athabasca River, 4, 11, 15, 22
Australia
  cultural and race studies, xliiin7
  Lebanese asylum-seekers (Pacific Solution), xix–xx
  postnational citizenship, 40
  pre-colonial Aboriginal land rights, xlivn12
Azadgarh colony, Calcutta, West Bengal, 163, 167
Azimuth Theatre, 1

Badil Resource Center, 60
Bahuguna, Nitin, 137
Bakan, Abigail, 40, 42, 47, 51
Bakhtin, Mikhail, 209–13, 220–21, 233n5, 234n9
Balibar, Étienne, 44–45
Bammer, Angelika, xliin3
Banerjee, Paula, 137
Bangalore, India, 115–17, *116*
Bangladesh, 170
Baruah, Sanjib, 122, 124, 127, 134
Basha, Kamel, 96, 100
BDS. *See* "Boycott, Divestment, and Sanctions"
Bedouin refugees, 70, 72
Belgium, theatre, 87–88
Belur Camp, West Bengal, 156–57
Bengal, East. *See* East Bengal
Bengal, West. *See* West Bengal

Benhabib, Seyla, 48–49, 113
Bertell, Dr. Rosalie, 9–10, 11
Bhabha, Jacqueline, 37, 40
Bhagat, Ram, 142
Bil'in, West Bank, 77–78, 80
bituminous sands. *See* oil sands
The Blue Room (Agger), 206
borders
    borderscapes, xx
    everyday life and non-status immigrants, xiii, 34, 44
    fear and, xviii–xix, xxix
    "hard" and "soft" borders, xvii–xviii, xx, xxxvi, xliii$n$9
    human needs and challenges to, xxiii
    ideological borders, 34
    Lebanese asylum-seekers (Pacific Solution), xix–xx
    "no border" movements, xxiii, xxv–xxvii
    See also citizenship studies and migrant illegality; displacement; refugees and asylees
"Borders" (King), xliii$n$9
Bosniak, Linda, xvii–xviii, 37–38, 40, 42, 47–48, 51, 52
Bott, Robert, 6, 7, 15, 16, 24, 26
Bourdieu, Pierre, habitus, 95, 103–04, 112
"Boycott, Divestment, and Sanctions" (West Bank wall), 77, 81–83, 85
Bunta Singh, 141–42
Burton, Antoinette, 54
Burtynsky, Edward, 17
Busby, Colin, 4, 26

Calcutta, West Bengal, xi, 157, 159–61t, 162, 164–65, 169
    See also West Bengal, squatter settlements
Canada, immigration in
    global capitalism and, 35
    immigration legislation and policies, 33, 35
    live-in caregivers, xxxiv–xxxvii, xl–xli, xlvinn27–28
    non-status Algerians in Montreal, xxvi
    sanctuary city movement, 56
    See also citizenship studies and migrant illegality; "Don't Ask, Don't Tell" campaign, Toronto; No One Is Illegal movement; Sudan: women refugees
Canada, Indigenous peoples. *See* Indigenous peoples, Canada
Canada's First Nations (Dickason), 202n10
"Canada's Oil Sands" (Bott), 6, 7, 15, 16, 24, 26
Canadian construction companies, West Bank, 80
Canadian Museum of Civilization, Gatineau, Quebec, xxxi–xxxiii
Cardinal, Douglas, architecture, xxxi–xxxiii
Carter, Jim, 16
Caruth, Cathy, 212
C.D. Howe Institute, 4
Chamberlin, J. Edward, 202n8
Chatterjee, Partha, 121, 122–23
Chow, Rey, 119
Chowdhury, Neerja, 139
citizenship studies and migrant illegality, 31–57

citizenship, definitions, 42
denationalized citizenship, 40–43
deportability and detainability,
    48–50
destabilization of categories,
    50–51, 55
everyday life and, xiii, xvii–xviii,
    32–34, 38, 43–46, 55, 56n1
exclusive/inclusive paradox of, 34,
    36–40, 50–56
global apartheid (Sharma), 35–36,
    40, 50
global capitalism and, 31, 35,
    50–51, 55
global migration, 34–35
illegalization, definition, 33
labour and, 34, 36, 40, 41–42, 44,
    47, 48, 55
mental health issues, 46
national sovereignty and, xvii, 36,
    38–40, 49–50
overview of, x, 31–32
postnational citizenship, xxiii,
    xxv–xxvi, 40–43
precarious immigration status,
    definition, 33
qualitative research, 46
racialization and, 33, 50, 52–53, 55
refugees and asylees, privileging
    of, 48–49
sans-papiers movement, France,
    xxv, 44–45
status as fluid process, 47, 54, 57n3
unauthorized and recognized/
    unrecognized, 45
See also borders; "Don't Ask, Don't
    Tell" campaign; No One Is
    Illegal movement

"Citizenship Studies and Migrant
    Illegality" (McDonald), x, 31–57
Cleto, Petronila, xxxiv–xxxv, xl–xli,
    xlvn24
Coleman, Daniel, 261
Columbus, Christopher,
    quincentenary, 183, 193
Communist Party of India, 153, 164,
    170, 172, 173, 175n8
Conceptual Practices of Power (Smith),
    92–93
Cosmopolitanism (Appiah), 90–91,
    97, 113
Coutin, Susan Bibler, 48, 53–54
"Creativity as a Form of Resilience
    in Forced Migration"
    (Hajdukowski-Ahmed), 205–35
Crowfoot, as literary character, 6–8,
    19, 27
cultural studies, xii–xiv
Curthoy, Ann, xliiin7
Curtis, Edward Sheriff, 180, 201n5
Cyrulnik, Boris, 210, 216, 220, 221,
    234n10

De Genova, Nicholas, 36, 39, 44, 47,
    50–55
Democratic Republic of Congo,
    xlivn21
Dench, Janet, 215–16
Devi, Manorama
    killing of, 138–41, *141*, 146, 147
    protests about killing of, 115–18,
    116, 138–41
Diab, Amr, xxxviii
The Dialogic Imagination (Bakhtin),
    211
Dickason, Olive, 202n10

"The Displaced Person" (O'Connor), xlivn13
displacement, xiv–xxix
    agency and, xxiii–xxix
    countering displacement, xli
    countering displacement by creativity, xxix–xxx
    definition of, xiv, xliin3
    history of, xv–xvi
    Indigenous and refugee studies, xiii–xvii
    internal displacement, xliiin4, 142–43
    language and, 201n3
    live-in caregivers, xxxiv–xxxvii, xl–xli, xlvinn27–28
    public engagement with, 92–94, 106
    sans-papiers movements, xxv, xxix, 44–45
    theatre groups and, 89–90
    youth displaced from violent areas, 118–19, 142
    See also "Displacements: Borders, Mobility, Statelessness" (2008 conference); Indigenous peoples and displacement; refugees and asylees; *and specific places and groups*
"Displacements: Borders, Mobility, Statelessness" (2008 conference)
    overview, xv, xliiin5
    performances at, xv, xxxiv–xli, xlvn26
    See also *Finding Our Song*; *Operetang Maynila*
"Displacing Oil: Towards 'Lyric' Re-presentations of the Alberta Oil Sands" (Gordon), ix–x, 1–30
Dodds-Round Hill power plant, 6–7
Dolendru, Thonjum, 140, 147
domestic abuse and migrant illegality, 38
"Don't Ask, Don't Tell" campaign, Toronto, Ontario
    mandate of, 38, 51–52
    overview of, 32–33
    residency and citizenship, 42, 45, 56
Doxtater, Michael, 181
Dugard, John, 84
Duggan, Peter, 16
Dum Dum, West Bengal, 160, 161t
Dumoulin, Philippe, 88, 89–90, 91–92, 96, 97
Dyer, Simon, 5–6, 16–17, 29n2

East Bengal, 154–56, 158, 160, 164
East Pakistan, 128, 152–53
El Boubsi, Soufian, 88–89

Fanon, Franz, 201n6
Far as the Eye Can See: A Play (Wiebe)
    as alternative narrative, 2
    coal mining, 3, 6
    Crowfoot as character in, 6–8, 19, 27
    lyric thinking (Zwicky) in, 4
    Peter Lougheed as character in, 3, 8–9, 19, 26–27
    Princess Louise as character in, 6–7
    synopsis of, 3
    William Aberhart as character in, 6–7, 19

Festival du Théâtre Action, Belgium, 87
Filipina Live-In Caregivers, Toronto, xxxiv–xxxvii, xl–xli, xlvi*nn*27–28
films
    "flipping the gaze," 180–81, 192, 201*n*6
    See also *It Starts With a Whisper*; *Overweight With Crooked Teeth*; *Suite: INDIAN*
Finch, David, 4–5
Finding Our Song (Jamjoum), xxxiv, xxxvii–xl, xlvi*nn*29–30
Fleischmann, Aloys, xlii*n*2
Fort Chipewyan, Alberta, 11
Fort McMurray, Alberta
    Indigenous peoples, 6–8
    See also oil sands
France, *sans-papiers* movement, xxv, 44–45
Frank, Arthur, 112
Fraser, Nancy, 94

Gabriel, Ellen, 191–92
Gagnon, Annette, 222–23
Gagnon, Madeleine, 231–32
Gandhi, Indira, 170, 171
Gandhi, Rajiv, 171
Gangte, Gin, 143
Ganguly, Indubaran, 163
Gaza Strip. *See* Israel and Palestine
gender
    citizenship and illegal migrants, 33, 35, 39, 51, 52, 56
    sexual violence and women refugees, 212–14, 217*t*
    See also Meira Paibis; refugees and asylees, women's mental health
Ghosh, Subhasri, 261
    on refugees and government in West Bengal, x–xi, 151–75
Gilman, Sander, 179, 201*n*5
Glanville, Erin Goheen, 261–62
global apartheid (Sharma), 35–36
Gordon, Jon, 262
    on oil sands, ix–x, 1–30
Graham, Catherine, 262
    on theatricality and exposure of exclusion, x–xi, 87–114
Grant, George, 10–12, 15, 22, 26
Grant, Jennifer, 5–6, 16–17, 29*n*2
Gronau, Anna, 201*n*2
Grossberg, Lawrence, xii, xiii
Grundy-Warr, Carl, xx
Guiding Principles on Internal Displacement (Kälin), 142–43

Hajdukowski-Ahmed, Maroussia
    "A Dialogical Approach to the Identity of Refugee Women," 212
    career, 262
    on creativity as resilience, xi–xii, 205–35
    on non-verbal communication, 214
    Not Born a Refugee Woman, 227
Hamdan, Naim, 96, 100
Harper, Elijah, 183, 193, 196, 200, 202*nn*9–10
Hasan, Wafaa, 262–63
Hatch, Christopher, 18
Haudenosaunee people
    condolence ceremony, 203*n*13

displacement and media, 178–81
humour and parody, 200
traditional culture *vs.* materialism, 194–95, 197–99
See also Iroquois Confederacy
"Healing from Torture" project, 207–08, 221–23, 226
Henderson, James (Sákéj) Youngblood, xix, xxi
Hermans, Hubert, 212
Higginson, Catherine, 201n4
Hitchcock, Peter, 205
Hobbes, Thomas, xviii–xix
Holston, James, 37, 46–47
Honey Moccasin (Niro), 193
human rights
    citizenship and personhood, xvii, 36–43, 47–48
    displacement and, xvii
    in North-East India, 145–47, 149n13
    West Bank wall and, 61, 69, 84–85
    See also Israel, West Bank wall
humour and parody
    in Shelly Niro's films, 178, 182–83, 186, 193–95, 202n7
    survival and, 201n1
Hunter, William M., 9
Hutcheon, Linda, 194

ICJ. *See* International Court of Justice
Immigrant and Refugee Protection Act (Canada), 33
Imphal, Manipur, India, 117, 127, 129
India
    caste system and displacements, 142
    partition of Pakistan and India, 151–56, *152*, 153t–155t, 159
India, North-East
    displacement of youth, 118–19, 129
    economic development, 127–29
    history of, 120–24
    imagined community, 122–23
    militarization of, 124–27
    overview of, 119
    political formation and resistance, 117–18, 119–24
    rights *vs.* security, 126–27, 129
    states and territories, 119–21, 124
    See also Armed Forces (Special Powers) Act; East Bengal; Manipur; West Bengal
Indigenous peoples and displacement, xiv–xxii
    agency of, xxiii–xxv, xxix
    alternate narratives, xv
    historical examples of refugees and, xv–xvi
    land and, xiv, xix
    language and displacement, 201n3
    lawfulness and, xviii–xix
    losses and, xvi–xvii, xix
    refugee studies and, xiii–xvii, xv
    rejection of nation-state, xxi–xxii, xxiii–xxv
    universal human rights, xvii
    See also displacement
Indigenous peoples, Canada
    Cardinal's architecture, xxxi–xxxiii
    migrant justice movement, Toronto, 52
    oil sands and, 6–8, 11, 13
    See also Niro, Shelly, works

Indigenous peoples, Middle East. *See* Israel, West Bank wall; Israel and Palestine
Indigenous peoples, North America
   American Romanticism and, 180
   government and legal systems, xviii–xix
   language and displacement, 201n3
   nation-to-nation relations as goal, xxi
   See also Niro, Shelly, works
Indigenous peoples, North-East India. *See* East Bengal; Manipur; West Bengal
Internal Displacement Monitoring Group, 60
International Cities of Refuge Network, xlivn17
International Court of Justice, West Bank wall
   on displacements, 60, 75
   on illegality of wall, 79–80, 81, 82, 86n7, 86n13
   on Israeli settlements, 64
   on route and security objectives, 67
International Resilience Project, 211
Iroquois Confederacy, 177, 185, 188, 191, 203n14
   See also Haudenosaunee people
Isin, Engin, 46–47
Israel, West Bank wall
   "Ariel Finger" deviation, 66
   closed zones, 70–73
   comparison to South Africa, 67, 81, 83, 86n8
   displacements and, 60–65, 69–75
   everyday life and, 66, 69–75
   Green Line and, 65–66, 70, 86n9
   indirect displacement, 73–75
   Israeli settlements and, 60, 64
   Jerusalem area, 66
   overview of, 65–69
   permit system in closed zones, 71–74
   political rationale for, 61–65, 67–69, 72
   population, 63
   psychological effects, 72
   research on, 60–61, 71, 72, 74–75, 77
   segregation system, 63–64, 66–69
   unemployment and, 74–75
   See also International Court of Justice; Israel and Palestine
Israel, West Bank wall, resistance
   boycott, divestment and sanctions campaign, 77, 81–83, 85
   committees, 59, 77–78
   history of, 75–77, 81–83
   Israeli retaliation, 78–79
   legal action, 76–77, 79–80, 86n12
   non-violence, 59, 76, 78–79
   overview of, 75–77, 85
   popular organizing, 77–79
   remaining on land as, 61
   women's participation, 77
   See also *Les Murs Tombent, Let Mots Restent*
Israel and Palestine
   1948 population transfer, xxxviii, 61–63, 64, 85n1
   1967 war, 63, 86n6
   dual citizens Canada/Palestine, xxvii–xxix
   Eretz Yesra'el (right to all of Palestine), 68
   Gaza Strip, 69

Green Line, 65–66, 70, 86n9
history of, 61–65, 75–77, 86n6
Israeli self-definition and, 67–68, 68–69, 72, 84
one-state solution, 64–65, 67, 69
Palestinian actions in Israeli courts, 79–80, 86n12
Palestinian resistance, 62–63
segregation policies, 63–64
settler society *vs.* indigenous population, 61–63, 85n2
two-state solution, 64–65, 69, 86n8
Zionism and, 61–64, 72, 85n3–4
"Israel's Wall, Displacement, and Palestinian Resistance in the West Bank" (Masri), x–xi, xlivn11, 59–86
It Starts With a Whisper (film)
displacement in, 182–83, 197
fire imagery, 177–79, 182, 183–84, 199–200
humour and parody in, 182, 193
Matriarchal Aunts, 178, 182–84, 190–91, 193, 197, 200
overview of, 182–84
production and distribution, 201n2, 202nn11–12
quincentenary of Columbus, 183, 193
spirituality and traditional culture, 183–84, 196, 199–200
stereotypes, 188–90, 197
water imagery, 20, 183–84, 197

Jadavpur area, Calcutta, West Bengal, 161t, 162, 163
Jamjoum, Hazem, xxxiv, xlvn25
Jayyus, West Bank, 73–74

Jerusalem area, 60, 66
Johnson, Pauline, 201n4

Kälin, Walter, 142–43
Kanehsatake people
Oka Crisis, 189–90, 191–92, 203n16
Karnad, Raghu, 143
Katinas, Tom, 22
Kertzer, Jonathan, 19
Keung, Nicholas, 38
Khirbet Qasa, West Bank, 73
King, Thomas, xliiin9, 2, 180, 201n5
Klaszus, Jeremy, 11
Kolkata, West Bengal. *See* Calcutta, West Bengal
Kramer-Hamstra, Agnes, 263
on Shelley Niro's films, xi, 177–203
Kroetsch, Robert, 20

Laishram Achaw Singh, 126
language
settlers, Indigenous people and, 202n8
Les Murs Tombent, Let Mots Restent (Walls Fall, Words Live On) (play), 87–114
actors and director, 88, 96
art as a new way to see life (Appiah), 90–92, 97, 112–13
audience engagement, 90–94, 99–101, 106
cultural styles of exclusion, 94–96, 98, 101, 104–5
displacement and mobility, 87–88, 106, 109
habitus (Bourdieu) and social pressures, 95, 103–04, 112

Index   273

production challenges, 87–89, 96, 112–13
staging, movement, and sound, 96–100, 107, 110–11
story of European journalist and translator, x, 90, 91–92, 97–112
story of translator, 90, 106–12
synopsis, x–xi, 90
wall representations in, 108–9
Levant, Ezra, 12–13, 15, 22
literature. *See* art, culture, and displacement
Live-In Caregiver Program, Canada, xxxiv–xxxvii, xl–xli, xlv$n$26, xlvinn27–28
Longjam, Ibotombi, 135
Lougheed, Peter, as literary character, 3, 8–9, 19, 26–27
Loughry, Maryann, 228
lyric thinking. *See* Zwicky, Jan, lyric thinking

Mahaffy, Cheryl, 11, 13
Malaysia, citizenship and immigration, 47
Manipur, India
  alternative histories, 130
  displacement of youth, 118–19, 129, 141–44
  drug and alcohol use, 135, 137
  economic development, 127–29, 141–42
  ethnic and religious groups, 119–20, 130–33, *136*, 137
  history of, xi, 121, 127–32, 134–35
  human rights, 145–47, 149n13
  information availability, 147n3
  militarization of, 126–27, 129–30, 133, 141, 146

nationalism and socialism, 131–34
underground groups, 124, 132, 148n5, 149n20
women's organizations, 134–37, *136*, 149n19
See also Armed Forces (Special Powers) Act; Devi, Manorama; Meira Paibis
Manomohan Singh, 133–34, 144–45
"Mapping Manipur" (Narayanan), x–xi, 115–49
Marsden, William, 16
Masri, Mazen, 263
  on Israel's wall, displacement, and Palestinian resistance, x–xi, xliv$n$11, 59–86
Maurer, Bill, 54
McCarroll, Cody, xlii$n$2
McDonald, Jean, 263
  on citizenship studies, x, 31–57
McMaster, George, 199
McNevin, Anne, 36
media
  "fact packages," 92–94, 105–6
  ideal human figures, 202n7
  journalist as literary character, 90, 91–92, 97–112
  reductive definitions of displaced people, xii, xxii, xxx–xxxi, 210
  spectacle (Ndebele), 190
  stereotypes of Indigenous peoples, 179–81, 188, 190–92, 198
  terminology for persons with precarious status, 57n3
Meech Lake Accord, 183, 193, 202n10
Meghalaya, India, 121
  underground groups, 124
Meira Paibis, Manipur, India
  alternative histories, 130

demonstrations by, 117, 127, 133, 134, 138–41
  as grassroots women's organization, xi, 118, 134–39, 136
Mexican immigrants. *See* United States, immigration
migrant illegality. *See* citizenship studies and migrant illegality
Mizoram, India, 121–22, 124
"Modern Parody and Bakhtin" (Hutcheon), 194
Mod'in 'Illit, West Bank, 80
Mohapatra, Manas, 124–25, 148n6
Mohawk people
  assimilation and autonomy of, xxiv
  Oka Crisis, 189–90, 191–92, 203n16
  sisterhood in Niro's photography, 201n4
Mohawks in Beehives (photography), 190, 201n4, 203n17
music and song
  Arab youth theatre, xxxiv, xxxvii–xl, xlvinn29–30

Nafi, Ayman, 59
Nagaland, India, 120–21, 124, 125, 132
Narayanan, Pavithra, 263
  on Manipur, x–xi, 115–49
Narratives of Citizenship (Fleischmann, Van Styvendale, McCarroll), xliin2
nationalism
  imagined community (Anderson), 122–23
nation-states
  citizenship paradox, 37–39

definition of nation-state, xlivn15
human rights and, xvii, 38–39, 47
Indigenous peoples' rejection of nation-state, xxi–xxii, xxiii–xxv
postnational citizenship, xxiii, xxv–xxvi, 40–43
See also borders; citizenship studies and migrant illegality
natural disasters and refugees, 234n8
Nazlet Issa, West Bank, 70
Ndebele, Njabulo, 190
Nehru, Jawaharlal, 120–21, 154, 159
Nehru-Liaquat Pact, 158
Netajinagar Colony, Calcutta, West Bengal, 166–67
Ni'ilin, West Bank, 59, 78–79
Nikhil Banga Bastuhara Karma Parishad, 164
Niro, Shelly, works
  Columbus's quincentenary celebrations, 183, 193
  contemporary and traditional culture, 178–80, 182, 193, 194–95, 197
  displacement in works, 200–01, 202n9
  everyday life, 178, 190–92, 200
  fire imagery, 177–79, 182, 183–84, 188, 199–200
  "flipping the gaze," 179–81, 192, 201n6
  humour and parody in, 178, 182–83, 186, 193–95, 202n7
  lyric thinking (Zwicky), 178, 195–99
  objectivity and, 180–81
  photography, 179, 180–81, 190, 192, 201n4

Index   275

spirituality, 183–84, 195–99
stereotypes, xi, 179–81, 185–86, 189–92, 193–94, 197, 201n5
water imagery, 183–84, 197–98
See also *It Starts With a Whisper*; *Mohawks in Beehives*; *Overweight With Crooked Teeth*; *Suite: INDIAN*
"The Non-Verbal Forms of Communication of Refugee Women Survivors of Torture" (Hajdukowski-Ahmed), 214
No One Is Illegal movement, x, 32–33, 45, 52, 56, 56n2
North-East India. *See* Assam; East Bengal; India, North-East; Manipur; West Bengal
Not Born a Refugee Woman (Hajdukowski-Ahmed et al.), 227
Nupi Lan movement, Manipur, India, 134–35, 149n18
Nyers, Peter, xviii, xxv–xxvii, xxix, 37–38, 49–50, 55

Occupied Palestinian Territory. *See* Israel, West Bank wall; Israel and Palestine
O'Connor, Flannery, xlivn13
"Ode" (Johnson), 201n4
oil sands, 1–30
"acceptable" trade-offs, 9–12
duck deaths, 1, 12–13, 15, 22, 28, 30n7
extraction as analysis, 14–16, 18, 24
extraction processes, 4–5, 29n2
health problems of local residents, 29n4

Indigenous peoples and, 6–8, 11, 13, 29n4
public survey on, 27
reclamation of land, 5–6, 14, 16–18
representations, alternative, 2, 18, 27–28
representations, dominant, 4, 6–9, 12–14, 19
statistics on, 5
sustainable development and, 2, 11–12, 18, 24, 26
tailings ponds, 1, 4–5, 23
wilderness and, 17, 28
See also "The Angel of the Tar Sands"; Zwicky, Jan, lyric thinking
Oinam, Bhagat, 130, 149n19
Oka Crisis, Quebec, 189–90, 191–92, 203n16
Ong, Aihwa, 41, 47
Onkwehonwe peoples, xxiv
See also Mohawk people
Ontario, challenge to migrant illegality. *See* "Don't Ask, Don't Tell" campaign, Toronto, Ontario
Operetang Maynila (Cleto), xxxiv–xxxvii, xl–xli, xlvn26, xlvinn27–28
Our Fair Share (Alberta Royalty Review Panel), 9
Overweight With Crooked Teeth (film), 180–81, 186, 193, 198, 202n7

"Pacific Solution" (Australia's treatment of Lebanese asylum-seekers), xix–xx

Pakistan
    partition of Pakistan and India,
        151–56, 152, 153t–155t, 159
Pakistan, East, 128, 152–53
Palestine Liberation Organization,
    76, 83
Palestinian Campaign for the
    Academic and Cultural Boycott
    of Israel (PACBI), 81–83
Palestinians
    dual citizens Canada/Palestine,
        xxvii–xxix
    See also Israel and Palestine
Palestinians, West Bank. See Israel,
    West Bank wall
parody. See humour and parody
Peace, Power and Righteousness
    (Alfred), 203*n*13
Pembina Institute, 5–6, 29*n*3
People of the Longhouse. See
    Haudenosaunee people
Perera, Suvendrini, xix–xx
Permanent Working Group on Forced
    Displacement, 60–61
Peutz, Nathalie, 51, 53, 57*n*4
Phanjoubam, Pradip, 143, 147*n*2,
    148*n*8
photography
    Curtis's stereotypes of Indians,
        180, 201*n*5
    "flipping the gaze," 179–81, 192,
        201*n*6
    Niro's works, 179, 180–81, 190,
        192, 201*n*4
Pond, Myrna, 223
"Portrait of the Artist Sitting with a
    Killer Surrounded by French
    Curves" (photograph), 192
Price, Matt, 18

prostitution, 11, 13, 158, 230
Pylee, M.V., 123

Qalqilya, West Bank, 70, 72–73

race and racism
    immigration policies, 33, 35, 50,
        52–53
    Israeli treatment of Arabs, 89
    racial discrimination in India, 143
Rajaram, Prem Kumar, xx
Ramani, Ima, 138–39
"The Refugee and the Government"
    (Ghosh), x–xi, 151–75
refugees and asylees
    agency of, xxv–xxvi
    definitions, xiv, xviii, xxv, xlii*n*1,
        xliii*n*4
    fear and, xviii–xix, xxix
    human rights, xvii
    identity and creativity, 215–16,
        230–32
    impact of 9/11 terrorist attacks
        on, 229–30
    Indigenous peoples and, xiii–v
    privileging of, 48–49
    statistics and causes, 234*n*8
    See also displacement
refugees and asylees, women's mental
    health
    agency as individual and societal
        relationship, xii, 211–12, 216,
        230, 234*n*10
    body memory and, 212–14
    conference participation (Saying
        "I"), 209, 225
    creativity and resilience, 206, 209,
        215–19, 217t–218t, 220–28,
        230–32

dialogics and identity, 205–06,
209, 215–16, 232n1
dialogism and resilience
(Bakhtin), 209–13, 220–21,
233n5, 234n9
economic hardships, 217–20,
217t–218t
identity and creativity, 215–19,
217t–218t, 230–32
mainstream institutions and,
217–20, 217t–218t
medicalized trauma discourse,
205–06, 219, 228–30
nonverbal communication, 213–
14, 228–30, 234n7
overview of, 205–10
research approach, 206, 209–12,
227–30, 232n1, 234n7
sexual violence, 212–14, 216, 217t,
230
shared narratives, xxii, 220, 221,
225–28
stigmatization, 216, 220, 229–30
torture, 207–08, 221–23, 226
victim and survivor discourse,
205–06, 210, 213, 216, 228–30
See also "Healing from Torture";
resilience and women refugees;
"Saying 'I' " (refugee women's
mental health); Sudan: women
refugees and mental health
resilience and women refugees
creative activities, 207–08, 221–24,
233n3
creative activities, benefits of,
223–24, 228–32
creativity and resilience, 206, 209,
220–28, 230–32
definitions of resilience, 211–12

factors that hinder and enhance,
217–20, 217t–218t
family and social relations, 217–
20, 217t–218t, 233n3
holidays and celebrations, 208, 222
hope and patience, 217–20,
217t–218t, 224
painting, 208–09, 223–24, 224, 227
religion, 218t, 219, 228
Sudanese refugee study, 217–20,
217t–218t
Rice, Ryan, 177
Ricoeur, Paul, xxi–xxii, xxxi, xxxix–xl
Routray, Bibhu Prasad, 134
Rowe, Stan, 15–16
Roy, B.C., 154
Ruffo, Armand, 201n6
Ryan, Allan, 201n1

Sachdeva, Gulshan, 128, 129
Sahidnagar Colony, Calcutta, West
Bengal, 167
Said, Edward, 201n6
Salameh Theatre Troupe, Mississauga,
Ontario, xxxiv, xxxvii–xl,
xlvinn29–30
sanctuary zones, xlivn17, 45, 56
sans-papiers movements, xxv, xxix,
44–45
Sassen, Saskia, 34–35, 39, 42–43,
45–47
"Saying 'I' " (refugee women's mental
health), 208–09, 223–28
"Saying 'I': Refugee Women Reclaim
their Identity" (conference),
209, 225
Sen, K.K., 128
sexual violence and women refugees,
212–14

Sharma, Nandita, 35–36, 40
Sharmila, Irom, 144, 149n17
Shiell, Leslie, 4, 26
Shimray, U.A., 143–44
Shohat, Ella, 147
Sierra Club, 11
Sikkim, India, 122
Simpson, Audra, 200
Sitting Bull, 181, 187, 195, 196, 198–99
Six Nations peoples
    artists and artisans, 177
    Hiawatha and Peacemaker, 184–85, 203n15
    history of, 177, 185, 195, 203nn13–14
    Iroquois Confederacy, 177, 185, 188, 191, 203n14
    matriarchies, 191–92
    stereotypes, 179–81, 189–92
    See also Haudenosaunee people; Niro, Shelly, works
Smith, Dorothy, 92–93, 105
Smith, Santee, 186, 203n18
Soguk, Nevzat, xxiii
South Asia Terrorism Portal (SATP), 124
Soysal, Yasemin, 40–42
spirituality
    Cardinal's architecture, xxxi–xxxiii
    renewal of Indigenous spirituality, 195–99
    See also Zwicky, Jan, lyric thinking
Spivak, Gayatri, 2, 18, 28
"The Standard Is Zero" (Bertell), 9–10
Stasiulis, Daiva, 40, 42, 47, 51
Stelmach, Ed, 11, 27
stereotypes
    Canadian Indigenous peoples, 179–81, 188–90

    humour and, 193–94
    photography of Indigenous peoples, 180, 192, 201n5–6
"Stirring the Cultural Fire" (Kramer-Hamstra), 177–203
Sudan
    civil wars, 233n4
    women refugees and mental health, 209, 217–20, 217t–218t
"Sui Generis and Treaty Citizenship" (Henderson), xxi
Suite: INDIAN (film)
    condolence ceremony in, 184–85, 197, 203n13
    cultural appropriations, 187–88
    dance and music, 186–87, 194, 203n18
    displacement and homelessness, 187–88, 197
    fire imagery, 177–79, 182, 183–84, 188, 199–200
    Hiawatha and Peacemaker as characters, 184–85, 197, 203n15
    overview of, 184–88
    parody and humour in, 186, 193–95
    spirituality, 197–99
    stereotypes, 185–86, 197
    traditional culture vs. materialism, 186–88, 194–95, 198–200
Suncor Energy Inc., 23, 25
    See also oil sands
Swallow (play), 1, 9
Syncrude Canada Ltd.
    autonomy of, 18
    Indigenous peoples and, 7
    oil mining plant, 25
    reclamation, 16

tailings ponds, 1, 12–13, 22, 23, 30n7
   See also oil sands

Taft, Kevin, 27
tar sands. *See* oil sands
Taruni, Keisam, 137, 138
Taylor, Charles, 226
Technology and Justice (Grant). *See* Grant, George
Territory, Authority, Rights (Sassen), 45
Thangjam, Homen, 138
Theater for Everybody, 87, 88–89, 90, 114n3
   See also Les Murs Tombent, Let Mots Restent
theatre
   art as a new way to see life (Appiah), 90–91, 97, 113
   expert opinion and public debate, 92–94, 106
   presentation of cultural styles of exclusion, 94–96
   as public arena for bodies and voices, 87, 112–13
   See also Far as the Eye Can See: A Play; Les Murs Tombent, Let Mots Restent; Operetang Maynila; Swallow
Théâtre du Public, 87, 88, 90, 114n3
   See also Les Murs Tombent, Let Mots Restent
"Theatricality and the Exposure of Exclusion" (Graham), 87–114
A Time of Visions (Niro), 190, 193
Toronto, Ontario
   Sanctuary City movement, 56

   See also "Don't Ask, Don't Tell" campaign, Toronto
Torpey, John, 53
torture and refugee women's mental health, 207–08, 221–23, 226
The Trickster Shift (Ryan), 201n1
Tripura, India, 121, 124
The Truth About Stories (King), 2, 180

Ungar, Michael, 210, 211–12, 229
United National Liberation Front, Manipur, 132
United Nations Centre for Human Settlements
   squatter settlements, definition of, 160
United Nations Office of the Coordination of Humanitarian Affairs, 66, 71, 72
United Nations Relief and Works Agency for Palestine Refugees in the Near East, 71, 72
United States, immigration
   citizenship, personhood, and nationalism, 42, 44, 45
   Mexican migrants, 44, 50–51, 52–53
Upadhyay, R., 132
USA PATRIOT Act, 148n6

Van Styvendale, Nancy, xliin2
Varsanyi, Monica, 40, 41–42

Walls Fall, Words Live On (play). *See Les Murs Tombent, Let Mots Restent*
Wasáse (Alfred), xxiii–xxiv, 195, 197–99
West, Amy R., xxv, xxxiv

West Bank. *See* Israel, West Bank wall; Israel and Palestine
West Bengal, 151–75
  colony committees, 159–60, 163
  government (1960–1980s), 170–71
  migrations, 151–54, 152, 153*t*–154*t*, 154–56, 170
  relief for migrants, 154*t*–155*t*, 156–59, 157*t*
  riot (1950) in East Bengal, 158, 164
  See also Calcutta, West Bengal
West Bengal, squatter settlements
  arpanpatras (for authorized occupants), 168–69
  colony committees, 159–60, 163
  definition of squatter, 160
  history of, 158–72, 161*t*, 162
  jabardakhal (forcible seizure), 151, 160
  land ownership and leases, 168, 170–74, 174*n*6
  law and order, 161–67
  legislation and policies, 164–68
  political impact of, 171–74
  refugee councils (UCRC), 164–69
  regularization of colonies, 167–71, 175*n*7
  settlements as resistance, 163, 167
  squatters (migrants), 151, 153
  women's resistance, 167
Wiebe, Rudy
  on land and literature, 19
  on oil sands, 6–7
  See also "The Angel of the Tar Sands"; *Far as the Eye Can See: A Play*
Williams, Raymond, xii, xiii
Workers Arts and Heritage Centre, Hamilton, Ontario, 208
Woynillowicz, Dan, 5–6, 16–17, 29*n*2

Yaeger, Patricia, 17
Yngvesson, Barbara, 54
"You're Not the Indian I Had in Mind" (King), 180
"Youth on the Move" (Shimray), 143–44

Zehle, Soenke, xxv
Zhang, Benzi, 144
Žižek, Slavoj, 24
Zionism, 61–64, 72, 85*n*3–4
Zwicky, Jan, lyric thinking
  analysis and technocracy, 3, 5, 14–15
  awareness of possibilities, 27–28
  interconnectedness and, 4–5
  language and separation, 20–21
  longing and, 178
  lyric and integration, 17, 19–22
  meaning of *lyric*, 3–4, 14–15, 30*n*6
  metaphors and, 26
  Niro's works and, 178, 195–99
  Rudy Wiebe's works and, 4, 20–22, 28, 30*n*8

Other Titles from The University of Alberta Press

Narratives of Citizenship
Indigenous and Diasporic Peoples Unsettle the Nation-State
ALOYS N.M. FLEISCHMANN, NANCY VAN STYVENDALE & CODY MCCARROLL, *Editors*
408 pages | Introduction, notes, bibliography, index
978-0-88864-518-0 | $39.95 (T) paper
Cultural Studies/Literary Criticism/Citizenship

The Man in Blue Pyjamas
A Prison Memoir
JALAL BARZANJI
SABAH A. SALIH, *Translator*
JOHN RALSTON SAUL, *Foreword*
288 pages | 34 B&W photographs, translator's preface, foreword, map
Wayfarer Series
978-0-88864-536-4 | $24.95 (T) paper
Memoir/Human Rights/Kurdistan

Building Sustainable Peace
TOM KEATING & W. ANDY KNIGHT, *Editors*
504 pages | Index, bibliography
Copublished with United Nations University Press
978-0-88864-414-5 | $39.95 (S) paper
Political Science/Peace Studies